Evangelistic Preaching 101

Evangelistic Preaching 101

Voices of the Past and Present on Preaching Effectively

By

Frank Shivers

LIGHTNING SOURCE
1246 Heil Quaker Blvd.
La Vergne, TN

Unless otherwise noted, Scripture quotations are from
The Holy Bible *King James Version*

Library of Congress Cataloging-in-Publication Data

Shivers, Frank R., 1949–
Evangelistic Preaching / Frank Shivers
ISBN 978-1-878127-10-5

Library of Congress Control Number:
2008911239

Cover design by
Tim King

For Information:
Frank Shivers Evangelistic Association
P.O. Box 9991
Columbia, South Carolina 29290
www.frankshivers.com

To

Dr. Bailey Smith

For outstanding example to pastor and evangelist in the evangelistic sermon and invitation and unrelenting passion to preach to win souls. Your tenacity in service, heart of humility, soundness in theology, and life of integrity serve as a model for us all.

Dr. Jim Palmer

A pastor with a heart for the vocational evangelist's support, stability, service, and success. Thank you, Jim, for the many years of friendship, encouragement, and partnership in evangelistic ministry.

CONTENTS

Preface

Evangelistic preaching is seldom heard in our churches in these modern times. Roy Fish said, "I wonder, have we stopped preaching evangelistic sermons because lost people are not coming to our services like they once did? Or maybe it's the other way around. Maybe we stopped preaching evangelistic messages, and God stopped bringing lost people to our services to hear them."[1] Personally, I believe the latter to be the case.

It is not my purpose in this volume to defend evangelistic preaching against its gainsayers. It needs no defense. Its track record over the years of being used by God to win millions from the jaws of Hell substantiates its power and place in the pulpit, and this is confirmed by Christ's own endorsement. My intent is rather to incite the divinely called preacher boldly to engage in evangelistic preaching more regularly and preparedly. In 2008, Southern Baptist Convention churches baptized fewer people for the fourth year in a row, and the SBC reported its lowest level of baptisms since 1987.[2] Additionally, membership in SBC churches suffered a decrease of nearly 38,400 members from 2007.[3] This alarming news should serve as a clarion call to evangelistic preaching in our churches.

Regarding the pastor, C. E. Matthews stated, "He should strive constantly to improve his preaching from every standpoint that would enable him to be more effective in

---

[1] Koonce, "Fish: Evangelistic Preaching."
[2] Finch, "Baptisms Again Dip."
[3] Ibid.

winning the lost. He should take advantage of every opportunity to learn new methods in soul winning, in giving an invitation at the close of the message...."[4] Matthews' directive is also applicable for evangelists, missionaries, and all who desire to preach to win souls; and it is more timely now than when first issued. The preacher must never cease tooling and sharpening evangelistic sermon preparation and delivery. The best evangelistic sermon has yet to be preached by you or anyone else.

Evangelistic Preaching 101 is designed to enhance the preacher's content, structure, and delivery of the evangelistic sermon, that he may be more effective in winning souls through preaching. In this endeavor I have drawn not only from thirty-six years of personal evangelistic ministry but heavily from preachers like C. H. Spurgeon, Adrian Rogers, Stephen Olford, W. A. Criswell, Roy Fish, Billy Graham, Faris Whitesell, Robert E. Coleman, L. R. Scarborough, George Sweazey, C. E. Matthews, Gipsy Smith, J. C. Ryle, C. E. Autrey, John Bisagno, Warren Wiersbe, E. J. Daniels, John R. Rice, and George W. Truett who are/were extremely successful evangelistic preachers.

Hopefully every preacher who visits these pages will leave with fresh desire to preach evangelistically more regularly and passionately and with tools to do so more effectively.

---

[4] Matthews, *Southern Baptist Program,* 117–118.

"There has been a dearth of evangelistic preaching. I'm not sure when it began, but it's almost like it's a taboo."[5]—Roy Fish

"Sorrowfully, there is a modern tendency to turn aside from evangelistic preaching, as though the people outside the church could be reached by lowering our standards and changing our eternal message. The spirit of compromise, secularism, and ecumenism are seen everywhere. It is more dialogue without decision, communication without conversion, universalism without personal salvation. This is not the method of the New Testament (Acts 2:40). The apostles preached for a verdict."[6]—W. A. Criswell

---

[5] Koonce, "Fish: Evangelistic Preaching."
[6] Criswell, *Criswell's Guidebook for Pastors,* 233–234.

1
Subject

What is evangelistic preaching?

Alan Walker states, "Evangelical preaching is preaching for a verdict. Its conscious purpose is to win an immediate commitment to Jesus Christ. Its aim is conversion. It seeks to make disciples, setting them on the road to maturity and holiness."[7]

V. L. Stanfield, my homiletics professor in seminary, declared evangelistic preaching "is the proclamation of the good news concerning the redemptive acts of God in Christ, by one who experientially knows Jesus Christ, in order to lead others to receive Christ as their Savior and Lord."[8]

"An evangelistic sermon aims to help people decide for Christ by clearly presenting the gospel story in the power of the Holy Spirit."[9]

Roy Fish surmised, "Evangelistic preaching majors on the message of Jesus, particularly on his redemptive deeds. That is the subject. The object of evangelistic preaching is to lead people to make an initial commitment to Jesus. It's preaching for a verdict."[10]

Billy Graham said regarding preaching content, "None matters as much as the Gospel of forgiveness for sin through Christ's death on the cross and the gift of eternal life through His resurrection. Wherever I have gone, that single message has been my preaching theme."[11]

---

[7] Larsen, *The Evangelism Mandate*, 100.
[8] Stanfield, *Effective Evangelistic Preaching*, 11.
[9] Lorentzen, ed., *Evangelistic Preaching*, 23.
[10] Koonce, "Fish: Evangelistic Preaching."
[11] Lorentzen, *Evangelistic Preaching*, Foreword.

Robert E. Coleman defines evangelistic preaching as "the proclamation of the Gospel in the power of the Holy Spirit with the aim of a clear decision for Christ in the hearers."[12]

W. A. Criswell declared, "The aim of the preacher is primarily the conversion of his hearers. The seeking note ought to be heard and felt in every sermon. Jonathan Edwards in his pulpit sought a verdict. Charles G. Finney expected results, and he had them. C. H. Spurgeon ended his sermons with an appeal to the lost. Even the sermon preached primarily for edification ought to have in it saving features."[13]

Faris D. Whitesell wrote, "Evangelistic preaching differs from other preaching....Evangelistic preaching is preaching at its best. It is preaching adapted to the highest ends of the Gospel—turning men from sin and darkness to salvation and light. Evangelistic preaching is preaching with a mission—winning a verdict in favor of the Lord Jesus Christ. The evangelistic sermon is an all-out effort to bring the lost to Christ." Whitesell continues, "A devotional or inspirational sermon with an evangelistic kite tail attached is not an evangelistic sermon. A sermon with a mild evangelistic strain or color running through it is not an evangelistic sermon. These sermons may be good and perfectly appropriate for many occasions, but such preaching ought not to be called evangelistic preaching."[14]

The Urgency of Evangelistic Preaching

The urgency of preaching evangelistically is due to man's eternal peril apart from Christ and the glory of God. It is urgent in that the preacher possesses the only remedy that heals the spiritually blind, deaf, dumb, lame, and dead which sit before him on Sunday and Wednesday. In an hour in which it may be estimated that 160,000 people die daily without Christ and with thickening spiritual darkness encompassing our world, Holy

---

[12] Douglas, ed., *Work of the Evangelist*, 135.
[13] Criswell, *Criswell's Guidebook for Pastors*, 234.
[14] Whitesell, *Evangelistic Preaching*, 28.

Spirit anointed evangelistic sermons must be thundered from the pulpit making plain the need, means, and urgency of salvation.

L.R. Scarborough, in describing man's lostness, underscores this urgency in evangelistic preaching: "There is no way of understanding that scripture (Luke 15:11–24) unless you say that God is there trying to tell and describe the spiritual condition before God of every unsaved man. He said the boy was "dead." There is no evidence in that parable that the boy had been actually dead and buried. He is talking about the condition of his soul. He said he was "lost" and is found. There is no evidence in the parable the boy was lost from human habitation. The fact is he had too much company of the bad sort. He is describing the spiritual condition of his son. The word I want to talk to you about tonight, descriptive of the spiritual condition of every man and woman who has not trusted Jesus Christ as his Savior, is that little word "*Lost*"—L-O-S-T—"Lost"....It means separation from God. It means eternal dwelling in the land of eternal punishment. It means the opposite of Heaven. It means the extreme opposite of righteousness. It means Hell. It means no peace. It means no happiness, no joy. It means separation from the good and companionship with evil. It means all there is that is wrapped up in darkness into which no sun shines. It means the starless night of eternity. It means sunless day forever and ever. It means all there is in the punishment of sin, in the wrath of God, in the indignation of a wrathful sovereign. Lost! Lost! Lost!"[15]

Basil Manly, Jr., (1825–1892), in "The Wisdom of Winning Souls," paints a picture of the unsaved and the minister's tremendous difficulty in winning them. "We have to overcome entire indifference. The souls that are to be won care nothing for spiritual blessings, having lost, through the fall, the right sense of such things. We are proposing to make those serious who have given all their days to levity and amusement, and

---

[15] Scarborough, "Lost!" 1.

those spiritual who have been entirely engrossed in worldly care....But we have to encounter the hostility of the heart, and not its indifference and reluctance merely. We have, as our first business, to fasten the charge of guilt upon men, to make them not only acknowledge, but feel their utter sinfulness and degradation in God's sight, to produce a sense of condemnation and self-abhorrence where self-complacency had filled the mind and love of pleasure ruled the life. Our efforts are opposed by the passions of men, too, as well as by their pride. Sins dear as a right eye must be renounced, and evil habits cherished as the right hand must be cut off. The interests also of men as regards this life are frequently opposed to our errand. Gainful as well as pleasurable sins must be abandoned. In fact, the whole nature must be changed. Our effort is nothing less than to win a wholly perverted and depraved soul back to purity and fit it for dwelling with God."[16] How might this monumental task be accomplished? Manly suggests, "The instrumentality proposed is the truth of God made effective by the Spirit of God."[17] Scarborough and Manly statements cite an irrefutable case for the point, place and priority of evangelistic preaching.

Evangelist Lester Roloff saw how vital evangelistic preaching is: "Oh, my preacher brother, if there is any hope left for the pew, it will have to come out of flaming pulpits."[18]

A story is told about a French surgeon who described to an English physician a new and extremely delicate operation he had performed. The Englishman asked the surgeon how the patient was doing, to which he replied, "Oh, he died. But it was a beautiful operation."[19] Evangelistic preaching, regardless of its beauty and literary excellence, is of little value if it fails to

---

[16] Nettles, *Ready for Reformation?*, 31.
[17] Ibid.
[18] Roloff, "The Family Altar," Number 3, 2.
[19] Bodey, *Inside the Sermon*, 130.

impact lives for time and eternity. The test of the evangelistic sermon is to ask in its aftermath, "What did it accomplish?"

Opposition to Evangelistic Preaching

As previously stated, the purpose of this volume is not to *defend* evangelistic preaching but to *underpin* it. It really needs no defense to those who embrace its biblical mandate, as echoed by C. H. Dodd, and its very meaning as defined in the Greek word *kerygma* (see below). Therefore, simply a quick overview of the objections to evangelistic preaching will be presented with pointed rebuttal. The opposition to evangelistic preaching enters from five primary courts: its biblical mandate, simplicity, relevancy (value), misuse, and emotional appeal.

Unbiblical Objection

According to C. H. Dodd, New Testament preaching is evangelistic preaching. He stated that "preach" in the New Testament always means "to evangelize" and that *kerygma*, or "preaching," always refers to speaking to the unsaved. Much of our preaching in the church at the present day would not have been recognized by the early Christians as *kerygma*. It is teaching or exhortation (*paraklesis)*, or what they called *homilia,* addressed to a congregation already established in the faith."[20]

Harper's Bible Dictionary says *kerygma* has to do more with the content of preaching than its act: the "Good News" of redemption through the death, burial and resurrection of Jesus Christ. *Tyndale Bible Dictionary* says *kerygma* is the "basic evangelistic message proclaimed by the earliest Christians. More fully, it is the proclamation of the death, resurrection, and exaltation of Jesus that leads to an evaluation of His person as both Lord and Christ, confronts one with the necessity of repentance, and promises the forgiveness of sins." J. Henry Jowett remarked that, "The ultimate aim of all true preaching is

---

[20] Sweazy, *Effective Evangelism*, 159.

the salvation of men. Salvation from what? Salvation from sin? Yes. Salvation from hellfire? Yes. Salvation from infirmity? Yes. From moral stuntedness and spiritual immaturity? Yes. From all arrested growth in the direction of the divine? Yes. The strenuous purpose of all vital preaching is to lift men out of the bondage of sin and dwarfhood and to set them in the fine spacious air and light of the free-born children of God."[21]

Jesus preached evangelistic sermons (Matthew 4:17); Philip preached evangelistic sermons (Acts 8:12); Paul preached evangelistic sermons (I Corinthians 1:17–18; Galatians 1:16). Paul exhorts all ministers, "Preach the word *[kerygma]*; be instant in season, out of season; reprove, rebuke, exhort with all longsuffering and doctrine. For the time will come when they will not endure sound doctrine; but after their own lusts shall they heap to themselves teachers, having itching ears; And they shall turn away their ears from the truth, and shall be turned unto fables" (II Timothy 4:2–4).

Simplicity Objection

Evangelistic preaching by virtue of its objective (win the unsaved) must be simple, and this spurs protest among Bible students in the church who want the "meat and potatoes," not the "milk and toast" of the Gospel. This being said, *simple* preaching need not be *shallow* preaching. W. A. Criswell's evangelistic sermon cited in Chapter 5 is certainly not shallow preaching, but it is simple. Simplicity and biblical substance can and should coexist in the evangelistic sermon, challenging both the mind to think and heart to act. Faris D. Whitesell stated, "The evangelistic sermon must be intellectually respectable. Too much so-called evangelistic preaching has been shallow, partisan, and emotional without much thought content. The evangelistic sermon should be as thought-provoking as any other sermon. It should be the result of hard and careful preparation and much prayer—but the evangelistic message must not be so profound that it cannot be understood. Above all

---

[21] Jowett, *Apostolic Optimism*, Chapter 20.

other types of preaching, it must be clear and easily followed if it is to be fruitful."[22]

Irrelevancy Objection

Some pastors don't preach evangelistically due to a "Christian only" audience in their church. Is this a valid reason not to preach evangelistically? "Not quite," answers Myron Augsburger. He states that the evangelistic sermon remains necessary even in a "Christian" assembly for three reasons: "(1) It helps believers clarify how they can present the Gospel to their friends during the week. (2) It gives relatively nonverbal members an opportunity to share the Gospel with their friends without saying a word! (3) People who regularly come to church don't necessarily have a personal relationship with Christ."[23] Elton Trueblood estimates that two-thirds of the members of American churches know nothing about personal conversion.[24]

I add a fourth reason, which is that evangelistic preaching keeps man's lost estate and need of salvation in focus in the minds of the saints. In hearing evangelistic sermons, believers are reminded of the spiritual condition of a friend, family member, classmate, fellow worker or neighbor who is apart from Christ and their eternal doom in Hell unless they repent and believe. This reminder may inflame the heart to go and tell the unreached about Jesus Christ.

Manipulation Objection

I must regrettably attest that some evangelistic (and pastoral) preaching is manipulative, but this is not how it is designed, nor is it the norm. Evangelistic preaching is prompting the unsaved to realize personal sinfulness, separation from God, and the possibility of salvation through the blood of Jesus Christ, and pleading for immediate decision. The evangelistic

---

[22] Whitesell, *Evangelistic Preaching*, 34–35.
[23] Augsburger, "Preaching Evangelistically."
[24] Ibid.

preacher must realize there is a marked line in preaching and extending the invitation which must not be crossed—the line between the passionate appeal to the unsaved to be reconciled to God willingly and that of coercion. Evangelistic preaching has gotten a bad rap because of preachers who push the envelope too far instead of allowing the Holy Spirit to do the drawing.

Emotionalism Objection

Biblical evangelistic preaching is a balanced blend "between the heart and the head so as to avoid the extremes of dry intellectualism and excessive emotionalism."[25] Emotions aroused in true evangelistic preaching are those which the Holy Spirit initiates from within as the Word is expounded regarding "sin, and...righteousness, and...judgment," not from without by a preacher's theatrics or tear-jerking stories. One must not equate true New Testament evangelistic preaching with the latter.

Understanding the essential of passion in sermon delivery, W. A. Criswell said, "Let not the pastor be afraid of emotion in preaching. True eloquence flows out of deep feeling. Jonathan Edwards appealed to the emotions. He believed that the passions are the prime movers in life. He was not afraid to appeal to the elementary instincts of fear, love, hope, deliverance, security. He believed that unless a man is moved by some affection, he was by nature inactive."[26] "The sermon," continued Criswell, "is no essay to read for optional opinion for the people casually to consider. It is a confrontation with the Almighty God. It is to be delivered with a burning passion in the authority of the Holy Spirit."[27]

Curtis Hutson reminds preachers that "men are not only loved into Heaven; they are warned into it. 'Noah...moved with fear, prepared an ark.' Dr. Bob Jones, Sr., once said, 'What America needs most is about six months of red-hot

---

[25] Gugliotto, *Handbook for Bible Study*, 149
[26] Criswell, *Criswell's Guidebook for Pastors*, 53.
[27] Ibid.

preaching on Hell by men who are half mad when they preach it. Love alone won't get the job done.' Eighty brilliant law, medical, or engineering students at a Christian fellowship meeting were asked, 'How many of you gave your hearts to Christ simply through your great love for God?' Not one hand was raised. Next they were asked, 'How many of you gave your hearts to Christ because you knew there was an awful Hell from which to flee and that without a Sin-bearer you would be eternally lost?' Every hand was lifted."[28] The preaching of biblical, doctrinal truth about Hell, judgment, Heaven, the Second Coming, and the wrath of God stirs the emotions of fear, guilt, and sorrow, and rightfully they ought (Jude 23)!

Sadly, due to abuse by some evangelists and pastors, the place and priority the evangelistic sermon once possessed in the pulpit has diminished. "But none of these abuses," George Sweazey states, "has any sort of necessary connection with the method. The finest things always have the worst perversions....A study of sermons of some of the church's most effective evangelists gives plenty of evidence that it still pleases God 'by the foolishness of preaching to save' (I Corinthians 1:21)."[29] Despite the ill manner in which some have used evangelistic preaching, its time-tested method in reaching the unsaved is divinely authorized and assigned by Jesus (Luke 24:45–47).

It is easy to get man saved; the hard part is to get him lost. Nothing short of preaching that exposes sin in man's heart, its consequences, and the solitary provision for deliverance through Jesus Christ's work on the Cross, energized by the Holy Spirit, can accomplish this task. This is the role of evangelistic preaching commissioned by our Lord in the New Testament to His minister. Discard it, and the pulpit sounds an "uncertain sound" (I Corinthians 14:8).

---

[28] Hutson, ed., *Great Preaching on Hell,* preface.
[29] Sweazey, *Effective Evangelism*, 161, 171.

Let the critic of evangelistic preaching sound his protest upon deaf ears. Such live in a different spiritual sphere and march to a different drumbeat from us. C. T. Studd wrote of the startling contrast in a poem entitled "I'm Not Going Your Way," a frank conversation between a young, modernist preacher and an old-time Bible preacher.

I'm Not Going Your Way
"You're just out of date," said young Pastor Bate
  To one of our faithful old preachers
Who had carried for years in travail and tears
  The Gospel to poor, sinful creatures.

"You still preach on Hades and shock cultured ladies
  With your barbarous doctrine of blood!
You're so far behind, you will never catch up—
  You're a flat tire stuck in the mud!"

For some little while, a wee bit of a smile
  Enlightened the old preacher's face.
Being made the butt of a ridiculous cut
  Did not ruffle his sweetness and grace.

Then he turned to young Bate, so suave and sedate,
  "Catch up, did my ears hear you say?
Why, I couldn't succeed if I doubled your speed;
  My friend, *I'm not going your way!*"[30]

Neither criticism nor culture must be allowed to dictate to the preacher the *what* of proclamation ("Jesus Christ, and Him crucified") or its *how* ("Preach")! Stay vigilant and don't let 'em make a nominal or theologically unsound preacher out of you.

---

[30] Criswell, *Criswell's Guidebook for Pastors*, 232.

"Evangelistic preaching is the most important of all preaching when we consider what it seeks to do. It puts the Gospel to its highest test; it applies the Gospel to the end for which it was created—the conviction and the conversion of sinners."[31]—Faris Whitesell

"If the truth were known, many sermons are prepared and preached with more regard for the sermon than the souls of the hearers."[32]—George F. Pentecost

"Some preachers are like the Chinese jugglers. One stood against a wall and the others threw knives at him. They'd hit above his head, close by his ear, under his armpit, and between his fingers. They could throw within a hair's breadth and never strike."[33]—John R. Stott

[31] Whitesell, *Basic New Testament Evangelism*, 105.
[32] Pentecost, "Famous Quotes."
[33] Stott, *Between Two Worlds*, 135–136.

2
Sermon

Evangelistic preaching is communication of the Gospel of Christ and man's needed response. Every preacher wants to communicate this message in understandable terms. There are twenty-eight time-tested, proven traits of the evangelistic sermon that if appropriated will enhance its preparation, preaching, and profit.

Must Be Positive

L. R. Scarborough stated, "The lost sinner wants certainty, and the preacher must preach with conviction if he is to win by his message."[34] Curtis Hutson declares, "People are moved by men who are sure of their ground and speak with authority."[35] Stephen Olford stated the reason why many churches are declining is that preachers are not preaching the authority of Christ in the power of the Holy Spirit. "Without that anointing, there is no purpose, no power, and no authority."[36] Billy Graham said, "Communicate the Gospel with authority. Preach it with assurance, remembering that 'faith comes from hearing the message, and the message is heard through the Word of Christ' (Romans 10:17). If I have one criticism of modern theological education, especially in Europe and America, it is this: I do not think we are putting enough emphasis on authoritative preaching. If you want God's best on your ministry, preach with power and authority."[37]

George W. Truett adds, "Let us who preach remember that we speak by divine authority; not theories, but facts; not what we don't know, but what our souls do know to their profoundest depths. I give it as the humble but deepest conviction of my heart that the overmastering necessity of the

---

[34] L. R. Scarborough, *With Christ*, 77.
[35] Curtis Hutson, "Evangelistic Preaching," 25.
[36] Doy Cave, "Preaching Is Much More."
[37] Douglas, *Work of the Evangelist*, 97.

modern pulpit is a return to that dogmatic tone of authority that characterized the apostles in the preaching of the Gospel and must be found in all effective preaching the world over.... There was an element in Paul's preaching that must needs be in all effective preaching. It was his tone of authority. He believed with all his heart his message, and as God's ambassador he delivered it without quailing for one moment under any fire. It is conviction that convinces. Earth's last place for stammering and indefiniteness is in the pulpit."[38]

James Stewart undergirds this truth of Truett: "The very terms describing the preacher's function—herald, ambassador—manifestly connote authority. Far too often the pulpit has been deferential and apologetic when it ought to have been prophetic and trumpet toned. It has wasted time balancing probabilities and discussing opinions and erecting interrogation marks, when it ought to have been ringing out the note of unabashed, triumphant affirmation—"The mouth of the Lord hath spoken it!"[39] Stewart suggests that this authority is derived from three sources: (1) the fact that it is God's Word, not our own, that we preach; (2) the testimony of pulpit giants of Christian centuries past such as Spurgeon, Augustine and Paul who back and reinforce our preaching; (3) the preacher's possession of the Word due to personal experience.[40]

Preach with confidence knowing that He who called you will enable the delivery and outcome. "When you stand before a group of people to give an evangelistic sermon, the strongest qualification you have, upon which all others rest, is the Spirit-endorsed assurance that you are *called* to do this, that you are doing exactly what the Lord wants *you* to do. In a less profound but equally true sense, you can identify with the words the Lord Jesus applied to Himself from the prophet Isaiah: 'The Spirit of the Lord is upon me, because he has anointed me to

---

[38] Truett, *We Would See Jesus*, 140, 139.
[39] Stewart, *Heralds of God*, 211.
[40] Ibid., 213–217.

preach good news to the poor' (Luke 4:18). If you can say that, what human argument or pressure can persuade you to do anything else?"[41] Always remember in evangelistic preaching that there is no demand upon your spirit that is not also a demand upon His Spirit in you.

One of Spurgeon's "preacher boy" students approached him for advice. "I have been preaching now for some months, and I do not think I have had a single conversion."

Spurgeon said to him, "And do you expect the Lord is going to bless you and save souls every time you open your mouth?"

"No, sir," he replied.

"Well, then," Spurgeon said, "that is why you do not get souls saved. If you had believed, you would have got the blessing."

He wrote, "I had caught him very nicely, but many others would have answered me in just the same way he did. They tremblingly believe it is possible by some mysterious method that once in a hundred sermons God might win a quarter of a soul. They hardly have enough faith to keep them standing upright in their boots; how can they expect God to bless them? I like to go into the pulpit feeling, 'This is God's Word that I am going to deliver in His name; it cannot return to Him void.' I have asked His blessing upon it, and He is bound to give it; and His purposes will be answered, whether my message is a savor of life unto life or of death unto death to those who hear it."[42]

W. B. Riley said, "I believe that the spirit of expectation is a psychological influence that reaches the minds and souls of men. I think that a great auditorium is moved when the lone man, the minister, entertains and expresses that spirit of expectation. I know that psychologically it is true that if he does not express it, their expectation is decreased to that extent; and if

[41] Lorentzen, *Evangelistic Preaching*, 121.
[42] C. H. Spurgeon, *The Soulwinner*, 1989, 58–59.

he does, it is accentuated. And what is expectation of results except another phrase for faith in God?"[43]

W. E. Sangster states that C. H. Spurgeon was the great preacher he was because he never entered the pulpit without remembering that it was through preaching he was saved. He always had the hope that as he opened the Holy Book and preached Christ, someone hearing him would do the same. Sangster concluded in saying, "Expectation filled him, and he took aim."[44]

As you preach, remember it was through preaching that you were saved and thus be reminded of the awesome biblical truth that "it pleased God by the foolishness of preaching to save them that believe" (I Corinthians 1:21). God honors biblically sound evangelistic preaching to the saving of souls. That's what God does. Sangster continues, "Grasp the fact that the heart of the Gospel is a meeting of God and man and preaching provides the best medium for that meeting."[45]

Must Be Biblically Sound

Roy Fish stated, "Much preaching has become the theories of men rather than the Word of God....Sermons have become psychological doses of uplift."[46] The preacher must proclaim the pure and unadulterated Word of God with boldness. "All the fundamental doctrines of the Christian faith have a place in evangelistic preaching."[47]

L. R. Scarborough said of evangelistic preaching, "Though not always consciously doctrinal, it is always latently and potently so. Present in every sermon to point men to God should be the fundamentals of divine truth: Christ's deity; His efficacious and life-giving death; His resurrection; His power now to save; sin, grace, sanctification; the inspiration and

---

[43] Riley, *"Soul-Winning Sermon,"* 19.
[44] Sangster, *Power in Preaching*, 25.
[45] Ibid., 21.
[46] Fish, "Roy Fish [Exhorts] Pastors."
[47] Whitesell, *Basic New Testament Evangelism*, 103.

authority of God's Word. They will give bone, sinew, meat, and vitality to his message."[48] An unknown speaker said, "We must not compromise our message in order to accommodate our method."

R. C. Campbell declared, "We must preach that sinners are doomed in sin and forever damned without Christ. We must, if we are true preachers, warn sinners to flee from the wrath to come. This is no day for a milk and water message. There is a tendency to substitute palatable platitude for probing preaching, formality for spirituality, discipline for diplomacy, organization for omnipotence, until many of us stand in our pulpits impotent paralytics instead of blazing prophets. Some of us are more apathetic than evangelistic, possessed more with the spirit of caution than with the spirit of conquest."[49]

John A. Broadus warns against revival preaching that is "mere claptrap and sensationalism, tirades of cheap wit and vulgar denunciation, extreme and one-sided statements, half-truths and specious errors—all these infect as a deadly poison a large proportion of what is called evangelistic preaching. An earnest and loving, but at the same time faithful and strong, presentation of pure Bible truth on the great matters of sin, judgment, atonement, salvation, regeneration, grace, repentance, and faith is the distinctive and emphatic need of the revival preaching of our age."[50]

"What the preacher says, regardless of how logical and dynamic, will not be as effective as the Word of God."[51] It is the preaching of the Word that is the "power of God unto salvation" (Romans 1:16). The Bible is a hammer that breaks (Jeremiah 23:29); a sword that cuts (Hebrews 4:12); a fire that burns (Jeremiah 20:9); and a light that illuminates (Psalm 119:105). Given the chance, the Word will break up the hardest

---

[48] Scarborough, *With Christ*, 77–78.
[49] Daniels, *Dim Lights*, 93.
[50] Broadus, *Preparation and Delivery*, 1898, 100.
[51] Autrey, *Basic Evangelism,* 120.

soil, cut the most stubborn heart asunder, burn and consume the dross of the most hideous sin, sift from one's life its every contaminant, and illumine the darkest mind of the need of Jesus. Preaching by whatever form must always be scriptural.

"A sin-sick soul needs a 'thus saith the LORD.'"[52] "To this end we shall continue to preach Christ crucified, because what is folly to the intellectualist and a stumbling block to the moralist remains the wisdom and the power of God (I Cor. 1:23–24).[53] R. G. Lee declared, "There is no Gospel if the atoning blood of Christ is omitted, the virgin birth denied, Christ's resurrection eliminated and justification by faith not proclaimed."[54]

Preachers would do well to tell their congregations what Spurgeon proclaimed to his in London, "Hold fast to the Word of God and nothing else; whoever he shall be that shall guide you otherwise, close your ears to him. If at any time, through infirmity or weakness, I should teach you anything which is contrary to this Book, cast it from you; hurl it away as chaff is driven from the wheat; if it be mine and not my Master's, cast it away. Though you love me, though I may have been the means of your conversion to God, think no more of what I say than of the very strangers in the street, if it be not consistent with the teachings of the Most High. Our guide is His written Word; let us keep to this."[55]

Vance Havner identified evangelistic preaching when he wrote, "We need a Whitefield, a Finney, a Moody who will preach the whole scale of Bible truth instead of sawing on one note, who will proclaim a solid, substantial message of sin black and Hell hot and judgment certain and eternity long and salvation free by grace through faith in Christ. There is too much back-fence haranguing and hairsplitting, peddling of

---

[52] Leavell, *Effective Evangelism,* 106.
[53] Stott, *Fundamentalism and Evangelism,* 37.
[54] Knight, *Knight's Illustrations for Today,* 247.
[55] Spurgeon, "Intelligent Obedience."

knickknacks and sandwiches, when men are dying for the meat of the Word."[56]

"Henry Moorehead, in hearing D. L. Moody preach, gave him solemn advice, 'If you will stop preaching your own words and preach God's Word, He will make you a power for good.' Moody took this advice to heart and from that day forward determined to devote himself to Bible study as never before. It had been Moody's practice to draw his sermons from Christian life experiences from the man on the street; now he would preach the Word."[57] O man of God, power is found in the Bible, so preach it.

Evangelistic preaching should include proclamation concerning sin, the law (Ten Commandments), repentance, the Cross, the resurrection, grace, and salvation. Messages on Hell, Heaven, Judgment, the New Birth, Baptism, and the Second Coming are always relevant. C. E. Autrey frankly stated, "We shall not see a revival of spiritual religion come to this earth until God's preachers and missionaries preach the truths that produce it. Justification must be declared with power. Forgiveness rather than a psychiatric treatment must be urgently advocated. Our sick and frustrated world needs a depth of therapy rather than an application of a skin ointment. Our problem is not one of nerves and psychological symptoms, but it is of the heart. It is sin eating away at the vitals of men. Men need forgiveness of sins. They need a real fellowship with the Creator."[58]

"The sermons that are the most likely to convert people," C. H. Spurgeon said, "seem to me to be those that are full of truth—truth about the fall, truth about the Law, truth about human nature and its alienation from God, truth about Jesus Christ, truth about the Holy Spirit, truth about the Everlasting Father, truth about the new birth, truth about obedience to God

---

[56] Havner, *Road to Revival,* 68.
[57] Larsen, *Company of the Preachers.*
[58] Autrey, *Evangelistic Sermons,* 46.

and how we learn it, and all such verities. Tell your hearers something, dear brothers, whenever you preach; tell them something; tell them something! If people are to be saved by a discourse, it must contain at least some measure of knowledge. There must be light as well as fire. Some preachers are all light and no fire, and others are all fire and no light; what we want is both fire and light."[59]

Must Be Personal

W. B. Sprague said, "It is only when men are made to feel that the Gospel comes home to their individual case, that they are themselves the sinners whom it describes, and that they need the blessings which it offers that they hear it to any important purpose."[60] Henry Ward Beecher said, "The longer I live, the more confidence I have in those sermons preached where one man is the congregation, where one man is the minister, where there is no question as to who is meant when the preacher says 'Thou art the man!'" C. H. Spurgeon could preach to audiences of 3,000 or 23,000 and make everyone present feel as if he were speaking to him personally.[61]

Daniel Webster declared, "When a man preaches to me, I want him to make it a personal matter, a personal matter, a personal matter!"[62] John Wesley "seemed to see into men's souls, putting his finger on hidden sins. People felt as if Wesley was speaking to them alone."[63] A person saved in a London crusade said of the preaching of Billy Graham, "I felt as though I was the only person in the arena and that every word was meant for me."[64]

Ralph Lewis states that directness in preaching greatly enhances it. "Some recent writers about preaching have warned

---

[59] Spurgeon, *The Soul Winner*, 90–91.
[60] Sprague, *Lectures on Revivals*, 65.
[61] Blackwood, *The Preparation of Sermons*, 163.
[62] Broadus, *Preparation and Delivery*, 1979, 165.
[63] Duewel, *Revival Fire*, 89.
[64] Long, *Legacy of Billy Graham*, 135.

against the minister's overuse of 'you' and 'I.' But I have come to agree with H. H. Farmer, the British writer on preaching, who says it is impossible to preach in the New Testament sense without coming to 'you' of direct personal application." Lewis adds that the word "you" or "your" is used or implied 221 times in the Sermon on the Mount and that in the Epistles a recurring concentration of "you" is used in direct address.[65] Lewis concludes, "Direct address is one of the most common characteristics of biblical preaching. And yet it is so often overlooked."[66]

I read the story of a preacher who told his congregation, "You are going to Hell because you are too generous. When I preach a sermon, you on the front row say, 'That is not for me' and pass it on to the second row. Those in the second row say, 'That is not for me' and pass it on to the third row. You folk pass it back behind you until the sermon is passed out the back door. No one feels it was for him." Evangelistic preaching is pointed, direct preaching to the unsaved, compelling them to face the urgent need of salvation.

To make the sermon personal, the evangelistic preacher, in addition to biblical substance and direct address, must utilize eye contact with the congregation.

Must Be Passionate

Richard Baxter said, "I preached as never sure to preach again and as a dying man to dying men."[67] The evangelist should preach likemindedly. Surely if the sermon does not evoke emotion in the evangelist, it will not with the congregation. G. K. Chesterton said, "It's a sin to present the Gospel—the greatest story ever told—in a dull, uninspired, joyless, and humorless manner."[68] Henry Ward Beecher commented, "If a man sleeps under my preaching, I do not send someone to

---

[65] Lewis and Lewis, *Inductive Preaching,* 142.
[66] Ibid., 143.
[67] Ryken, *Worldly Saints,* 107.
[68] John, "Evangelistic Preaching."

wake him up, but I feel someone needs to come and wake me up."[69] L. R. Scarborough said, "Any end of the Gospel is good, just so it's the hot end."[70] Preacher, preach the hot end!

"Theme, text, illustrations, will not make an evangelistic preacher. You may recall Bagehot's reflection upon Mr. Gladstone's oratory: 'A man must not only know what to say, he must have a vehement longing to get up and say it.'"[71] John Stott stated, "But we should not fear genuine emotion. If we can preach Christ crucified and remain altogether unmoved, we must have a hard heart indeed. More to be feared than emotion is cold professionalism, the dry, detached utterance of a lecture which has neither heart nor soul in it."[72] "A lot of preaching is motivated by love of preaching, not love of people."[73] It is he who speaks with a fire in his bosom and tears in his eye who is able to be used of God to draw men to Christ. Start low, aim high and catch fire as you move through the sermon.

A minister asked the actor Macready how he was able to attract great crowds by fiction, while he preached the truth without any crowds at all. "This is quite simple," Macready replied, "I can tell you the difference between us. I present my fiction as if it were truth; you present the truth as if it were fiction."[74] These chaffing words are sadly true regarding preaching today.

E. J. Daniels stated, "Even Bible truth must be on fire if it is to burn into the hearts of its hearers. The greatest theme is lifeless when delivered by a cold-hearted preacher. This explains why many highly educated ministers fail to warm the hearts of their hearers while some hot-hearted country parson can stir the

[69] Henry Ward Beecher, "If a Man Sleeps."

[70] John Rice, *Soulwinner's Fire*, 86–87.

[71] Coffin, *Evangelistic Preaching*, 36.

[72] Stott, *Preacher's Portrait*, 51.

[73] Havner, "Sermon Illustrations."

[74] Stott, *Between Two Worlds*, 284.

same listeners to tears and actions."[75] James Stewart declared, "There is something wrong if a man, charged with the greatest news in the world, can be listless and frigid and feckless and dull. Who is going to believe that the tidings brought by the preacher matter literally more than anything else on earth if they are presented with no sort of verve or fire or attack, and if the man himself is apathetic and uninspired, afflicted with spiritual coma and unsaying by his attitude what he says in words?"[76]

Must Be Plain

Perhaps the greatest compliment I have received in the aftermath of preaching an evangelistic sermon is, "Thank you for making it plain." C. H. Spurgeon commented, "When a man does not make me understand what he means, it is because he does not himself know what he means....It is not enough to be so plain that you can be understood; you must speak so that you cannot be misunderstood."[77]A veteran minister once gave some sound advice to a young preacher when he told him to keep preaching on the simple but great texts of the Bible, making it clear to people how to be saved. That's advice I have sought to heed throughout my ministry.

At Amsterdam '83, I heard John Wesley White state that Billy Graham preached a sermon to a native tribe in a third world country and then delivered the same sermon at Harvard. Graham knew the importance of keeping the message simple and clear. James Stewart said, "You never preach the Gospel unless you preach it with simplicity."[78] He said further, "If you shoot over the heads of your hearers, you don't prove anything except you have a poor aim."[79]

---

[75] Daniels, *Dim Lights,* 88.

[76] Stewart, *Heralds of God,* 41.

[77] Michael, *Spurgeon on Leadership,* 25–26.

[78] Douglas, *Work of the Evangelist,* 98.

[79] Ibid.

L. R. Scarborough said about the preaching of Jesus, "He never used big words. All of his illustrations were drawn from common life. He expounded the most mysterious doctrines, but always in the terms of common life. He always made himself understood when he sought to do it."[80] Billy Graham said, "I have never been able to find anyone who could write (sermons or speeches) for me. The sentences must be extremely brief, paragraphs brief and extremely simple. The average American has a working vocabulary of 600 words; the average clergyman has a vocabulary of 5,000 words. As I have grown older, I have had to study to be simple."[81]

In observing the North Greenville University choral practice prior to singing at the South Carolina Baptist Convention, the director cautioned its members, "What *you* hear is not what *they* hear." Great advice for the evangelistic preacher: What you hear yourself speaking is not necessarily what the audience hears. You hear yourself saying clearly, "Ye must be born again," but the Nicodemuses in the congregation hear you saying it is a must for them to be born of their mother a second time. What you hear is not necessarily what the audience hears, so work hard at laying aside the words of Zion for simpler words that bear the same meaning.

Vance Havner humorously said that a theologian was someone who took something simple and made it complicated. Evangelistic sermon preachers must avoid becoming "theologians" in this sense, determining ever to keep the message of the Gospel on the lowest rung so all can comprehend and respond. Curtis Hutson stated, "Good preaching is not complicating a simple matter but simplifying a complicated matter."[82] Hutson continues, "If you want results, say what a ten-year-old Sunday school child could understand."[83]

---

[80] Scarborough, *How Jesus Won Men,* 191–192.
[81] Graham, *Life Wisdom,* 117.
[82] Hutson, "Evangelistic Preaching."
[83] Ibid.

Billy Sunday said, "Put the cookies on the lower shelf so all can reach them."[84] L. R. Scarborough told of a great compliment he heard on a simple preacher when many were saved in a meeting in which he spoke. "In every sermon he makes the way and plan of salvation simple so that any sinner, young or old, can, if at all under conviction and attentive, find the way to Christ." Scarborough then stated, "We should never presume on the wisdom of sinners. We best regard the oldest and wisest of unsaved men as children and make the way of life plain and simple to everyone."[85]

> The plodding multitudes will never be benefitted by preaching which requires them to bring a dictionary with them to the house of God....The Reformation banished an unknown tongue from the reading desk; we need another to banish it from the pulpit.—C. H. Spurgeon[86]

"Deeply loved expressions which are full of meaning for church people may seem offensively hollow to those who have not learned their content. Technical terms in any field are the shorthand which must be written out in full for the uninitiated."[87] Roy Fish advises regarding the evangelistic sermon, "Study the people who will hear your message. As you're planning your preaching, jettison the jargon. Forget the 'language of Zion.' Be willing to be flexible in the use of terminology. You may have to think of another word for 'regeneration' or think of an illustration for redemption."[88] "Use language that connects."[89] Larry Sabotoe of the Center of Politics stated on Fox News, September 30, 2008, "Language matters vitally in politics." But it matters most in preaching.

---

[84] Streett, *The Effective Invitation,* 156.
[85] Scarborough, *How Jesus Won Men,* 190–191.
[86] Spurgeon, *Flashes of Thought,* 408.
[87] Sweazey, *Effective Evangelism,* 172.
[88] Koonce, "Evangelistic Preaching Is a Must."
[89] Augsburger, *Preaching Evangelistically.*

A cartoon depicts a dog sitting next to its owner with the caption, "What we say to dogs." The owner is reprimanding the dog for its bad behavior with phrases like, "Bad dog, Ginger. I have had it with you. From now on, you stay out of the dustbin. Do you understand me, Ginger? Do you?" The next scene has the caption "What dogs hear." What the dog is actually hearing is, "Blah, blah, blah, Ginger. Blah, blah, blah, blah. Blah, blah, blah, blah, Ginger." What the preacher says and what the people actually hear can be vastly different!

C. H. Spurgeon states, "My brethren, the preaching of the gospel minister should always have soul winning for its object. I have felt as though I could weep tears of blood that the time of the congregation on the Sabbath should be wasted by listening to wordy rhetoric, when what was wanted was a plain, urgent pleading with men's hearts and consciences."[90] Speaking of well-refined, polished ministers who speak with great eloquence but never win souls in their preaching, Spurgeon comments, "I know not how it is, but another man comes with his very simple language but with a warm heart and straightway men are converted to God."[91]

E. J. Daniels stated in regard to preaching, "Often in striving to be deep you only become difficult to understand. Many ministers who are said to be deep are just plain muddy—not clear!"[92] A great preacher was asked "If you were to put into one sentence a message of counsel to your brother preachers in England and around the world, what would it be?" This preacher responded, "It would be this: O brother preachers, make it plain to the people how they are saved."

---

[90] Spurgeon, *Spurgeon's Sermons on Soulwinning,* 99–100.
[91] Ibid., 16.
[92] Daniels, *Dim Lights,* 90.

Must Be Empowered by the Holy Spirit

Evangelistic preaching is Holy Spirit empowered preaching. It must cut to the quick of a man's heart and conscience leading him to see his sinful condition and need of salvation. Preaching that does not reach the conscience is futile, and only preaching endued from on high by the Holy Spirit can accomplish this. The apostle Paul declared, "Because the Good News we brought to you came not only with words, but with power, with the Holy Spirit, and with sure knowledge that it is true" (I Thessalonians 1:5 New Century Version).

Peter's sermon at Pentecost "pricked" the hearts of the hearers leading them to cry out, "Men and brethren, what shall we do? Then Peter said unto them, Repent, and be baptized every one of you in the name of Jesus Christ for the remission of sins, and ye shall receive the gift of the Holy Ghost" (Acts 2:38). The word "prick" means "to pierce slightly with a sharp point; to affect with anguish, grief, or remorse; to ride, guide, or urge on with or as if with spurs." Evangelistic preaching is 'pricking' preaching that penetrates the heart with conviction of sin, judgment and things to come. C. H. Spurgeon stated, "Spread your sail; but remember what you sometimes sing, 'I can only spread the sail; Thou must breathe the auspicious gale.' Only be sure you have the sail up. Do not miss the gale for want of preparation."[93]

John Stott stated, "But if human beings are in reality spiritually and morally blind, deaf, dumb, lame, and even dead, not to mention the prisoners of Satan, then it is ridiculous in the extreme to suppose that by ourselves and our merely human preaching we can reach or rescue people in such a plight. Only Jesus Christ by his Holy Spirit can open blind eyes and deaf ears, make the lame walk and the dumb speak, prick the conscience, enlighten the mind, fire the heart, move the will, give life to the dead, and rescue slaves from Satanic bondage.

---

[93] Spurgeon, *Morning and Evening*, Jan. 30.

And all this He can and does, as the preacher should know from his own experience."[94]

There is a difference between "soulish preaching" and "anointed preaching," according to Adrian Rogers. "Soulish preaching" (personality) is preaching that "does not cause fruit to remain, because man is preaching outside the anointing of God's Spirit." The "soulish preacher" attempts to persuade through human reason, but it will not ultimately change the individual, though it may be packaged with entertainment and information. "Anointed preaching" is the enlightening, empowering, and quickening of the preacher by the Holy Spirit. Rogers remarks that ministers can easily mistake "soulish preaching" for "anointed preaching."[95]

Greg Heisler, in *Spirit-Led Preaching,* comments, "If Spirit-empowered sermons are going to be preached, then a Spirit-led approach to preaching must be followed. Spirit-led preaching is more about a mind-set than a method. It is directed toward keeping our hearts aligned with the Spirit rather than just keeping our outlines in line with the same letter....The preacher who is Spirit-driven, Spirit-led, and Spirit-dependent will also be Spirit-empowered."[96]

The fourteenth-century preacher John Tauler was his generation's most powerful preacher, according to C. E. Autrey. There came a time in which he realized he preached to perform more than to bless and pulled away from the pulpit to pray long hours. On a Sunday when the crowds from all over Europe came to his church to hear him preach, he did not show. Attendants soon found him in his study upon his knees in prayer. When they urged him to preach to the waiting congregation, Tauler responded, "Go back and tell the audience I will not preach today. Neither shall I ever preach again unless God comes with me into the pulpit." Tauler continued his praying

---

[94] Stott, *I Believe in Preaching,* 329.
[95] Rogers and Patterson, *Love Worth Finding,* 157.
[96] Heisler, *Spirit-Led Preaching,* 4.

for days, not showing to preach to the crowds that continuously came to his church. Finally when he returned to the pulpit, he did so with such power that within a few minutes of his sermon many people were so convicted that they fell prostrate along the benches, in the aisles and upon the floor.[97] The evangelistic preacher must be of the attitude of Tauler, waiting for God's empowering from on High before entering the pulpit.

C. H. Spurgeon cautions, "A primary qualification for serving God with any amount of success and for doing God's work well and triumphantly is a sense of our own weakness. When God's warrior marches forth to battle strong in his own might, when he boasts, 'I know that I shall conquer; my own right arm and my conquering sword shall get unto me the victory,' defeat is not far distant. God will not go forth with that man who marches in his own strength. He who reckoneth on victory thus has reckoned wrongly, for 'it is not by might, nor by power, but by my Spirit, saith the Lord of hosts.'"[98]

John Piper chimes in on this same note in stating, "How utterly dependent we are on the Holy Spirit in the work of preaching! You wake up on Sunday morning, and you can smell the smoke of Hell on one side and feel the crisp breezes of Heaven on the other. You go to your study and look down at your pitiful manuscript, and you kneel down and cry, 'God, this is so weak! Who do I think I am? What audacity to think that in three hours my words will be the odor of death to death and the fragrance of life to life (II Corinthians 2:16)!'"[99] We all identify with Piper, do we not?

The Holy Spirit must seize the minister, giving divine light as he prepares the evangelistic sermon through study of the biblical text, commentary research, the gathering of the lumber to build the house, and its actual outline and content. The sermon once developed must be energized by the Holy Spirit in

---

[97] Autrey, *Basic Evangelism*, 68.
[98] Spurgeon, *Morning and Evening*, November 4.
[99] Piper, *Supremacy of God*, 37–38.

the preacher for effective delivery to the end souls may be saved. Thus with regard to preaching to win souls, the Holy Spirit must consume the preacher from start to finish.

Must Be Pointed

A young preacher asked a friend after one of his sermons, "Did I preach too long?" The friend responded, "You did not preach too long, but you talked too much after you stopped preaching." In the early church, sermons by the Latin Fathers were relatively short, lasting ten to fifteen minutes. Long sermons arrived upon the scene after the Reformation, especially among the Puritans, who counted preaching as the supreme devotional exercise. Length of preaching was an hour, gauged by the sandglass. Once the sand was expended, the preacher was to stop unless the audience would grant him "another glass."

Wesley rarely preached longer than thirty minutes; Whitefield advised a time frame for preaching of no more than forty minutes; McLaren seldom preached less than forty-five minutes. Spurgeon would tell his students, "Whatever else you preach about, preach about forty minutes!"[100] Adam Clarke stated, "It is not essential to a sermon that it be a half hour or an hour long. Some preach more in ten minutes than others in sixty."[101] "If you ask me," Spurgeon advised, "how you may shorten your sermons, I should say, *study them better.* Spend more time in the study that you may need less in the pulpit."[102] Martin Luther adds, "Some plague the people with too long sermons, for the faculty of listening is a tender thing and soon becomes weary and satiated."[103]

John Bisagno embraces the conviction that preachers should preach shorter sermons and give longer invitations.[104] Billy

---

[100] *Homiletic Review,* Vol. LIX, 456
[101] Adam Clarke, *Letter to a preacher,* 41.
[102] Spurgeon, *Lectures to My Students,* 135.
[103] Luther, Quotationsbook
[104] Bisagno, Personal Correspondence.

Graham was asked by the Religion News Service in 2005 what has changed in his sermon delivery over the years. Graham responded, "My sermons are shorter than they used to be."[105] Adrian Rogers stated, "A thirty-minute sermon is amply sufficient for today's society."[106] Woodrow Wilson's reply to a person who asked how long it took him to prepare a ten-minute speech was, "Two weeks"; to prepare an hour speech, "One week"; to prepare a two-hour speech, "I am ready now."[107]

Conciseness in the sermon requires more midnight toil than sermons akin to the energizer bunny that just go on and on, but the payoff is well worth the additional blood, sweat, and tears. The reduction of the *quantity* of the evangelistic sermon enhances the *quality* and effectiveness of the sermon, if prepared studiously.

Alice in Wonderland gives the preacher excellent advice regarding sermon length. "Where shall I begin, please your majesty?" she asked. "Begin at the beginning," the king said very gravely, "and go on till you come to the end; then stop."[108]

It's an old saying, but it bears truth to be heeded: "Stand up, speak up, and shut up."

Must Be Saturated with Prayer

Evangelistic preaching is dedicated *to* prayer (saturation); determined *by* prayer (subject); developed *through* prayer (structure); dependent *upon* prayer (success), delivered *in* prayer (strength) but is doomed *without* prayer. C. H. Spurgeon, in a sermon to his congregation, underscored the importance of prayer by the preacher for those to whom he was to speak: "Oh, if we (ministers) do not pray for you, my dear hearers, our preaching to you will be hypocrisy! We shall never speak to man with any power of *persuasion,* unless first we speak to God for men with power of *supplication!* Not without

---

[105] Adler, comp., *Ask Billy Graham,* 164.
[106] Rogers and Patterson, *Love Worth Finding,* 196.
[107] Stewart, *Heralds of God,* 136.
[108] Lewis Carroll, *Alice in Wonderland,* 180.

many a prayer and many a heaving of my heart in sighs have I come here to speak tonight. I believe that I am sent to find out some appointed for Christ in the divine purpose and covenant, and I pray my Master that there may be many such!"[109]

Pray for the evangelistic text for the sermon and preparation guidance. Pray for the people to whom you will speak. Pray that obstacles will be torn asunder and a bridge will be erected by the Holy Spirit over which you can walk with the Gospel. Pray distractions will not arise. Pray for divine sensitivity in preaching and pleading. Pray for receptivity to the Gospel. Pray for a warm heart and liberty in its delivery.

E. M. Bounds wrote, "The character of our praying will determine the character of our preaching. Light praying makes light preaching."[110] C. H. Spurgeon added, "If there be any man under Heaven who is compelled to carry out the precept 'pray without ceasing,' surely it is the Christian minister.... How much of blessing we may have missed through remissness in supplication we can scarcely guess, and none of us can know how poor we are in comparison with what we might have been if we had lived habitually nearer to God in prayer....The fact is, the secret of all ministerial success lies in prevalence at the mercy seat."[111] W. E. Sangster stated, "Unction comes only of praying....Able preaching can often reveal the cleverness of man. 'What clear distinctions! What dexterous use of words! What telling illustrations!' Unction reveals the presence of God."[112]

George W. Truett was pastor of the First Baptist Church in Dallas, Texas, and one of history's greatest evangelistic preachers. It was this man's holy habit to enter his library to study and pray daily from 7 P.M. until midnight.[113] In light of

---

[109] Spurgeon, "An Urgent Request."

[110] Wiersbe, "Your Preaching Is Unique."

[111] Spurgeon, *Lectures to My Students,* 42, 49.

[112] Sangster, *Power in Preaching,* 21.

[113] Rosscup, *How to Preach Biblically,* 56.

this, it is no wonder God used him so effectively in winning souls in the pulpit and in private.

Henry Holloman, professor of systematic theology at Talbot School of Theology, has said, "Behind every good biblical preacher is much hard labor in preparation. However, only prayer can assure that his work is not wasted and that his message will spiritually impact the hearers. As the biblical preacher interweaves prayer with his preparation, he should focus on certain petitions: (1) that he will receive God's message...in spiritual as well as mental *comprehension*,...(2) that's God message will first grip his own heart in strong *conviction*, (3) that he will clearly and correctly convey God's message in the power of the Spirit in effective *communication*, (4) that the Spirit will use the message to produce proper response and change...spiritual *transformation*,...and (5) that the whole process and finished product will accomplish God's purpose in *glorification* of God through Christ."[114]

W. E. Sangster declared, "The praying that affects preaching is the praying that has saturated its every part...From beginning to end preaching must be impregnated with prayer."[115] Spurgeon advises about praying, "One warm, hearty prayer is worth twenty of those packed in ice."[116]

Must Be Compassionate, Tender and Loving

It has been said that before a person will listen to what you have to say, they want to know how much you care. It is important that you preach from the heart, not just the head. People must come to realize that you are interested in their hurts, disappointments, struggles and failures and desire to help. A great preacher stated, "On every pew is a broken heart." Reach out to the unsaved with a tear in your eye (Psalm 126:5–6). Don't hide your emotions in preaching; let people hear and see the painful sorrow you bear for them. "We cannot

---

[114] Ibid., 58.
[115] Sangster, *Power in Preaching,* 98.
[116] Spurgeon, "Prayer-Meetings."

be priests on their behalf, unless like Aaron we wear their names upon our breasts. We must love, or we cannot bless... when love is gone; it is like a smith working without fire or a builder without mortar....Where there is no love, there will be no life."[117]

A biographer of Robert M. M'Cheyne stated that everywhere he stepped Scotland trembled and that whenever he opened his mouth a spiritual force seemed to sweep in every direction. A traveler, eager to see where M'Cheyne had preached, went to his old church. An old sexton agreed to give him a tour. In M'Cheyne's study, the old gentleman ordered, "Sit in that chair." Before him on the table was an open Bible. "Drop your head in that book and weep. That is what our minister always did before he preached," said the old man. He then led the visitor to the pulpit before another open Bible. "Stand there," he said, "and drop your head on your hands and let the tears flow. That was the way our minister always conducted himself before he began to preach!"[118] What a worthy example for preachers today!

C. H. Spurgeon, in his sermon "When the Preacher Has No Burden for the Souls of Men," stated, "And what shall I say of the unfaithful preacher, the slumbering watchman of souls, the man who swore at God's altar that he was called of the Holy Ghost to preach the Word of God, the man upon whose lips men's ears waited with attention while he stood like a priest at God's altar to teach Israel God's law, the man who performed his duties half asleep in a dull and careless manner until men slept too and thought religion a dream? What shall I say of the minister of unholy life whose corrupt practice out of the pulpit has made the most telling things in the pulpit to be of no avail, who has blunted the edge of the sword of the Spirit and turned the back of God's army in the day of battle? Ay, what shall I say of the man who has amused his audience with pretty things

---

[117] Spurgeon, *Come Ye Children*, 28–29.
[118] Michael Tan, *Hearts Aflame*, 12.

when he ought to have aroused the conscience, who has been rounding periods when he ought to have pronounced the judgment of God, who has been preaching a dead morality when he ought to have lifted Christ on high as Moses lifted the serpent in the wilderness? What shall I say of the men who out of the pulpit have made a jest of the most solemn things, whose life has been so devoid of holy passion and devout enthusiasm that men have thought truth to be fiction, religion a stage play, a prayer a nullity, the Spirit of God a phantom, and eternity a joke?

"If I must perish, let me suffer anyhow but not as a minister who has desecrated the pulpit by a slumbering style of ministry, by a want of passion for souls. God knoweth how oftimes this body trembles with horror at the thought lest the blood of souls should be required at my hands. I cannot understand that lifeless performance of duty, that cold and careless going through of services which, alas, is too common. How shall such men answer for it at the bar of God—the smooth things, the polite and honeyed words, the daubing of men with untempered mortar of peace, peace, when they should have dealt with them honestly as in God's name."[119]

General William Booth was notified by one of his captains that the work was so difficult that no progress had been made. Booth replied with two words, "Try tears." Success soon was known in the work.[120] As we preach, may we do as Fanny Crosby in the hymn "Rescue the Perishing" suggests and "weep o'er the erring one, lift up the fallen" and "tell them of Jesus the mighty to save."[121]

Must Be Pressing

The evangelistic message must be delivered with a sense of urgency. When I was a young evangelist, a pastor told me prior to a service, "Frank, preach as if I was lost and to die at the end

---

[119] Spurgeon, "Preacher Has No Burden," 412.
[120] Taylor, *Why Revival Still Tarries,* 18.
[121] Crosby, *Songs of Devotion.*

of the service." In reality, for all we know a lost soul sits before us as we preach, hearing his last sermon. May we preach as if it was so!

A preacher was to speak to inmates at a large prison. The afternoon prior to the day he was to speak, he visited the prison. The warden guided him to the chapel where he would soon speak. "It will be full tomorrow morning, sir," said the warden. The preacher noted two front chairs draped in black and asked why they were so draped. The warden replied, "The two men who will occupy those seats tomorrow are under sentence of death. On Monday they go to the electric chair!"

The preacher inquired, "Do I understand that this will be the last service they will ever attend?"

"Yes sir," was the reply. "Your sermon will be the last one they will ever hear."

The preacher went home and tore up the sermon he had prepared feeling it would not meet the need. Upon his knees, he prayed, "O God, give me a message for those two men who will be sitting in those draped chairs."[122] The evangelistic preacher must prepare adequately and preach urgently due to the many chairs blackly draped in the church in which he preaches.

History sadly reminds us of the time that the great evangelist D. L. Moody failed to give an invitation, wanting to give the people time to think over their decision. He had preached on the subject *What Shall I Do Then with Jesus Who Is Called the Christ?* That night (October 8, 1871), the great Chicago fire spread through the city, and by the next day the city lay in ashes. Moody said failing to give an invitation that night was his greatest mistake. In his message "The Fire Sermon," which he preached over twenty years later on the anniversary of that awful night, he said, "I have never seen that congregation since. I have hard work to keep back the tears

---

[122] Raymond Barber, "Ready to Preach."

today…but I want to tell you one lesson I learned that night which I have never forgotten, and that is, when I preach, to press Christ upon the people then and there and try to bring them to decision on the spot. I would rather have that right hand cut off than to give an audience now a week to decide what to do with Jesus."[123] Moody's words, "…when I preach, to press Christ upon the people then and there and try to bring them to decision on the spot," speak of the urgency necessary in preaching evangelistically.[124] The evangelistic message rings the bell of immediate decision for Christ (II Corinthians 6:2).

Must Be Pertinent for the Audience

The evangelistic sermon must be relevant to the people it addresses. It would be inappropriate to preach a scorching sermon on Hell to children. Shape the evangelistic message for the targeted audience. Stuart Briscoe, referring to the importance of the proper site for the sermon, shared what he called a bizarre example. "Imagine," he said, "what it would be like to transport Chicago office workers to India and Indian pilgrims to Chicago. This would have been necessary if careful site selection had not been made in the case of the Taj Mahal and Sears Tower…but [that would be] not much more bizarre than some sermons which have been erected on most unsuitable sites."[125]

C. H. Spurgeon states, "The Holy Spirit can convert a soul by any text of Scripture, apart from your paraphrase, your comment or you exposition. But you know there are certain Scriptures that are the best to bring to the minds of sinners."[126] Ask the Holy Spirit to guide in the selection of the evangelistic text, its preparation and presentation. Solomon declares, "A word fitly spoken is like apples of gold in pictures of silver" (Proverbs 25:11). Henry Ward Beecher, in his book *Lectures*

---

[123] Gunther, "The Fire Sermon," 7–8.
[124] Ibid.
[125] Bodey, *Inside the Sermon*, 44.
[126] Spurgeon, *The Soulwinner*, 84.

on Preaching, stated, "Preaching will be proper or improper, wise or successful, in proportion as it adapts itself to the special want of the different peoples and the different classes of people in any one time."[127]

The words of John Calvin regarding pastoral preaching apply to evangelistic preaching equally, "What advantage would there be if we were to stay here half a day and I were to expound half a book without considering you or your profit and edification?…We must take into consideration those persons to whom the teaching is addressed.…For this reason let us note well that they who have this charge to teach, when they speak to a people, are to decide which teaching will be good and profitable so that they will be able to disseminate it faithfully and with discretion to the usefulness of everyone individually."[128]

Must Be Illustrated

C. H. Spurgeon remarked, "A sermon without illustrations is like a house without windows." Andrew Blackwood cautioned, "Sometimes windows in a building weaken the walls and mar the design."[129] The preacher must use discernment as to the usage of illustrations. Lionel B. Fletcher stated, "The illustration must grip you, or it will not grip through you. The preacher must live the story, or he will not make the story live before the people."[130] "When good illustrations are used, the sermon is presented in pictures. And it is important to make men see as well as hear the sermon."[131]

Haddon Robinson underscored the importance of illustrations in this manner, "When preachers stand up in the pulpit, they face audiences with their guard up. A few in the congregation wait eagerly for the sermon to begin. Most wait eagerly for the sermon to conclude. Like Nathan before them, the preach-

---

[127] Beecher, *Lectures on Preaching,* 230.
[128] Adam, *Speaking God's Words,* 132–133.
[129] Blackwood, *Preparation of Sermons,* 159.
[130] Fletcher, *The Effective Evangelist,* 212.
[131] Hutson, "Evangelistic Preaching."

ers have to smash through barricades erected by indifference, confusion, comfort, and guilt. Preachers must turn ears into eyes and free listeners to think with pictures in their heads. Appropriate illustrations do that....Effective preachers stalk and store illustrations to tell the truth in fresh ways."[132] Work hard in the evangelistic sermon to provide "bridges" to comprehension through storytelling, illustration, and example.

Jesus utilized stories to drive home a doctrinal or practical point. "It is important to underscore that Jesus' stories were never utilized as an end in themselves. His stories were strategic. They were a means to an end. It is increasingly popular these days to equate biblical preaching with mere storytelling. While stories are important, we must know how they function. The Bible and its preachers utilized stories for life-changing purposes, and we should do the same....If we are to enlist stories and illustrations in our preaching, they must be employed to give life to the principles we are expounding."[133]

John Bisagno writes, "Ninety-five per cent of the preachers I listen to are telling me stories from Scotland or England and France about Lord Chancellery, vicar of England, or Baron 'Von Whosoever' of Scotland in the seventeenth century. Get rid of those old sermon illustration books and get into life. Read today's authors. Read modern books of sermon illustrations. Read *People, Time, Newsweek, USA Today*, and your local newspaper. Listen to the radio. Listen to television, particularly the evening news. Get among your people. Get out into the real world and find real, live, relevant illustrations."[134]

Perry and Whitesell cite ten purposes of the illustration in the sermon: to illustrate the subject, to obtain and hold interest, to establish rapport with the audience, to rest the audience, to strengthen argument, to bring conviction of sin, to persuade, to aid the memory, to ornament the sermon, and to stimulate the

---

[132] Green, ed., *Illustrations for Biblical Preaching,* 7.
[133] Fabarez, *Preaching That Changes Lives,* 107–108.
[134] Bisagno, *Letters to Timothy,* 159.

hearers' imagination.[135] Haddon Robinson cautions, "If an illustration has to be explained, don't use it."[136]

Authenticate the truthfulness of the illustration or statistic. Don't let a great evangelistic sermon be undermined by an incorrect fact or untrue illustration. As a rule, it is best to select short illustrations over longer ones. A final caution regarding use of the illustration in preaching comes from the pen of Stephen Olford, "To tell a story or anecdote simply for the sake of humor or dramatic effect is unpardonable for the consecrated and conscientious evangelist."[137]

Must Be Properly Packaged

The type of packaging utilized with the evangelistic sermon must "fit" the preacher. Styles of packaging the evangelistic sermon include expository, biographical, narrative, textual, topical, and testimonial. Regardless of the style (pattern) of preaching utilized, the evangelistic sermon must be founded in Holy Scripture and flow from start to finish building one point upon another until the crucial appeal of invitation is extended. "Sermon style is to be your servant, not your master. Whatever pattern you use, it must help accomplish your single aim to make the Gospel clear so that sinners will come to Christ when you invite them. You want people to leave the meeting praising the Savior, not complimenting your style."[138]

John Bisagno exhorts, "If you want a hearing, be yourself. Don't act like a preacher, don't look like a preacher, and don't talk like a preacher. Someone said, "So live that no one will suspect you're a preacher but if they find out you are, they won't be surprised." If preaching is a symphony, it should always be played in the key of "B natural."[139]

---

[135] Perry and Whitesell, *Variety in Your Preaching,* 111–117.
[136] Robinson, "Preaching the Old Testament."
[137] Douglas, *Work of the Evangelist,* 778.
[138] Lorentzen, *Evangelistic Preaching,* 112.
[139] Bisagno, *Letters to Timothy,* 163, 162.

When you're trying to reach people in the community, you can't yell at them. The reason preachers yelled 100 years ago was they didn't have public address systems. If they wanted to talk with a person in the back row, they had to yell so they could be heard. In some traditions, yelling is equal to preaching....[The] conversational element in delivery is far more appealing to people today.—Haddon Robinson[140]

Manner (packaging) of preaching can and should vary with regard to type and place of audience. As an evangelist, the theme of my preaching (evangelistic services) never changes, but the form of delivery does to fit the audience (children, student, adult) and place (church, camp, classroom, conference).

Must Be Freely Proclaimed

In the evangelistic sermon delivery, the preacher should take every measure to insure he is not encumbered by manuscript or notes. This is not to state that notes are not to be used, but if they are used, they should be used discreetly and unobtrusively.

Must Be Priority in Service

The evangelistic sermon is not to take back stage to singing, testifying, or announcements. It is the pivotal part of the service and must be given prime time. The evangelistic preacher ought to be in the pulpit no later than twenty-five minutes from the starting time, and sooner if possible.

Must Be Practiced

One pitcher may earn over $2 million a year for delivering a baseball across home plate, while another pitcher at the same time is delivering the same priced baseball to the same plate for $50,000 a year. The difference is not the baseball, but its

---

[140] Robinson, "Interview."

delivery.[141] Sadly, too many pastors and evangelists fail to deliver their message effectively. "Their material is excellent; the delivery is poor."[142] The great pitchers practice continuously throwing a baseball. Practice preaching and delivering the evangelistic sermon. I have rehearsed my sermons before the ocean, stars, mirrors, and cow pastures, seeking to burn them in my heart and improve delivery in the church. I have found it profitable to rehearse them time and again upon my knees before God. I am not the preacher I used to be, and by God's grace and my practice, I'm not the preacher I am going to be. The evangelist must continuously work at improving the delivery of the sermon. In the delivery of the evangelistic sermon, work hard not to have it just in hand and head, but in heart.

Must Be Persuasive

It is the goal of evangelistic preaching to persuade men to be reconciled to God. At the beginning of the sermon and interwoven throughout the sermon the invitation to be saved should be clearly stated. "And he (Paul) reasoned in the synagogue every sabbath, and *persuaded* the Jews and the Greeks" (Acts 18:4, italics ours). The meaning of *persuade* is "to induce one by words to believe." Matthew Henry remarks regarding this text, "He did not only dispute argumentatively with them, but he followed his arguments with affectionate persuasions, begging of them for God's sake, for their own soul's sake, for their children's sake, not to refuse the offer of salvation made to them...the good effect of his preaching. He persuaded them; that is, he prevailed with them—so some understand it. *In sententiam suam adducebat—He brought them over to his own opinion.* Some of them were convinced by his reasonings and yielded to Christ."[143]

---

[141] Bisagno. *Power of Positive Evangelism,* 8.
[142] Ibid.
[143] Henry, *Commentary,* Acts 18:1–6.

Evangelistic preaching is persuading (not manipulating) sinners both to examine and to respond to the claims of Christ without delay. C. E. Autrey states, "Evangelistic preaching is searching. It reaches the conscience. It brings men face to face with God, with themselves, and with their needs. It lays bare the soul. It discovers sin in the life. It is convincing."[144]

C. H. Spurgeon, in a lecture to ministerial students, said, "We must cultivate *persuasiveness*. Some of our brethren have great influence over men, and yet others with greater gifts are devoid of it. These last do not appear to get near to the people; they cannot grip them and make them feel. There are preachers who in their sermons seem to take their hearers one by one by the buttonhole and drive the truth right into their souls, while others generalize so much and are so cold withal, that one would think they were speaking of dwellers in some remote planet whose affairs did not much concern them. Learn the art of pleading with men. You will do this well if you often see the Lord."[145] "A man can be moved to action if his mind can be convinced that the action is reasonable and if his heart can be convinced that the action is necessary. You must therefore bring your hearer to the point where he says, "I *can* be saved (mind). I *must* be saved (emotions). I *will* be saved (will)."[146]

Must Be Polite

In evangelistic preaching, it is imperative to exhibit a spirit of gentleness, kindness, and approachability. The preacher must cautiously avoid appearing pushy, overly aggressive, manipulative, and insensitive. C. H. Spurgeon stated, "When you preach, speak out straight, but be very tender about it. If there is an unpleasant thing to be said, take care that you put it in the kindest possible form."[147] The preacher must ever be

---

[144] Autrey, *Basic Evangelism*, 120.
[145] Spurgeon, *Lectures to My Students*, 210.
[146] Streett, *Effective Invitation*, 159.
[147] Spurgeon, *Soul Winner*, 78.

cautious that he does not demean or embarrass any person in preaching.

Must Be Preached Humbly

Pride can lead the evangelistic preacher to "manufacture" decisions by manipulation and perversion of the condition for salvation. Pressure to "produce" placed upon the evangelistic preacher by pastors, religious leaders, and church members must not in any way jeopardize his preaching and ministry. G. Campbell Morgan stated, "The true evangelist will be very careful to avoid the possibility of a passion for numbered results spoiling his message. I sometimes fear lest the desire to have large statistical returns may tend to make a man make the way of salvation unduly easy. We have been preaching 'believe,' and we have not sufficiently said 'repent, repent, repent'; and we have still to preach this truth, that unless a man will turn to God from idols, then his faith, though he boast of it, is dead and worthless."[148] Evangelistic preaching must never become "number driven."

Additionally the preacher must guard against arrogance and egotism, ministering both in humility and sympathy. "There is a special danger which comes to those who have done well in evangelism. They are likely to grow less dependent on the sort of anxious prayer which comes from fear and the knowledge of inadequacy....When evangelism becomes merely a matter of well-polished methods, it is finished."[149] John Bunyan once preached an especially powerful sermon. The first person he spoke to afterward told him so. He said, "Yes, I know. The Devil told me that as I walked away from the pulpit." "George H. Morrison was right: 'Preach, not for the salvation of your sermon, but for the salvation of souls.'"[150]

Adam Clarke advised a young preacher, "Never assume an air of importance in the pulpit; you stand in an awful place, and

---

[148] G. Campbell Morgan, *Evangelism,* 82–83.
[149] Sweazey, *Effective Evangelism*, 53.
[150] Wiersbe and Wiersbe, *Elements of Preaching*.

God hates the proud man. Let your demeanor prove that you feel you are speaking before Him who tries the spirit and to whom you are responsible for every word uttered."[151] Leonard Ravenhill declared, "The successful preacher does not end his sermon with the congregation on its feet applauding *him;* but rather, he leaves it on its knees adoring *Him.* "[152]

"'You cannot at the same time give the impression that you are a great preacher [or theologian or debater or whatever] and that Jesus Christ is a great Savior,' [said] James Denney. If you call attention to yourself and your own competence, you cannot effectively call attention to Jesus and his glorious sufficiency."[153]

C. H. Spurgeon, in the sermon *The Approachableness of Jesus,* spoke regarding preacher pride and arrogance: "Oh, dear, dear, the lofty ministerial airs that one has seen assumed by men who ought to have been meek and lowly! What a grand set of men some of the preachers of the past age thought themselves to be! I trust those who played the archbishop have nearly all gone to Heaven, but a few linger among us who use little grace and much starch. The grand divines never shook hands with anybody except, indeed, with the deacons and a little knot of evidently superior persons. Amongst Dissenters it was almost as bad as it is in most church congregations, where you feel that the good man, by his manner, is always saying, 'I hope you know who I am, Sir; I am the rector of the parish.' Now, all that kind of stuck-upishness is altogether wrong."[154]

Must Be Discerning As to a Divine Change

Prepare the evangelistic sermon for its delivery, but ever be sensitive to the Holy Spirit's leadership in changing or altering the message in the eleventh hour. C. H. Spurgeon identified with the struggle of changing messages in the midst of a

---

[151] Clarke, *Letter to a Preacher*, 34–35.
[152] Ravenhill, *Heart Breathings.*
[153] Packer, *Your Father Loves You.*
[154] Spurgeon, "Approachableness of Jesus."

service: "The people were singing, and I was sighing. I was in a strait betwixt two, and my mind hung as in the balances. I was naturally desirous to run in the track which I had carefully planned, but the other text would take no refusal and seemed to tug at my skirts, crying, 'No, no, you must preach from me. God would have you follow me.' I deliberated within myself as to my duty, for I would neither be fanatical nor unbelieving, and at the last I thought within myself, *Well, I should like to preach the sermon which I have prepared, and it's a great risk to run to strike out a new line of thought; but still, as this text constrains me, it may be of the Lord, and therefore I will venture upon it, come what may.*" Spurgeon concluded, "Anything is better than mechanical sermonizing in which the direction of the Spirit is practically ignored. Every Holy Ghost preacher, I have no doubt, will have such recollections clustering his ministry."[155]

This certainly has been my experience on occasions. In preaching I have discovered it is best to focus most on outcome, not outline, yielding to the Holy Spirit's lead. In regard to evangelistic messages, John Bisagno advises, "There may be reasons why you will need to change, and we must be sensitive to the Holy Spirit as to what to preach. Don't be averse to changing at the last minute."[156]

Must Be Preached with Integrity

Sincerity and integrity must mark the evangelistic preacher. David Hume, referring to the preaching of John Brown of Haddington, said, "I like that man, for he preaches as if Christ were in the pulpit with him."[157] Spurgeon added, "May we never be priests of God at the altar and sons of Belial outside the tabernacle door.... We do not trust those persons who have two faces, nor will men believe in those whose verbal and

---

[155] Spurgeon, *Lectures to My Students*, 91–92.
[156] Bisagno, *Power of Positive Evangelism*, 11.
[157] Autrey, *Basic Evangelism*, 67.

practical testimonies are contradictory....It is a horrible thing to be an inconsistent minister."[158]

The preacher in private and in the pulpit must heed Paul's admonition to Timothy, "If you keep yourself pure, you will be a utensil God can use for his purpose. Your life will be clean, and you will be ready for the Master to use you for every good work" (II Timothy 2:21 NLT). Haddon Robinson certainly is correct in stating, "Time has changed the way people view pastors [and I add evangelists]. Perhaps we're not lumped with scam artists or manipulative fundraisers, but we face an Olympic challenge to earn respect, credibility, and authority."[159]

In light of this truth, the preacher must all the more live a separated and guarded life. Matthew Henry cautions, "Ministers must preach not only in the pulpit, but out of it; their converse must be a constant sermon, and in that they may be more particular in the application and descend to persons and cases better than they can in their public ministry."[160]

Robert Murray M'Cheyne, giving counsel to a young minister prior to his ordination, declared, "Do not forget the culture of the inner man—I mean of the heart. How diligently the cavalry officer keeps his sabre clean and sharp; every stain he rubs off with the greatest care. Remember you are God's sword, His instrument—I trust a chosen vessel unto Him to bear His name. In great measure, according to the purity and perfections of the instrument will be the success. It is not great talents God blesses so much as a great likeness to Jesus. A holy minister is an awful weapon in the hand of God."[161]

Must Be Preached Periodically

The problem in the church is that too little strictly evangelistic preaching is being done. As stated in the introduction, Roy

---

[158] Spurgeon, *Lectures to My Students,* 17.
[159] Hybels, Briscoe, and Robinson, *Mastering Contemporary Preaching,* 140.
[160] Henry, *Young Christian,* 9–10.
[161] Rosscup, *How to Preach Biblically,* 70.

Fish said, "I wonder, have we stopped preaching evangelistic sermons because lost people are not coming to our services like they once did? Or maybe it's the other way around. Maybe we stopped preaching evangelistic messages, and God stopped bringing lost people to our services to hear them."[162] Sadly, in some churches preacher and parishioner do not know what an evangelistic sermon "looks" like.

How often should a pastor preach a solid evangelistic sermon to his congregation? Most likely more than he does presently. G. Campbell Morgan, addressing this very question, suggests, "The presence in our congregations of those not actually and personally submitted to Christ must always create the necessity for such service. Nothing can be more paralyzing to the life of a minister himself or to the congregation that assemble regularly to hear him as he preaches the Word than that he should come to think, or should preach as to make people think, that definite decision for Christ is not important in every individual life. There is a danger that we take too much for granted about the people to whom we preach, and if we are not careful we shall drift into the opinion that because these people are attending services, therefore there is no need for the direct appeal of the evangel to be made to them." Morgan continues, "There must be occasionally some message, some appeal, some opportunity given to those who sit under *your* ministry to make an immediate decision and a definite confession of Jesus Christ."[163]

C. H. Spurgeon states, "We must have Christ in all our messages, no matter what else is in them or not in them. There ought to be enough of the Gospel in every message to save a soul."[164] Regarding this sermon criterion of Spurgeon, do you hear the Lord saying, "Weighed in the balance and found wanting?"

---

[162] Koonce, "Fish: Evangelistic Preaching."
[163] G. Campbell Morgan, *Evangelism,* 65–66.
[164] Spurgeon, *Soulwinner,* 100.

Sermon

The Text and Topic Selection Are Pivotal

In my thirty-six years in evangelism, the sermons that have been used by God to win souls the most are those prepared and delivered to that end. These are sermons that from start to finish have a "harpoon" in them for the souls of lost men and women.

C. H. Spurgeon states, "As to which messages are most likely to be blessed to the conversion of those to whom they are preached, I would say that first are those sermons which are distinctly aimed at the conversion of the hearers."[165] Spurgeon shared an experience of hearing a preacher pray for God to save souls by the sermon he was to preach. Regarding this preacher's sermon, Spurgeon said, "I do not hesitate to say that God Himself could not bless the message to that end unless He made the people misunderstand all that the preacher said to them, because the whole message was apt to harden the sinner in his sin rather than to lead him to renounce it and to seek the Savior....So, if you want your hearers to be converted, you must see that your preaching aims directly at conversion, and that it is such that God will be likely to bless to that end. When that is the case, then look for souls to be saved, and look for a great number of them, too."[166]

Revisit Sermons That Are Profitable

Preach over and over sermons that God uses to win souls. Prior to Billy Graham's San Diego crusade in 2004 he stated, "I'll be preaching some of the same sermons I preached in 1949. The Gospel hasn't changed, and people's hearts haven't changed."[167] J. Harold Smith preached the sermon "God's Three Deadlines" hundreds of times, resulting in an estimated 1.5 million public professions of faith. George W. Truett preached some of his revival sermons in his church over and

---

[165] Ibid., 84.
[166] Ibid., 84–86.
[167] Adler, *Ask Billy Graham*, 164.

over for more than thirty years.[168] E. J. Daniels preached four sermons over five hundred times each ("The Four Greatest Truths in Heaven or Earth"; "The High Cost of Being Lost"; "Gambling with Destiny"; and "The Secret of Success in Every Realm"), likewise with great success. Daniels states, "Every minister has found that God blesses certain messages He has given to him more than others. Although I do not use a manuscript, nor even notes, I do use the same texts, illustrations, and general development in these sermons. Because I believe they contain God's Truth, my soul is set on fire each time as I preach them."[169]

Personally I have preached one sermon over five hundred times, and upon each occasion, almost without exception, someone has professed faith in Christ. The key in revisiting a sermon is the prompting of the Holy Spirit. Billy Sunday stated that regardless of the many times he preached the same sermon he always "soaked" it in prayer.[170] Prayer infuses life and fire into the sermon.

W. E. Sangster stated, "Some men think it is dishonoring to God not to prepare a new sermon every time they mount the pulpit steps, but that is a rule that I find unconvincing. Having blessed the message to one congregation, God can bless it to another."[171] Professor James Denney of Glasgow stated that Jesus probably repeated Himself more than five hundred times. Commenting on this statement, Billy Graham said, "That is encouraging to every evangelist. The Gospel at times seems 'old' to us. But repeat and repeat and repeat it."[172] C. E. Matthews stated, "We sing the same songs over and over. A person may have heard 'Amazing Grace' a thousand times and

---

[168] Matthews, *Church Revival,* 69.

[169] Daniels, *Fervent, Soul-Stirring Sermons,* Foreword.

[170] Whitesell, *Evangelistic Preaching,* 35.

[171] Sangster, *Craft of the Sermon,* 201.

[172] Douglas, *Work of the Evangelist,* 98.

love it better every time he hears it. What is true of a genuine gospel song is true of a genuine gospel sermon."[173]

At a Criswell College luncheon in the aftermath of Criswell's death, Junior Hill cited his first and fondest memory of Criswell. Hill said that while upon a flight to Atlanta, "he tapped me on the shoulder and said, 'Lad, may I ask you a question?' And I thought, *Boy, do I wish I had a tape recorder. Dr. Criswell was asking me a question.*" Criswell told Hill he had "'thousands of sermons, thousands…but now that I am out here on the road, traveling around and preaching, I find myself coming back to the same two or three. Is that all right, Son?' And I thought, *Can you imagine, a great man of God asking a redneck Alabama evangelist if that's all right?*"[174]

A word of caution is in place. I heard E. J. Daniels state that once a sermon lost its fire he threw it into the fire. That is great advice for pastor and evangelist to heed. Avoid preaching sermons that have lost freshness, vitality and power.

Must Be Decision Driven

Evangelistic preaching provokes a response to the Gospel "then and there." It always provides people the opportunity to respond to the invitation of Christ to be saved. In my book *The Evangelistic Invitation 101,* I cite 150 helps in giving the invitation at the climax of the sermon.

The sinner must be brought to realize that "tomorrow" may be too late to be saved. It is the preacher's task under the anointing of the Holy Spirit to show people the deadly danger of delay and thus the need to be saved immediately. "The little word 'now' is often on the evangelical preacher's lips: 'Now is the accepted time. Now is the day of salvation. Accept Christ now lest you go to Hell.' The word asks, 'Why live another day without the joy, the inner peace, the fulfillment which Christ

---

[173] Matthews, *Church Revival,* 69.
[174] Norm Miller, "Warren on Criswell."

can bring?' So there is calling for an answer now."[175] The evangelical preacher must call sinners to repentance and faith in Christ with soul urgency each time the invitation is extended! It may be their last chance to come. Spurgeon stated, "When anyone dies, I ask myself, 'Was I faithful? Did I speak all the truth? And did I speak it from my very soul every time I preached?'"[176] Every preacher should ask these questions personally. In Chapter Four, I deal exclusively with the invitational appeal.

Must Be Preached Boldly

William Gurnall remarked, "A minister without boldness is like a smooth file, a knife without an edge, a sentinel that is afraid to let off his gun. If men will be bold in sin, ministers must be bold to reprove."[177] The most effective evangelistic preaching is that which causes the sinner to face personal sin (transgression of the law), feel its guilt (godly sorrow and brokenness), foresee and fear its consequences (present and eternal separation from God) and focus on its only remedy (Jesus Christ).

John R. Rice, in writing about the kind of preaching needed, remarked frankly, "The preachers today who plead that they must preach only 'a positive message,' that preaching against sin is a 'negative message,' certainly do not follow the pattern of this great man of God (John the Baptist), one of the greatest ever born of women, as Jesus said. John the Baptist preached against sin, against particular sins. And he did it boldly. He hurt people's feelings; he made people angry; he caused a disturbance. But he was faithful to God and to the Bible.... Young preacher, do not be taken in by the sophistry of the time-serving preachers who do not preach against sin....The preacher who never has a word to say against drunkenness and adultery and lewdness and covetousness and blasphemy is a

---

[175] Walker, *Standing Up to Preach*, 61.
[176] Comfort, *Evidence Bible*, 504.
[177] Edwards, *Dictionary of Thoughts* (online), 437.

dumb dog who cannot bark. He is a Balaam preaching for profit."[178] Preach against sin, particular sins, Rice urged, with love and compassion.

C. H. Spurgeon declared, "There are more souls won by wooing than threatening. It is not Hell, but Christ we desire to preach. O sinners, we are not afraid to tell you of your doom, but we do not forever choose to be forever dwelling on that doleful theme. We rather love to tell you of Christ and Him crucified. We want to have our preaching rather full of frankincense of the merits of Christ than of the smoke and fire and terrors of Mt. Sinai..."[179] Billy Sunday once was reprimanded for preaching too strongly in a crusade and was urged to tone down his preaching on sin. One man said, "Billy, you are rubbing some of the cats the wrong way." Sunday responded, "Then let the cats turn around."[180]

Must Be Conscience Targeted

Bradley Miner in his sermon *The Duty of Preaching to the Conscience* declared, "The man who preaches to the conscience has the greatest power over his hearers. Preaching to the conscience is essential to success. The design of preaching is to bring guilty men to repentance and faith and holy living. One may preach to the other faculties and do some good, but the ambassador for Christ has not gained his object until the sinner repents and cordially receives Christ to reign over him. He may appeal to the passions, to the hopes, the fears, the love, the hatred of his hearers, if through these he reaches the conscience."[181]

Faris Whitesell stated, "The route to the will usually runs through the emotions and conscience. When the emotions have been aroused, then we should pass right to the conscience and seek its condemnation of the sinner. Conscience rests upon and

---

[178] John Rice, "Preaching We Need."
[179] Spurgeon, *Spurgeon's Gems,* 204.
[180] Sunday, *Sword of the Lord,* 3.
[181] Whitesell, *Evangelistic Preaching,* 106.

follows our judgment of what is right and wrong. Conscience will excuse sin when dormant and wrongly informed, but when the conscience is illuminated by divine truth it accuses the sinner. We must appeal to the conscience for conversions."[182]

Must Be Authentic

A key to effective evangelistic preaching is cited frankly by C. H. Spurgeon: "Be yourself, dear brother, for if you are not yourself, you cannot be anybody else; and so, you see, you must be nobody....Do not be a mere copyist, a borrower, a spoiler of other men's notes. Say what God has said to you, and say it in your own way; and when it is so said, plead personally for the Lord's blessing upon it."[183] Listen to effective evangelistic preachers and learn from them, but do not endeavor to be "them." David could not fit into Saul's armor, nor can we in another man's.

Martin Luther gave these ten qualifications for the preacher:

1. He should be able to preach plainly and in order.
2. He should have a good head.
3. He should have good power of speech.
4. He should have a good voice.
5. He should have good memory.
6. He should be sure of what he means to say.
7. He should be ready to stake body and life, goods and glory on its truth.
8. He should know when to stop.
9. He should study diligently.
10. He should allow himself to be vexed and criticized by everyone.[184]

---

[182] Ibid., 36.
[183] Spurgeon, *All Around Ministry*, 67.
[184] Luther, "Qualifications for Preaching."

Faris Whitesell said it best, "Our day needs New Testament evangelistic preaching—Spirit-empowered preaching, bold preaching, doctrinal preaching, Biblical preaching, relevant preaching, persuasive preaching, pungent preaching, preaching full of the love of Christ supported by transformed lives."[185]

"True preaching is the sweating of blood."[186]—Joseph Parker

"A sermon has a flow of thoughts, an emotional as well as logical development. All sermons have tension that is best created in the introduction and with each point. The moment you lose the tension, the sermon is over."[187]—Haddon Robinson

"In a sense, God's expositor is all at once an explorer, a detective, a historian, a tracker, and a prospector. In searching out God's message, he is a Columbus navigating the expansive seas of Scripture to bring news of a fairer world. He is a Sherlock Holmes poking for clues that will cause God's truth, justice, and mercy to prevail. He is akin to Catton, who, in his famous Civil War trilogy, delved into history and cast events in their original light. Again, he is comparable to Tom Tobin, scout and expert in Colorado trail signs, who could find clues most men had missed....For the sake of others, he serves as a prospector who pans for gold in the streams of living water, the Word."[188]—James E. Rosscup

"He who has ceased to learn has ceased to teach. He who no longer sows in the study will no more reap in the pulpit."[189]—C. H. Spurgeon

"Biblical preaching's authenticity is significantly tarnished by contemporary communicators who are more concerned with personal relevance than with God's Revelation."[190]—Richard Mayhue

"The average preacher has been taught to do everything but preach and yet, the most important thing in the world is the preaching of the Gospel."[191]—Lester Roloff

---

[185] Whitesell, *Basic New Testament Evangelism,* 106.
[186] Ravenhill, *Why Revival Tarries,* 64.
[187] Robinson, "Interview," (audio workshop).
[188] Rosscup, *How to Preach Biblically,* 93.
[189] Vines and Shaddix, *Power in the Pulpit,* 82.
[190] MacArthur, *Rediscovering Expository Preaching,* 3.
[191] Roloff, "The Family Altar," Number 3, 1.

3
Structure

Gladstone stated, "Eloquence [I adapt to say *"Preaching"*] is the pouring back on an audience in a flood what is first received from them as a vapor."[192] The contribution of a receptive and responsive hearer to the power of the preacher is something the laity has not yet fully grasped. There is something to be said of the value of the "Amen Corner" in the delivery of the sermon.

Content of the Sermon

The evangelistic sermon should be constructed according to the general principles of preaching as with any sermon. This chapter is not intended fully to address this subject (the preacher has hundreds of resources that do that) but simply and concisely to deal with its main components. Alexander Gregg surmises that "there are three things to aim at in public speaking: first, to get into your subject; then, to get your subject into yourself; and, lastly, to get your subject into your hearers."[193] In a nutshell, that is the goal of evangelistic preaching, with the exception that it also includes pleading for a public response.

Text

"That is my text. I am now going to preach. Maybe we'll meet again, my text and I; maybe not." Regrettably this approach to preaching, that came from an unknown source, is that of far too many preachers. Henry Ward Beecher said he regarded "a text as simply the entrance into a pasture; the bars once down and he once in, he had a right to walk all over the pasture and browse where and on what he chose."[194]

Spurgeon, when asked how to select a text, told his students, "Cry to God for it."[195] Spurgeon added, "Many ministers

---

[192] Funk and Wells, ed. *The Homiletic Review,* 64.
[193] Edwards, *Dictionary of Thoughts,* 543.
[194] *Homiletic Review,* Vol. XLIX, 109.
[195] Spurgeon, *Lectures to My Students,* 86.

appear to think that they are to choose the text; they are to discover its teaching; they are to find a discourse in it. We do not think so....devout minds evermore desire that the choice of the text should rest with the all-wise Spirit of God and not with their own fallible understandings, and therefore they humbly put themselves into His hand, asking Him to condescend to direct them to the portion of meat in due season which He has ordained for His people."[196] Spurgeon, though a master preacher, admitted that his greatest difficulty was finding texts for his sermons to fit the subjects he wanted to preach.[197] In this difficulty he does not stand alone.

Adrian Rogers stated, "The proper selection of a text is a matter of great significance. Good sermon preparation requires taking a passage of Scripture and analyzing it, organizing it, illustrating it, and then applying it to everyday living. The text is to be understood, believed, and applied to both personal and social needs....Yes, it must always be a biblical text."[198]

Albert Mohler stated, "Moreover, because the Bible is the inerrant and infallible word of God, the shape of the biblical text is also therefore divinely directed. God has spoken through the inspired human authors of Scripture, and each different genre of biblical literature demands that the preacher give careful attention to the text, allowing it to shape the message. Far too many preachers come to the text with a sermonic shape in mind and a limited set of tools in hand. To be sure, the shape of the sermon may differ from preacher to preacher and should differ from text to text. But genuine exposition demands that the text establish the shape as well as the substance of the sermon....The preacher rises in the pulpit to accomplish one central purpose—to set forth the message and meaning of the biblical text. This requires historical investigation, literary discernment, and the faithful employment of the *analogia fidei* to

---

[196] Ibid., 85–86.
[197] *Homiletic Review,* Vol. XLIX, 110.
[198] Rogers and Patterson, *Love Worth Finding,* 196.

interpret the Scripture by Scripture. It also requires the expositor to reject the modern conceit that what the text *meant* is not necessarily what it *means*. If the Bible is truly the enduring and eternal word of God, it means what it meant as it is newly applied in every generation."[199]

> First, I read my Bible until a text gets hold of me. Then I go down to the James River and walk in it. Then, I get into my pulpit and preach it out.—John Jasper (Slave Preacher)[201]

Topic

"What do hearers remember about a sermon? Often the topic! In the history of preaching almost every message that has lived has done so partly because of its name....If the layman is to remember your next sermon, he will associate it with a subject. Why not give it a name that he will recall with ease....In naming sermons, therefore, never lose sight of the man in the pew."[201] "Payday Someday" immediately comes to mind at the mention of the name R. G. Lee, as does "God's Three Deadlines" with the name J. Harold Smith.

Remembrance of a sermon title often brings recall of sermon substance to some measure, which allows it yet to live long after it is proclaimed. Jerry Vines and Jim Shaddix caution regarding the selection of the title, "Do not promise more than you can give in a message....Some preachers have lost credibility because the substance of their sermon did not fulfill the enormous claims of the title."[202]

The Proposition Sentence

The proposition sentence is a concise sentence that states the essence of the sermon. It is the "hub" from which the spokes (preaching points) develop. The proposition is the gist of the

---

[199] Mohler, "Recovery of Christian Worship, (Part 2)."
[200] Day, *Rhapsody in Black*, 116.
[201] Blackwood, *Preparation of Sermons*, 91, 96.
[202] Vines and Shaddix, *Power in the Pulpit*, 141.

sermon, the sermon condensed into one sentence, the spinal column running through the message. It is the thing a lawyer states when he begins his plea with a jury; it is the thing the legislator states when he begins to plead for the passage of a favorite measure. "The proposition should have a valid and vital relationship to the central idea of the text. To ensure unity in the sermon structure, the proposition should include a plural noun that relates to each of the main points in the sermon ("Ways," "Steps," etc.)"[203] Fred Craddock states, "No preacher has the right to look for points until he has the point."[204]

John A. Broadus stated, "The proposition deserves more attention than is given by many preachers. It is a statement of the subject as the preacher proposes to develop it. It is the subject (idea) and predicate. The subject answers the question, What is the sermon about? The proposition answers the question, What is the sermon? Its form should be one complete declarative sentence, simple, clear, and cogent."[205] The proposition serves as the determinant with regard to what biblical material is necessary for a sermon and what should be laid aside. According to Vines and Shaddix, answering the following question throughout the analysis stage of your sermon preparation will keep you on keel with the sermon's purpose.[206]

THE CONTENT QUESTION:
IS THIS INFORMATION ABSOLUTELY NECESSARY OR EXTREMELY HELPFUL IN SUPPORTING THE PROPOSITION OF THIS SERMON?

---

[203] Thad Dowdle, Personal Correspondence, 4 March 2009.
[204] Duduit, ed., *Handbook of Contemporary Preaching,* 163.
[205] Broadus, *Preparation and Delivery,* 1979, 54–55.
[206] Vines and Shaddix, *Power in the Pulpit,* 175.

The Objective Sentence

The objective sentence concisely states the purpose of the sermon; that which you hope to accomplish in its delivery.

The Transitional Sentence

The introduction transitional sentence is like a hitch on a train engine that hooks it to the cars it is to pull. It is the major connector from introduction to the body of the sermon. The transition sentences within the body of the sermon hook main point to main point and then to the invitation. Thad Dowdle advises, "Transition sentences should be worked out to clarify movement from each main point in the sermon to the following main point."[207]

The Body of the Sermon or Outline

The body of the sermon contains an introduction, two or more points, illustrations and invitation (conclusion) all built around the evangelistic text selected.

<u>Introduction</u>

"The introduction would do well to relate some life issue to the main idea of the text and to the main point of the sermon."[208] The introduction is critical in capturing the congregants' attention. Mark Galli testifies, "A good introduction arrests me. It handcuffs me and drags me before the sermon, where I stand and hear a Word that makes me both tremble and rejoice."[209] I prefer short introductions capsulating the substance and purpose of the sermon.

V. L. Stanfield stated that the "introduction should be fairly brief. The entire sermon should not be 'long.' Therefore, only limited time can be spent in the sermon introduction. When your friends visit, they do not like to stay on the porch. When people hear a sermon, they do not want to stay in the introduc-

---

[207] Dowdle, Personal Correspondence, March 4, 2009.
[208] Ibid.
[209] Fabarez, *Preaching That Changes Lives*, 28.

tion. Move quickly into the sermon!"[210] Michael Fabarez undergirds Stanfield's remark in declaring, "The sermon's sense of urgency must be evident right out of the gate. Those critical opening moments of the sermon provide us the opportunity to give our listeners a whiff of why this message is so important."[211] John Ogilvie adds, "The first three minutes of the sermon determine the effectiveness of the whole message. Whether we preach twenty minutes or a half-hour, during these three minutes of the sermon it is crucial to 'set the hook.'"[212] Warren Wiersbe stated, "I try to hit the pulpit running. When you're preaching for eternity, time is precious, and we can't afford to waste it chatting about the weather."[213]

In regard to the introduction, C. H. Spurgeon stated, "It is always a pity to build a great porch to a little house."[214] In the aftermath of my preaching of an evangelistic message, a man looked me in the eyes and said, "I like how you get straight to the point." My experience reveals it is expedient for the preacher not to ramble on about things that do not relate to the message but to stay honed in on it from start to finish for effectiveness.

An old lady told John Owen, the Puritan preacher, that he took so much time spreading the table that she lost her appetite.[215] Austin Phelps stated, "Don't let the introduction be a piece of dead timber nailed to a living tree."[216] The introduction "should be simple, direct, appropriate for the sermon, modest, and fairly brief. The two most important parts of the introduction are the beginning and the end. The first sentence in the introduction should be striking. Eliminate all false starts

---

[210] Stanfield, *Effective Evangelistic Preaching*, 23.
[211] Fabarez, *Preaching That Changes Lives*, 101.
[212] Cox, *Handbook on Contemporary Preaching*, 176.
[213] Bailey and Wiersbe, *Black and White*, 86.
[214] Spurgeon, *Lectures to My Students*, 133.
[215] Perry and Whitsell, *Variety in Your Preaching*, 155.
[216] Ibid.

such as apologies, anecdotes, puns, and inane remarks."[217] The introduction is to be prepared at the climax of the sermon development.

<u>Body of the Sermon</u>

The body of the sermon flows from the analysis of the text. Paige Patterson suggests four hermeneutical principles that will enable the preacher to interpret and apply the text rightly.

1. The Principle of Divine Illumination.

The most important of all principles was given by the Lord when He promised the arrival of the Comforter, the Holy Spirit: "But the Helper, the Holy Spirit...will teach you all things" (John 14:26). Any believer (preacher) who will ask the Author of the Bible to be his personal teacher will experience astonishing insights into God's Word.

2. The Principle of Contextual Interpretation.

No verse should be interpreted in isolation from its context. Both the immediate context and the larger context may need to be carefully considered.

3. The Principle of Clarity.

Difficult and apparently ambiguous verses should always be understood in the clear light of the many verses that are perfectly clear.

4. The Principle of the Grammatical-Historical Method.

Every effort should be made to understand precisely what the words mean as they are employed by the authors. The historical situation which produced the writing must also be the subject of careful investigation.[218]

Commenting on Patterson's point of Divine Illumination, Thad Dowdle stated, "I have found that the illumination of the

---

[217] Whitesell, *Evangelistic Preaching,* 43.
[218] Criswell, ed., *Criswell Study Bible,* 20–21.

Holy Spirit especially makes clear the relationship between the truth of Scripture and the issues of life today."[219]

The preaching points should flow easily one to the other, building upon the "preaching point" of the sermon and progressing toward the invitational appeal. The outline of the sermon should be easy to follow. James Cox states, "The most important single device for achieving boldness of attack in preaching is a well-constructed outline."[220] C. E. Autrey wrote, "...an outline is like a peg to hang one's hat upon. It helps one remember a line of thought."[221]

Regarding the number of headings or preaching points, Stephen Olford warns, "The number of headings and subheadings depends upon the text and cannot be predetermined. But here it is important to major on clarity rather than on complexity. It is possible to have so many points that a sermon ends up with no points at all—especially from the listener's perspective."[222] Instead of rushing through a lengthy discourse, "it is best to repeat a few essential points...often so they can be easily remembered...and avoid overwhelming people with a 'mass of matter' which in reality buries the truth."[223]

Donald McDougall adds, "Communicate the message; don't just outline it. Concentrate on the communication of the message, not just the outline. We have such a penchant for nice, pat outlines. Having an outline is not bad, nor is it bad to have an outline that people can remember, but creating an outline that inadequately reflects the passage's meaning is terrible."[224]

Donald G. Miller writes of the sermon outline comparing it to the automobile transmission prior to the invention of automatic transmissions. "There was no question as to when each

---

[219] Dowdle, Personal Correspondence. 4 Mar 2009.

[220] Cox, *Handbook of Contemporary Preaching*, 163.

[221] Autrey, *Evangelistic Sermons*, 87.

[222] Douglas, *Work of the Evangelist*, 777.

[223] Gugliotto, *Hand-Book for Bible Study*, 149.

[224] Rosscup, *How to Preach Biblically*, 192.

stage gave way to the next, and every passenger in the car knew exactly in what gear the car was functioning. The automatic transmissions which have overcome this may be an automotive gain. It is questionable, however, whether there has been a parallel gain through silent-transmission homiletics. While riding in a car it may not be imperative that the rider know in what gear the mechanism is moving. But listening to a sermon ought not to be such a passive experience. Listening to a sermon involves conscious thought. It is impossible, therefore, for any automatic procedure of which the listener is not conscious to carry his thought forward from stage to stage and to get him from the starting point of the sermon to its goal. If the listener has to spend time wondering whether the preacher has completed the stage of thought with which he began and has moved on to something else, or whether what he is saying at the moment is still relevant to the first stage of the sermon, confusion is bound to result, and the final impact of the sermon be weakened."[225] Thad Dowdle cautions "that announcing the number of major points in the sermon introduction may be a hindrance to continued attention."[226]

Alliteration

I heard Junior Hill state that the man in the pew is clueless about what sermonic alliteration means. He is correct. Alliteration is more important to the preacher than the parishioner. As many ministers, I have found myself at times searching the dictionary for one more "c word" to fit my alliterated outline. When it could not be found, it *forced* a change in approach. Alliteration is good if it serves its purpose well—to aid one's memory in preaching, to make transition from point to point smooth, to aid the listener's comprehension of the message and enhance its remembrance. Alliteration must be biblically true to the text and never forced upon a text. Warren Wiersbe said, "I used to think that every sermon had to be alliterated. Several

---

[225] Donald Miller, *Way to Biblical Preaching*, 95.
[226] Dowdle, Personal Correspondence, 4 Mar 2009.

of the preachers I admired when I was young followed that pattern. I've moved away from that. Now I alliterate only if it comes naturally and helps the sermon. Lloyd Perry, who taught me in seminary, would say to us, 'Gentlemen, remember, alliteration will sell you short every time.' And it will."[227]

How to Outline the Sermon

Every preacher has to find the method that is comfortable and most effective in regards to the preparation of the sermon outline. Personally I choose to fold in half a piece of white computer paper and jot my outline on its front and back (not inside, due to possible bleed through). At the top of the first page I write the sermon title (underlined) with the scripture text reference underneath. Under the heading "Intro" (introduction) I write the introduction (abbreviated if possible) and the transition sentence to the body of the sermon. My main points normally are three, each of which are written in large letters underlined in a different color ink for easier sighting. The abbreviation "Ill." is used for the spot in the sermon where illustrations are to be shared. I jot down just enough of the illustration for recall. My subpoints are numbered, and these help me stay on track. I circle in red ink key words in the subpoints that trigger my memory regarding a matter I want to emphasize. Regarding the transition from the body of the sermon to the invitation I write down the transitional sentence that soars me into the invitation. I prepare my sermons in manuscript form but wait until the day prior to preaching or the same day of preaching (if possible) to jot down the outline so it will be fresh in my mind.

Bridge to the Invitation

The transitional sentence between the preaching points and the invitation connects the sermon to the salvation decision desired. It is helpful either to memorize this sentence or have it clearly written for recall at this point in the sermon delivery.

---

[227] Bailey and Wiersbe, *Black and White*, 95.

Examples of the invitation transitional sentence are shared in the following chapter.

Billy Graham states, "Several things distinguish evangelistic preaching, but one of the most important is that it includes an appeal for decision—an appeal for men and women to decide for Christ."[228] Sadly, many ministers preach powerfully but summon weakly. It is here that great evangelistic sermons often fall flat, ending with little or no fruit. Advance preparation and practice of the evangelistic appeal emboldens and equips the preacher to share it effectively. The subject of the sermon invitation will be considered more fully in chapter four.

Preparation and Delivery of the Sermon

Pray It Down

Cry out to God for divine leadership in the selection of the subject and text.

Study It Through

Avoid eisegesis and engage in studious exegesis. Search out the biblical background and the meaning of the text and its application. Rudyard Kipling provides the preacher a launch pad in text interpretation and application:

I kept six honest serving men;

> They taught me all I knew.

Their names were What and Why and When

> And How and Where and Who."[229]

Dwight L. Moody once mumbled while Henry Weston was speaking, "There goes one of my sermons." Weston stopped and asked what he meant. Moody replied that another of his sermons had just been ruined by an interpretation that proved his own wrong.[230] Make sure what you preach is true to the scriptural text.

---

[228] Douglas, *Work of the Evangelist*, 171.

[229] Kipling, *Just So Stories*, 81.

[230] Miller, *Way to Biblical Preaching*, 8.

Work It Out

Develop the "preaching point," the objective of the sermon, and the preaching points. Write the sermon down in manuscript form.

Burn It In

Rehearse the sermon before the Lord until it possesses you. No preacher dare enter the pulpit with sermon in hand but not ablaze in his heart. The text must inflame the preacher. R. G. Lee was known for "picturizing" his sermons, envisioning them before their proclamation. This task required great mental discipline on Lee's part.[231]

Speak It Full

Plead for the fullness of the Holy Spirit's power to proclaim the message to the salvation of souls. The last thing John Calvin did before entering the pulpit to preach was to pray, "Come, Holy Spirit, come."[232]

Keep It Clear

Haddon Robinson, paraphrasing a Russian proverb, says, "It is the same with men as with donkeys; whoever would hold them fast must get a very good grip on their ears....If a preacher will not—or cannot—think himself clear so that he says what he means, he has no business in the pulpit. He is like a singer who can't sing, an actor who can't act, an accountant who can't add."[233]

Be Yourself

"The fact is that this whole matter of delivery," says James Stewart, "can be resolved into two precepts which are not so paradoxical as they appear: Be yourself—forget yourself. God has given to each man his own individuality, and standardization is emphatically no part of the divine intention for your ministry. How intolerably dull it would be if every preacher

---

[231] Gericke, *Adorning the Doctrine,* 127–129.

[232] Stanfield, *Effective Evangelistic Preaching,* 25.

[233] Robinson, *Biblical Preaching,* 39, 161.

had to be cut to the same pattern! You are to give free rein to your personality....Be yourself. And do not complain if you cannot be someone else...but also forget yourself. You are to use for the delivery of the Word every faculty God has given you; and simultaneously you are to renounce yourself utterly, so that in the end the messenger shall be nothing, the message everything. You are not to cramp or stifle your individuality; but you are to offer it so completely to God upon the altar that, when the service closes, the dominating thought in the worshippers minds will be not of any obtrusive human proficiency or cleverness, but only this—'The Lord was in His holy temple today!'"[234] Stewart states also, "Every sermon must have something of your own lifeblood in it. It is your personal act of witness....To say the preacher's sermon should be his own does not at all mean the obtruding of self into the picture."[235]

The Sermon Style

The preacher must jealously guard the selected text from preconceived ideas or notions, allowing the Holy Spirit to grant illumination through reflection and diligence in study into its primary teaching and application. He has no discretionary authority to "add to or take away" from the biblical text but is to proclaim all it dictates tactfully, passionately and lovingly. Stephen Olford at Amsterdam '83, which I attended, stated "I am convinced that all evangelistic preaching should be basically expository preaching. Whether or not we expound the Bible topically or textually, we still need to exegete the Scriptures if we are going to validate what we are going to say as God's truth. We must ever remember those famous words of Augustine, 'When the Scriptures speak, God speaks.'"[236]

John Stott sums up who the preacher is and his purpose: "The expository preacher is a bridge builder, seeking to span the gulf between the Word of God and the mind of man. He

---

[234] Stewart, *Heralds of God*, 186–187.
[235] Ibid., 174.
[236] Douglas, *Work of the Evangelist*, 776.

must do his utmost to interpret the Scriptures so accurately and plainly, and to apply them so forcefully, that the truth crosses the bridge."[237] Tom Johnston, associate professor of evangelism at Midwestern Baptist Theological Seminary, adds, "The Holy Spirit is a pretty good bridge builder, as He is able to divide soul and spirit and judge the thoughts and intentions of the heart."[238] Andrew Blackwood cautions the preacher to remember that the good cook prepares the meal in the kitchen and serves it in the dining room, leaving the pots and pans in the kitchen. Just so, the preacher should prepare the sermon in the study and deliver it in the pulpit, leaving the "pots and pans" of its development in the kitchen.[239]

The story is told of a teenage boy who asked his buddy, "What's the best way to kiss a girl?" This friend replied, "There ain't no bad way."[240] In referring to the best way to prepare a sermon, John Bisagno stated, "It is *your way* and *God's way*. Don't walk in Saul's armor at this point. Be yourself. Find what fits you, determine what is comfortable, and go with it."[241] In evangelistic preaching, the target is to reach the spiritually blind, deaf and lame; therefore, it is essential, regardless of sermon pattern, that the message be biblically sound, clear, passionate and decision driven.

Evaluating the Evangelistic Sermon

Robert E. Coleman suggests seven questions in evaluating the evangelistic sermon.

1. Is the sermon Christ exalting? (I Corinthians 1:23; II Corinthians 4:5; Acts 5:42) "The first measure of a sermon's power is the degree to which it exalts Christ and makes men aware of His claims upon their lives."

---

[237] Stott, *Preacher's Portrait*, 25.
[238] Johnston, Personal Correspondence, 19 May 2009.
[239] Dowdle, Personal Correspondence, 4 Mar 2009.
[240] Bisagno, *Letters to Timothy*, 155.
[241] Ibid.

2. Is the sermon scriptural? (John 20:31; II Timothy 3:16; Romans 10:17) "Preaching that brings men to the Savior is subject to the spirit and letter of God-breathed Scripture."

3. Is the sermon soul searching? (John 15:22) "To meet human need, a sermon must strike hard at the problem of sin."

4. Is the sermon logical? "The sermon must be built on a convincing course of logic."

5. Is the sermon simple?

6. Is the sermon experiential? "A living, personal, certain experience of salvation is the object of the message."

7. Is the sermon demanding a verdict? (Romans 10:13; II Corinthians 6:2; 5:11) Preaching calls for a verdict that is logically and clearly stated.[242]

The Absence of Holy Spirit Conviction

Carl Bates in his sermon "Greatness in the Church" stated, "I have often had people say to me, as I greet them after a service on Sunday morning, 'I cannot understand why people are not being convicted in our church.' I can understand why! There is no conviction because we have not met these New Testament qualifications (Acts 2: 37–47). When the preacher is filled with the Spirit of God, when the people let Christ, the living Lord, exercise control in their lives, when the ordained body of leaders in the church stand together, when the preacher proclaims the Word of God in the midst of the people, the same thing that happened (Acts 2:37) will happen again....We may erect our beautiful buildings, call our brilliant preachers, hear our finely trained choirs, and glory over our perfectly organized groups, but if we miss these qualifications, we have failed and shall fail. This is why there is no conviction under the preaching of God's Word."[243]

Sermon preparation involves hours of tedious study, research, and prayer. I read the story of a preacher who never

---

[242] Douglas, *Work of the Evangelist*, 136–137.
[243] Stanfield, *Effective Evangelistic Preaching*, 62.

prepared his sermon during the week but waited until he was on the platform Sunday morning to do so. As the church sang hymns, he desperately would pray, "Lord, give me your message. Lord, give me your message." One Sunday while praying, "Lord, give me your message," he heard the Lord say, "Ralph, here's My message. You're lazy."[244] May that statement never be sounded from the Lord's lips to us!

C. H. Spurgeon reminds the preacher, "Sermons should have real teaching in them, and their doctrine should be solid, substantial and abundant. We do not enter the pulpit to talk for talk's sake; we have instructions to convey important to the last degree, and we cannot afford to utter pretty nothings."[245] "God has not called us to *create* sermons but to *convey* sermons He has given in His Word."[246]

---

[244] "The Preacher."
[245] Spurgeon, *Lectures to My Students,* 70.
[246] Whitsett, Evangelism Conference.

"Come needy, come guilty, come loathsome and bare;

"You can't come too filthy—come just as you are."—J. Hart[247]

"The most important thing in preaching is the listener's verdict."—Hershel Hobbs[248]

"How disappointing to bring an audience by prayer, study, and preaching to the door of eternal life and not allow them a chance to enter."—George Sweeting[249]

"The true evangelistic sermon is a planned, organized, and concentrated drive toward the goal of decisions for Christ."—Faris Whitesell[250]

"Evangelistic preaching is urgent. The appeal is to the will. The will is the entire personality in action. One seeks to win the hearer as a man, soul and body, for time and eternity....Whatever the tone-color of the sermon, the aim is to move the will of the hearer Christward."—Andrew Blackwood[251]

"We'll know that we're in the last days of effective evangelism in America when we give up our deep conviction about giving a strong invitation for people to come to Christ."—Wayne Bristow[252]

"All successful preaching is bringing the human soul to know God as he has revealed Himself to us. It is thus that 'deep calleth unto deep,' the human and the divine meet, and the emptiness of the human heart finds its satisfaction in Him who is 'all in all.'"—Harry E. Knott[253]

"Laymen frequently stand nonplussed at the close of a sermon, not knowing what they are to think or what they ought to do."—Charles E. Jefferson[254]

---

[247] Gadsby, *Things Most Surely Believed,* 157.

[248] Bodey, *Inside the Sermon,* 130.

[249] Koessler, *Moody Handbook on Preaching,* 86.

[250] Whitesell, *Evangelistic Preaching,* 28.

[251] Blackwood, *Home Church,* 88.

[252] Bristow, "Full-Time Evangelists."

[253] Knott, *Prepare an Expository Sermon,* 73.

[254] Jefferson, *Quiet Hints,* 87.

4
Summons

The invitation at the climax of the sermon is criticized as to its place in the church by some, jeopardized by ignorance of its purpose by others, and sadly all too often nullified of its effecttualness due to its misuse by most. C. E. Matthews stated, "It might be said that the majority in the congregation and many of our ministers have little or no concept of the seriousness of the inexpressible importance of the invitation. This fact is revealed in the thing witnessed again and again at the conclusion of the preaching service—a good sermon but no appeal."[255] In stressing the importance of a good invitation, Matthews continues, "When the service is concluded and the congregation stands for the invitation, the moment has struck for the consummation of everything that has been done in the name of the Lord up to that hour for that one thing. All the work in preparation—the census, the contacts in visitation, the publicity, the prayer meetings, money contributed, everything—was for that invitation. All that has transpired in that particular service—the sermon, the praying, the music, the time spent by the congregation in worship—everything has been done to make ready for that invitation."[256]

Dr. Len G. Broughton stated: "I remember a few years ago, when I had not as much experience as I have now and when my enthusiasm perhaps was not as well balanced as it is now, I had been invited to preach in one of the leading churches in one of the great cities. I went into the pulpit conscious that God was with us in a very peculiar sense, and when I finished my sermon, the one thing on my mind was the salvation of souls. I did not know whether they had ever had an invitation given there for the confession of Christ, but I did not stop to ask. I stepped down and extended the invitation to any who would

---

[255] Matthews, *Program of Evangelism,* 93.
[256] Ibid., 92–93.

accept Jesus then and there to come to the front. Immediately a strong, able-bodied man got up and, with tears streaming down his face, came to the front and took my hand; then another man came. Fourteen grown people confessed Christ that morning. As we went out of the church, the wife of one of the officers, who was also a Sunday school teacher, spoke to an officer of the church and said: 'I greatly enjoyed the sermon until the last, but I do not think that a man should disarrange the order of the service for the sake of having a few people come to the front.' The first one who came forward was a railroad engineer who was killed in a wreck that Sunday night."[257] Despite its opponents, the invitation must be extended, giving man a means to respond to God's offer of eternal life.

George Sweeting wrote, "I'm aware of the struggles that some have concerning any form of invitation. Yet evangelistic preaching calls for a decision. Jesus emphatically said, 'Whoever acknowledges me before men, I will also acknowledge him before my Father in heaven. But whoever disowns me before men, I will disown him before my Father in heaven' (Matthew 10:23–24). The reasons for a public decision are many. First, we owe it to Jesus. Jesus died publicly on the cross for our sins, and we are required to acknowledge Him publicly. Secondly, we owe it to others. We are to confess Him 'before men' (10:32). Third, we owe it to ourselves. A public decision puts a person on record and brings out the best in him. It's a constant reminder of what we have decided and helps fortify our faith."[258]

The evangelistic invitation is clearly mandated in Scripture as a means to call lost man to salvation through repentance and faith. The Bible is a Book of invitations. God extended the first invitation in Scripture to Adam and Eve after their sin when He cried out to them, "Where art thou?" (Genesis 3:9). Moses issued an invitation at the base of Sinai when he said to a

---

[257] P. L. Tan, *7700 Illustrations,* No. 5314.
[258] Koessler, *Moody Handbook on Preaching,* 86.

multitude of people, "Who is on the Lord's side, let him come unto me" (Exodus 32:26). Joshua extended an invitation to the Israelites in stating, "Choose you this day whom ye will serve" (Joshua 24:15). Isaiah was God's man to issue the invitation to Judah when he said, "Come now, and let us reason together saith the Lord: though your sins be as scarlet, they shall be as white as snow; though they be red like crimson, they shall be as wool" (Isaiah 1:18). Paul extended the invitation to the Philippian jailer to be saved; Peter extended it to the crowd at Pentecost. Jesus in the New Testament extended the invitation to Simon and Andrew when He said, "Come ye after me, and I will make you to become fishers of men" (Mark 1:17). He issued an invitation saying, "Come unto me, all ye that labor and are heavy laden, and I will give you rest" (Matthew 11:28). In Revelation 3:20, Jesus issued the invitation again clearly, "Behold, I stand at the door, and knock: if any man hear my voice, and open the door, I will come in to him." The Bible not only opens with an invitation, but closes with one in Revelation 22:17, "And the Spirit and Bride say come. And let him that heareth say come. And let him that is athirst come. And whosoever will, let him take the water of life freely." In this text Jesus clearly commands and authorizes its issuance, ("I Jesus." v. 16).

C. E. Autrey comments, "In many of the cases in Scripture, the exact idea of the present-day type of invitation is not intended, but the germinal idea is there. In some cases the basis for the modern invitation is there beyond any doubt."[259] "C. H. Spurgeon earnestly exhorted those who had accepted Christ as their Savior to come forward amongst his people and avow their attachment to His person and name. Words of kindly encouragement and of loving persuasiveness were addressed to the timid and retiring ones who feared to avow themselves to be the Lord's lest they should fall back into sin and dishonor His name. This was followed by an appeal to those who had

---

[259] Autrey, *Basic Evangelism*, 127–128.

confessed the name of Jesus—an appeal of so stirring and searching a nature that many must have felt constrained to say, 'Lord what wilt thou have me to do?' Prayer for more earnest living, abiding, practical godliness, followed this address."[260] So ministers, without apology, have good reason to give the invitation. The preacher is right to preach the Gospel and then exhort, invite, compel and plead with people to come to Christ at that moment.

Roy Fish stated, "Preaching evangelistically is woefully incomplete without an invitation to come to Jesus. In the New Testament it is obvious that evangelistic preaching and compelling invitations were virtually inseparable."[261] Jerry Vines declared, "At the end of every sermon I invite people to receive Jesus Christ as their Lord and Savior. I do so on very good Bible precedent."[262] Billy Graham, speaking to evangelists from around the world at Amsterdam '83, said, "Is it valid or legitimate to extend an invitation for people to come to Christ?" Then he answered this question with an emphatic, "Yes!"[263]

Renowned Southern Baptist "expert" in evangelism C. E. Autrey states regarding the sermon and invitation, "Every sentence and every paragraph should pull for a decision."[264] Faris D. Whitesell says, "Emotions aroused and desires stirred will soon pass away unless acted upon at once; good impulses are harder to generate the second time than they were the first time, if the first resulted in no action."[265] D. L. Moody stated, "I once heard someone in the inquiry room telling a young person to go home and seek Christ in his closet. I would not dare tell anyone to do that. He might be dead before he got home. If I read my Bible correctly, the man who preaches the Gospel will not tell

---

[260] Drummond, *Prince of Preachers,* 658.

[261] Fasol et al., *Preaching Evangelistically,* 76.

[262] Allen and Gregory, *Southern Baptist Preaching Today,* 410.

[263] Douglas, *Work of the Evangelist,* 171.

[264] Autrey, *Basic Evangelism,* 127.

[265] Douglas, *Work of the Evangelist,* 178.

me to seek Christ tomorrow or an hour hence, but now. He is near to every one of us this minute to save."[266]

A theological student from England was assigned the task of hearing a noted preacher. He reported back with disappointment and disgust saying, "That man didn't do anything but say, 'Come to Jesus.'"

The professor inquired, "Did they come?"

"Well, yes, they did," he replied.

The professor then said, "I want you to go back and listen to that man preach again and again until you can say, 'Come to Jesus' as he did and have people respond."[267] The invitation's purpose is to have hearers "come to Jesus." Its clear aim is to solicit positive response to God's call to be saved. For this purpose to be accomplished, the minister must work hard in perfecting its "extension."

Sound, Strong and Sure Invitations

C. E. Matthews hits the nail squarely in stating, "The matter of how the net is drawn probably is the chief difference between a preacher who is successful as an evangelist and one who is unsuccessful as an evangelist. Therefore, the greatest and most earnest thought and study humanly possible on the matter of the invitation should be made by every preacher of the Word of God."[268]

How can the preacher give a biblically honest and effective evangelistic invitation?

Give It Plainly

Clearly state the decision for Christ sought. Use terminology that connects with the unchurched in the pew. Billy Graham's appeal following his sermon *The Narrow Gate* serves as a pattern for clarity in appeal. "I'm asking you young people here tonight to give your life to Christ. Then you who are older,

---

[266] Moody, "Tomorrow."
[267] Fasol et al., *Preaching Evangelistically*, 75.
[268] Matthews, *Church Revival*, 99.

you have some gray hairs, and perhaps you think it is too late. But God has spoken to you again tonight, and He is giving you another chance. I'm asking you tonight, the old and the young, to get up out of your seats—hundreds of you right now—and come and stand right here in front of this platform and say by coming, 'I give my life to Christ. I want to follow His flag. I want to serve Him. I want to look at Him. I want Him to have all of me. I don't care what it costs.'"[269]

A minister ended his sermon with great concern and earnestness like this: "And now, my friends, if you do not believe these truths, there may be for you grave eschatological consequences."

Afterwards a layman asked the preacher, "Did you mean that they would be in danger of Hell?"

"Why, yes," he replied.

"Then why in the world didn't you say so?" the layman inquired.[270] Clarify simply what is necessary for salvation (Acts 20:21) and that which will transpire once they come to the altar. Do diligence not to equate or give the impression that "walking the aisle" is synonymous with salvation, detailing the need of repentance and faith.

Give It Passionately

Preach with soul urgency and then plead with soul urgency for man to be reconciled to God. Knowing the uncertainty of another opportunity to reach the sinner in the pew, seek his soul for Jesus Christ then and there with all earnestness. "Never be professional in the invitation. Pray over the lost until you can feel the pains of Hell laying hold upon them. Yearn for the salvation of the lost even as God yearns for them. Plead as constrained by the love of Christ. Very few men today can plead with power. It is a lost skill! We must pay the price. We cannot plead unless we bleed—bleed under the burden for

---

[269] Graham, "The Narrow Gate."
[270] Green, ed., *Illustrations for Biblical Preaching*, 286.

souls, bleed with compassion, bleed with tenderheartedness and melting love."[271]

Give It Politely

Permission evangelism is operative in the pulpit as it is in private. Be careful not to embarrass, threaten, or demean those whom you are seeking to win to Christ. John Henry Jowett advises, "We want more tenderness in our speech, the tones of love and of sensitive yearning. We want less scolding and more pleading, less driving and more wooing. *'Compel* them to come in' (Luke 14:23). I am glad that the somewhat harsh word has been excised from the Revised Version and that in its place we have the soft and welcome word 'constrain.' *'Constrain* them to come in.' Woo them into the kingdom!"[272]

Give It Positively

Expect people to respond. Don't bury your face in a hymnal, but look eagerly for the sinner's response. Instead of saying, "If anyone here needs to be saved," state, "For those here today who need to come to Christ..." Couch the appeal in the positive, not negative. "Dr. Matthews, Dr. Scarborough, Dr. Carroll, and, in fact, all effective soul winners never said, 'Is there one who will accept Christ today?' They would say, 'How many will now accept the Savior?' The preacher with poise will expect great things to happen every time he preaches Christ."[273] George W. Truett gave the invitation with confidence, saying, "You will come." Every preacher will do well to do the same.

Give It Persistently

Though the type of invitation may vary (altar call, raising of the hand, checking a decision card), it ought always to be issued. R. G. Lee stated, "Only a few times in my fifty-three years of preaching have I failed to give an invitation.

---

[271] Whitesell, *Sixty-Five Ways,* 29.
[272] Jowett, *Apostolic Optimism,* Chapter 20.
[273] Autrey, *Basic Evangelism,* 132.

Sometimes I have failed to get a large response. Sometimes hundreds have responded."[274]

Give It Patiently

Don't hurry the invitation to its conclusion. O. S. Hawkins is correct in his assessment of invitations that are rushed, "Hurried and haphazard appeals seldom result in positive response."[275] In the invitation period, the lost in the pew prayerfully are processing the message shared and the decision requested through (1) *Reflection,* "What am I being asked to do?" (2) *Inspection,* "Is this something I need to do?" (3) *Deliberation,* "Is this something I am willing to do?" (4) *Resolution,* "Will I do it here and now?" (5) *Application,* "I will receive Christ as Lord and Savior here and now." This process may take moments for some but minutes for others, necessitating patience. Billy Graham testifies that it was when Mordecai Ham extended the invitation hymn in a Charlotte crusade one more verse that he responded to the altar call to be saved.

Give It Persuasively (Acts 18:4)

Knowing what is man's lot presently and eternally without Christ motivates the minister to persuade the lost earnestly to be saved. He must persuade the sinner to choose life over death, Heaven over Hell, happiness over heartache, good over bad, and Jesus over the world, the flesh and the devil. The minister must bring the sinner to believe the claims of Christ are true and his need of salvation is absolutely necessary. C. E. Autrey states, "Lost men are under the wrath of God. They are not aware of their condition. The evangelist knows this and must, by his firm, tender pleas, lead the sinner to realize his guilt before God. Mere perfunctory concern in the evangelist cannot be used of God to bring a sense of dire need in the sinner's heart."[276]

---

[274] Lee, "Gospel Invitation."

[275] Hawkins, *Drawing the Net,* 64.

[276] Autrey, *Basic Evangelism,* 132.

Give It Prayerfully

Billy Graham states, "Every time I give an invitation, I am in an attitude of prayer inwardly, because I know I'm totally dependent on God....This is the part of the evangelistic service that often exhausts me physically....There is an inward groaning and agonizing in prayer that I cannot possibly put into words."[277] "The battle for the invitation is not won in the pulpit. It is won in the prayer closet. It is won in advance."[278]

Give It Periodically

The invitation should be interwoven throughout the sermon. The most effective evangelistic messages I preach appeal to the sinner to embrace Christ from start to completion. This appeal is not the full-blown type issued at the invitation time but simply one that keeps the sinner focused on the decision they will be asked to make at the sermon's conclusion. Leighton Ford stated, "An honest invitation, in my judgment, should begin at the outset of the message. People should know what is going to happen rather than having something sprung on them. Billy Graham begins giving the invitation with his opening prayer....Then the invitation is repeated throughout the message as the truth is applied. I do not mean people are told over and over to take some action, but repeatedly they are asked, 'Is this you? Has God been speaking to you about this and this? Are you sensing that God is calling you?'"[279]

Give It Preparedly

Effective invitations require planning in regard to substance and issuance. Matters such as transition from the body of the sermon to the invitation smoothly, invitational hymn, type of appeal, notification to musicians of approach, and actual appeal must be prayerfully planned well in advance. The minister should work hard in varying the approach to and method of the

---

[277] Douglas, *Work of the Evangelist*, 173.
[278] Bisagno, *Letters to Timothy*, 167.
[279] Berkley, ed., *Preaching to Convince*.

invitation to avoid "staleness." Keep it fresh. Don't let people get so accustomed to the manner in which you extend the invitation that it becomes mundane and a signal to ready for departure from the service. Andrew Blackwood stated, "The ineffectiveness of a man's closing words may spring from lack of variety."[280] Keep the invitation unpredictable.

Additionally, preparation with regard to the invitation is paramount with the host pastor, musicians, choir, and music leader to assure all are on the same page so that this key part of the service flows smoothly. Musicians need to know when to start playing; the host pastor needs to know when the service will be back in his charge; the music leader needs to know the form of invitation that will be used (instrumental or singing only or combination) and that he is to stand to the right or left of the pulpit to lead the invitation without hand motions.

Invitational Types

Basically there are five types of invitational methods from which others spring. The appeal for public decision for Christ, the appeal for decision for Christ in the pew by uplifted hand, the appeal for decision for Christ using a decision card, the appeal for decision for Christ by having sinners pray the "sinner's prayer" in the pew, and the appeal for decision for Christ in departure from the service. In my book *The Evangelistic Invitation 101,* I cite thirty variations of these types of invitations. Keep in mind as you utilize various invitational types the words of C. E. Autrey, "There is no sure-fire plan."[281] Preach evangelistically fervently, extend the invitation preparedly and passionately, but in all rely upon the Holy Spirit entirely.

Transitional Sentences to the Invitation

The transitional sentence from the body of the sermon to the invitation should be formed based upon the proposition (purpose) of the sermon and be written out, memorized and prac-

---

[280] Blackwood, *Preparation of Sermons*, 173.
[281] Autrey, *Basic Evangelism*, 131.

ticed. Its purpose is to reinforce pointedly the goal of the message and enable a smooth landing into the invitational appeal, keeping it from appearing to be a "tack on" to the sermon.

Examples of the Evangelistic Transitional Sentence

John R. Rice's invitational transition sentence in his message *What Must I Do to Be Saved?*: "Will you not right now, with the same simple faith of that young woman who takes a husband, accept Jesus as your Savior and say to Him, 'I do'?"[282]

Billy Graham's invitation transition sentence in his message *Heaven or Hell*: "How do you go to Heaven? Jesus said, 'I am the way, the truth, and the life' (John 14:6). The Bible says, 'There is [no] other name...given among men, whereby we must be saved' (Acts 4:12). You can't get there except through Christ. The Bible says it's a narrow road—very narrow. Jesus said. 'Except [you] repent, [you] shall...likewise perish' (Luke 13:3). Has there ever been a moment in your life when you really turned from sin to God? Has there ever been a moment when you really received Christ into your heart?"[283]

George W. Truett's invitation transition sentence to his message *The Door to Heaven:* "I have just one more word. Are you on the road that leads home to Heaven? You should be altogether sure about that. There ought not to be guesswork about that. Are you on that road to Heaven? There is just one road, just one."[284]

W. A. Criswell's transition sentence in his message *Saving Faith:* "And that's what that means there: *pisteuo epi*—'believe upon the Lord Jesus Christ.' Commit your life to Him. Trust Him for it. 'And thou shalt be saved.' And that's our invitation

---

[282] John Rice, *Revival Appeals,* 168.
[283] Graham, "Heaven or Hell."
[284] Truett, "Door to Heaven."

to your soul this day—a family you, a couple you, or just a one somebody you."[285]

Examples of the Evangelistic Invitation

B. H. Carroll issued the invitational appeal in this manner: "The most important question on this earth is the settlement of your relation with God. That takes precedence over everything. There is nothing to be mentioned in comparison with the settlement of this question. Come now or never. Not to come now is to be shut out forever."[286]

R. A. Torrey's invitation in his sermon *God's Blockades on the Road to Hell:* "Oh, men and women, listen! No man or woman here will go out of this place tonight refusing to accept Christ without trampling under foot the form of Him who was crucified on the Cross of Calvary for you, without trampling under foot the One who was wounded for your transgressions and bruised for your iniquities and upon whom the chastisement of your peace was laid....God has piled mountain high the obstacles that lie in the path of sin that you are persistently pursuing and that ends in an everlasting Hell. Don't try longer to surmount these obstacles. Turn back tonight. Yield to God. Turn out of the path of unbelief that leads to an eternal Hell and turn into the path that leads to eternal glory by accepting Jesus Christ as your personal Savior."[287]

D. L. Moody's invitation in his sermon *Tomorrow May Be Too Late:* "Now is a time of mercy. It may be I am talking to someone whose days of grace may be few, to someone who may be snatched away very soon, who may never hear another gospel sermon, who may be hearing the last call. My friend, be wise! Make up your mind that you will seek the kingdom of God now. 'Behold, now is the accepted time; behold, now is the day of salvation.' Christ is inviting you to come: 'Come unto me, all ye that labor and are heavy laden, and I will give

---

[285] Criswell, "Saving Faith."
[286] Lee, *Sermonic Library,* 27.
[287] Hutson, *Great Preaching on Hell,* 195–208.

you rest.' Oh, may we all find rest in Christ now! Do not let anything divert your mind, but make up your mind this hour that you will settle this great question of eternity."[288]

L. R. Scarborough issued this invitation at the climax of his sermon entitled *Lost*: "I want you to think for a moment of the seeking Savior. He is seeking you through your mother. He is seeking that unsaved man tonight by the godly life of his wife. He is seeking that wayward, wicked father by the life of his consecrated daughter or son. He is seeking you through this preacher, through these singers, through this sermon, through His divine Spirit. Why, this tabernacle and these lights are saying, 'Come to Jesus.' These Christian people say, 'Come to Jesus.' This civilization in which we live today says, 'Jesus is come to seek and save that which was lost.' He is seeking you, and He bids you seek Him. You are a sinner; He is a Savior. You are going to Hell if you hold on to your sins. He says, 'Hold on to Me. Trust Me. Give me your heart, and I will give you a heaven down here and a great eternal Heaven up yonder.'

"Oh, tonight let this Savior come into your soul by giving up your sins and trusting Jesus Christ as your Savior. Tonight, not on the church, not on the ordinances, though I love them; not on a moral life, though I prize it; not on liberality, though I bless God for liberality; but tonight on the two arms of the cross of Jesus Christ I swing out the hope of the world's salvation. 'There is no other name in Heaven or on earth whereby you must be saved.'

"Thirty-six years ago I trusted Him; and, thank God, though I have buried my loved ones, I have stood by the bedside of my sick wife and children and other loved ones, I have suffered, tonight I say, 'I do not want any other name.' Jesus Christ's name is sufficient. God help you tonight to let Jesus Christ

---

[288] Moody, "Tomorrow."

come to that dark world of your heart where it says 'Lost' and let the word 'Jesus' be written in its place."[289]

John R. Rice issued this invitational appeal at the climax of his sermon entitled *No Room for Jesus*: "Poor, lost sinner, is not your heart convicted of your terrible sin in crowding Jesus out? Will you go to Hell because you have no room in your heart for the Son of God? Will you spend eternity in torment because pleasure or self-will or sin in any form bars the door of your heart against Jesus? Oh! Let Him in! Let Him in today!

"Christ brings sweet peace. You can never have peace without Him. He brings salvation, but there is no other name given under Heaven among men whereby you must be saved. Christ gives everlasting life, but 'he that believeth not is condemned already.' Most of the world has no room for Jesus. But those few that received Him, how happy they were and how blessed! 'He came unto his own, and his own received him not. But as many as received him, to them gave he power to become the sons of God, *even* to them that believe on his name' (John 1:11, 12).

"Receive Him today! By faith take Him as yours. Open your heart and with tender love take Jesus in. You will never have a real Christmas without Him. But if you have Him, you can laugh at poverty; you can rejoice in adversity; you can look death in the face unafraid. If you have Jesus, you have all God can give a poor, rebellious race! Take Him today!"[290] (Rice then read the words to the song, *No Room in the Inn.*)

B. H. Carroll's invitation at the climax of his sermon *Saved from Sin:* "And all I ask you to do, so far as external motion is concerned, is just this: that while we sing a hymn you stand up for a moment. When you see that I recognize you, you may sit down. What do I mean by that? It is not an idle request. I mean that you thereby admit that you are a sinner. You admit you

---

[289] Scarborough, *Prepare to Meet God,* 39–41.
[290] John Rice, *Revival Appeals,* 168.

need a Savior. You intend by it that in your heart, not out loud with your mouth, but that in your heart today you will simply think this prayer, 'God be merciful to me a sinner.' I do not ask your lips to move. While there must be a confession, you may confess by an act. You stand up today under this invitation, and it says to God, 'I do confess I am a sinner. I confess it this day, I need a Savior. I am from today, from my heart, a suppliant for divine grace; and I say in my heart, *God be merciful to me a sinner.*'

"Now if you stand up, I want you to mean all this. And then I ask as we all kneel down to pray, you will turn the eyes of your mind, of your soul, to the One whom God hath sent forth to be the Savior, Jesus, and you will honor Him in your mind, look at Him and ask Him to save you. 'Lord Jesus, save me; save me. I accept salvation in Christ.' Will you do it? The standing up will reveal what God has been doing.

"I don't know who will stand; I don't know positively that there will be anybody, but I ask for a demonstration of what God's work has been, what He has wrought in this congregation today while I have been preaching. If one of you sitting up here in the choir has discovered that your soul is a lost soul and feel it, stand up today and confess it. Let there be a quietness here today that can be felt. Let a home feeling come over this audience—a feeling of domesticity, that this is a family of men and women akin to each other and we are here on a momentous matter. God is not in the whirlwind nor in the earthquake, but He is in the still, small voice. Now sing, and let convicted sinners stand up before God in confession of sin and as supplicants for life. Ah! There you stand. What hath God wrought!"[291]

Invitation Conclusion

Upon George W. Truett's being asked if there was a rule for deciding how long the invitation should be extended, He

---

[291] B. H. Carroll, *Evangelistic Sermons,* 42–44.

replied, "Yes. And it is very simple. If the Holy Spirit is working, we dare not quit. If not, we dare not presume."[292] Sensitivity to the work of the Holy Spirit in the pew by the minister is crucial to know when the invitation should conclude. The determination to stop or continue the invitation must not be based simply on little or no response to several verses of the decision hymn or upon time. John Bisagno stated, "Don't be afraid to give a long invitation....I have found that 90% of the converts come forward after the third verse of the invitation."[293] Plan the service and sermon to ease any time restraint for the invitation, granting the Holy Spirit total freedom to convict, convince and convert.

Never close an invitation without first giving people warning. Always say, "This next verse will be our final stanza of the invitation." This will prompt sinners who intend to come to move forward without further delay. At times the Holy Spirit will impress upon the minister the need to extend the invitation a verse beyond "the last stanza to be sung." Billy Graham testifies that it was when Mordecai Ham extended the invitation one more verse that he hit the sawdust trail and was saved. Dave Walton shares that during an invitation he wrestled with the issue of salvation finally deciding to respond "if they would sing one more stanza." It appeared this would not happen, when suddenly the pastor felt strangely warmed to extend the invitation one final verse. Dave Walton immediately responded, leaving a life of drugs, alcohol and wastefulness to live for Jesus Christ. Walton now serves God as a vocational evangelist. Thank God for the divine sensitivity of these two preachers to extend the invitation one more stanza!

At the formal invitation conclusion, inform people that the "offer still stands," that a minister or counselor will be available at the front of the platform to talk personally with all who desire to know Christ.

---

[292] Bodey, *Inside the Sermon*, 130.
[293] Bisagno, *Power of Positive Evangelism*, 22–23.

"It is more important clumsily to have something to say than cleverly to say nothing."[294]—Charles Koller

"We need more candid preaching and less can-died preaching."[295]—Herschel Ford

"There is not enough one-hundred-percent evangelistic preaching. Many preachers have never dared to preach thus. They have been afraid to let go and try. Oh, come, brother preacher, there never was a greater need for evangelistic preaching than now. Launch out and try your wings!"[296]—Faris D. Whitesell

"The word of God is too sacred a thing and preaching too solemn a work to be toyed and played with, as is the usage of some who make a sermon but matter of wit and fine oratory. Their sermon is like a child's doll from which if you take its dress the rest is worth nothing; unpin this story, take off that gaudy phrase, and nothing is left in the discourse."[297]—William Gurnall

"Every man who preaches should aim at preaching his best sermon every time he mounts the pulpit"[298]—C. H. Spurgeon

[294] Koller, *Expository Preaching without Notes*, 42–43.
[295] "Quotes on Preaching."
[296] Whitesell, *Evangelistic Preaching,* 41.
[297] Gurnall, *Christian in Complete Armour,* 622.
[298] Allen, *Exploring the Mind,* M-538.

5
Samples

All who preach would cherish the privilege to look in upon the master preachers in their study as they nestle with the Bible and reference books preparing a sermon. Such an experience would be more profitable than a manual on the "how to" of sermon preparation. In this chapter, I invite you to receive counsel from some renowned preachers past and present regarding the preparation and delivery of the sermon. Listen intensely to their advice. Look closely at their sermon method. Latch hold of their sermon passion. Muse over the two evangelistic messages cited by Gipsy Smith and W. A. Criswell. Warm your heart for effective evangelistic preaching by the fireplace of their souls. Grasp the burden these two men possessed in preaching to win souls. Study their messages until you catch the feel and flow of a biblical evangelistic sermon.

Great Preachers on Preaching

Jesus

In Jesus' Sermon on the Mount, a worthy pattern for preaching is charted. In this 18-minute, 2,130-word sermon, Jesus uses directness in address (221 times "you" or "your"); questions (19) and one-syllable words. In this sermon, Jesus uses 404 verbs for energy, 320 pronouns, and 20 clear contrasts coupled with many more comparisons and illustrations. He uses repetition throughout the sermon: "heaven" (18 times); "father" (17 times); "but I say" (14 times); "kingdom" (8 times); "you have heard" (6 times). Connective words are used extensively: "that" (51 times); "for" (24 times); "therefore" (13 times); "but" (8 times); "into" (59 times); "no," "not," "neither," "nor" (70 times).[299]

---

[299] Lewis, *Inductive Preaching*, 147.

C. H. Spurgeon

"I confess that I frequently sit hour after hour praying and waiting for a subject and that this is the main part of my study. Much hard labor have I spent in manipulating topics, ruminating upon points of doctrine, making skeletons out of verses and then burying every bone of them in the catacombs of oblivion, sailing on and on over leagues of broken water till I see the red lights and make sail direct to the desired haven. I believe almost any Saturday in my life I make enough outlines of sermons, if I felt liberty to preach them, to last me for a month.... Wait for the elect word, even if you wait till within an hour of the service. This may not be understood by cool, calculating men who are not moved by impulses as we are, but to some of us these things are a law in our hearts against which we dare not offend. We tarry at Jerusalem till power is given."[300]

"All through the week I am on the lookout for some material I can use on the Sabbath, but the actual work of arranging it is left till Saturday evening."[301]

"I had thought of giving one more answer to this question, but time fails me. The answer would have been somewhat like this—that to preach the Gospel is not to preach certain truths *about* the Gospel; not to preach *about* the people, but to preach *to* the people. To preach the Gospel is not to talk about what the Gospel is, but to preach it into the heart, not by your own might, but by the influence of the Holy Ghost; not to stand and talk as if we were speaking to the angel Gabriel and telling him certain things, but to speak as man to man and pour our heart into our fellow's heart. This I take it is to preach the Gospel, and not to mumble some dry manuscript over on Sunday morning or Sunday evening. To preach the Gospel is not to send a curate to do your duty for you; it is not to put on your fine gown and then stand and give out some lofty speculation. To preach the Gospel is not with the hands of a bishop to turn over

---

[300] Spurgeon, *Lectures to My Students,* 84–85.
[301] *Homiletic Review,* Vol. XLIX, 110.

some beautiful specimen of prayer and then to go down again and leave it to some humbler person to speak. Nay, to preach the Gospel is to proclaim with trumpet tongue and flaming zeal the unsearchable riches of Christ Jesus so that men may hear and, understanding, may turn to God with full purpose of heart. This is to preach the Gospel."[302]

"...the mass of people do not lay hold on what is said but on how it is said. And if it is said smartly and privily and said forcedly, that is enough for them, though it be a lie. But if the truth be spoken, that they will not receive unless it be attended by some graces of oratory or elegance. Now the Christian that has gone beyond babyhood does not care about how the man says it. It is the thing that is said that he cares about. All he asks is 'Did he speak the truth?'...he cares not for the trimming of the feast nor for the exquisite workmanship of the dish. He only cares for that which is solid food for himself."[303]

G. Campbell Morgan said of this great London pastor, "For many years Spurgeon fixed upon a text and then gave it to his secretary, who was a minister, in his great library, saying 'There is my text.' Then that minister went through Spurgeon's library, which he had indexed for him, and brought everything that had any bearing on that text and piled books all around him. Spurgeon took those books and read all those things and then made his outline. That was his method."

Spurgeon, as he lay on his deathbed, testified to a friend, "My theology now is found in four little words: 'JESUS died for ME.' I don't say this is all I would preach if I were to be raised up again, but it is more than enough for me to die upon."[304] In times when Spurgeon had nothing to say to his people, he would put himself in his gun and fire it off, tapping hold of his own inner life, the knowledge of the spiritual that God had place within his soul, the experience of answered

---

[302] Spurgeon, "Preach the Gospel."
[303] Spurgeon, "Search the Scripture."
[304] P. L. Tan, *7700 Illustrations,* No. 657.

prayer, rewarded service, compensated suffering, fruitful faith to illustrate the faithfulness of God and the high privilege of believers.[305]

William Gurnall

"Ministers have no ability of their own for their work. Oh! How long may they sit tumbling their books over and puzzling their brains until God comes to their help, and then—as Jacob's venison—it is brought to their hand. If God drop not down His assistance, we write with a pen that hath no ink; if anyone need walk dependently upon God more than another, the minister is he."[306]

Richard Baxter

"What skill doth every part of our work require, and of how much moment every part! To preach a sermon, I think, is not the hardest part. And yet what skill is necessary to make plain the truth, to convince the hearers; to let in the irresistible light into their consciences and to keep it there and drive all home; to screw the truth into their minds and work Christ into their affections; to meet every objection that gainsays and clearly to resolve it; to drive sinners to a stand and make them see there is no hope, but they must unavoidably be converted or condemned; and to do all this so for language and manner as beseems our work and yet as is most suitable to the capacities of our hearers. This, and a great deal more that should be done in every sermon, should surely be done with a great deal of holy skill. So great a God, whose message we deliver, should be honored by our delivery of it."[307]

"O sirs, how plainly, how closely, how earnestly should we deliver a message of such moment as ours when the everlasting life or everlasting death of our fellowmen is involved in it!…There [is] nothing more unsuitable to such a business than

---

[305] Funk and Wells, *The Homiletic Review*, 64.
[306] Spurgeon, *Lectures to My Students*, 86.
[307] Stewart, *Heralds of God*, 141.

to be slight and dull. What! speak coldly for God and for men's salvation? Can we believe that our people must be converted or condemned and yet speak in a drowsy tone? In the name of God, brethren, labor to awaken your own hearts before you go to the pulpit, that you may be fit to awaken the hearts of sinners....Oh, speak not one cold or careless word about so great a business as Heaven or Hell. Whatever you do, let the people see that you are in good earnest....A sermon full of mere words, how neatly so ever it be composed, while it want the light of evidence and the life of zeal, is but an image or a well-dressed carcass."[308]

Charles E. Finney

"I almost always get my (sermon) subjects on my knees in prayer; and it has been a common experience with me, upon receiving a subject from the Holy Spirit, to have it make so strong an impression on my mind as to make me tremble, so that I could with difficulty write....When subjects are thus given to me that seem to go through me, body and soul, I can in a few moments make out a skeleton that shall enable me to retain the view presented by the Spirit; and I find that such sermons always tell with great power upon the people....I believe that all ministers called by Christ to preach the Gospel ought to be, and may be in such a sense, inspired as to preach the Gospel *'with the Holy Ghost sent down from heaven'* (I Peter 1:12)."[309]

John Stott

"Exposition is not a synonym for exegesis. True biblical preaching goes beyond the elucidation of the text to its application. Indeed, the discipline of discovering a text's original meaning is of little profit if we do not go on to discern its contemporary message. We have to ask every Scripture not only 'what *did* it mean?' but 'what *does* it say?'...If we are to build

---

[308] Baxter, *Reformed Pastor.*
[309] "The Revival Labors" 9.

bridges for the Word of God to penetrate the real world, we have to take seriously both the biblical text and the contemporary scene and study both....On the one hand, we preachers need to be as familiar with the Bible 'as the housewife with her needle, the merchant with his ledger, the mariner with his ship' (Spurgeon). On the other, we have to grapple with the much more difficult—and usually less congenial—task of studying the modern world."[310]

"Writing out your sermon forces you to think straight and sufficiently. It exposes lazy thinking and cures it. After you are thoroughly familiar with your outline, reduce it to small notes. Pray that God will enable you to 'so possess the message that the message possesses you.'"[311] Stott emphatically remarked, "Preaching is indispensable to Christianity."[312]

W. A. Criswell

In his sermon "The Secret of a Preacher's Power," Criswell cites three characteristics of a great preacher: the preacher's dependence upon the Holy Spirit, the preacher's compassion for his people, and the preacher's life of deep and everlasting commitment.[313]

Charles Ryrie

"Second Timothy 2:15 instructs those who handle the word of truth to do it 'accurately.' The word means to 'cut a path so the traveler may go directly to his destination.' It also is used of a mason cutting stones straight so as to fit into their proper places. Thus we should handle Scripture in a straight manner; that is, correctly, soundly, and to the point."[314]

---

[310] Stott, "Paralyzed Speakers and Hearers," 44–45.

[311] Stott, *Between Two Worlds*, 216

[312] Mohler, "Recovery of Christian Worship, (Part 1)."

[313] Criswell, "Preacher's Power."

[314] Ryrie, *Practical Guide*, 72.

Roy Fish

"'Ministers must return to preaching Christ crucified and resurrected, avoiding theories that human beings conjure up.... This preaching helps humanity to know that Christ is acquainted with the suffering of humanity. If we show our people Calvary towering over the wrecks of time, our preaching will not be in vain....This message is not easily accepted by the lost of the world....Today's Athenians still mock the resurrection....' But he said that ministers shouldn't take insults to the Gospel personally, for a minister's first calling is not to *defend* the Gospel of Christ. His calling is to *preach* it."[315]

R.W. Dale

"Many young preachers, when they sit down to prepare a sermon, start like Abraham, who 'went out, not knowing whither he went.' The preacher who has a definite end to reach rarely loses any of the time which he gives to preparation; he sees in the distance the point to which he has to travel, and he either finds or makes a road to it."

Charles E. Jefferson

"A clear aim is the preacher's life preserver....No question should be oftener on the preacher's lips than, 'To what purpose is this?' That is the question with which he should begin every sermon. On the first page he should write in clean, terse Saxon the precise work this particular sermon is intended to do; and on the last page he should write his honest answer to the question: Is this sermon so constructed as to be likely to accomplish the result for which it has been written?"

Vance Havner

"Could it be that some preachers are decrying great preaching today because they can't do it? Could it be that we are trying to do by other methods what we can no longer do by

---

[315] Fish, "Roy Fish [Exhorts] Pastors."

preaching because we will not pay the price to be God-called, Bible-believing, Christ-centered, Spirit-anointed men?"[316]

George W. Truett

Truett, speaking to the Southern Baptist Convention in 1899, declared, "My brothers, we are not here to win men by cleverness of speech. We are to be concerned, not that men may see our handsome bow and arrows and our skillful use of the same, but that they may hear the cries of the wounded of the Lord: 'Men and brethren, what must we do to be saved?'... We should preach Christ and Christ only, because we have no warrant or authority for preaching anything else. Paul wrote to the Galatians: 'But though we, or an angel from heaven, preach any other gospel unto you than that which we have preached unto you, let him be accursed'....Ah, brethren, like Paul, we will have no 'other gospel,' for if salvation through the atonement of Christ shall fail, then all has failed, for this is the very ultimatum of God."[317]

John MacArthur

"The ideal in preparing a sermon would be to study a passage of Scripture, pick a unit of truth out of the text, develop the interpretation of it, get a good outline so people can follow the flow, create an introduction and a conclusion, and preach it. That is the ideal; that would be a real sermon....The objective is not to give you information in a perfectly clean little package that you will never forget, because you will forget!...It is designed to take you where you haven't gone in terms of your thinking and understanding of the Word of God. It is intended to create a spiritual response in that very moment and to deposit some things that will shape, over a long period of time, a fixed set of convictions in the fabric of your life."[318]

---

[316] Havner, *Sword of the Lord*, 3.
[317] Truett, *We Would See Jesus,* 146, 144.
[318] Rosscup, *How to Preach Biblically*, 313–314.

"Somewhere along the line you have to do the hard work. The difference between mediocre preaching and good preaching is effort....The struggle to understand the Bible is a struggle that basically you're willing to make or you're not. I think if you're serious about the Word of God—you believe it is the Word of God—you just pay the price. You just make the effort because you know that that is the priority of your life."[319]

"There is a science to preaching, and that's the science of interpretation. Interpretation of the Bible is done by fixed rules; in that sense it's a science. You don't have any latitude; you can't approach the Scripture any other way than by the legitimate fixed rules of biblical interpretation. So that's the science part of it. You work in the text; you deal with the syntax, lexicography, language; you get all the elements of the text in the original language. You work together with the relationship of words. You deal with context, history, whatever might inform that text. And that's the science part of it.

"And when you've done all of that and you've created this thing and you've got a good outline and flow and you've got an introduction (that's always right at the end because I can't introduce until I know what I'm going to say) and then you come up with a conclusion last of all, put the whole package together, and you've got a unit. Rarely ever am I able to preach that. And therein lies the other element of preaching. It's not just science; it's also art. It doesn't just depend upon fixed rules; it depends upon the experience of the very event itself."[320]

John Bisagno

"As a pastor, early in the week I determined the subject and began to read myself full, watching for illustrations from life, from the media, from every source, praying, mulling over and meditating about the subject for the following Sunday. By

---

[319] MacArthur, "Question and Answer Session."
[320] MacArthur, "Vilification of Jesus."

Wednesday or Thursday, the ideas began to crystallize, and I was ready to start putting my thoughts down on paper."[321] "Once you have determined the central idea and reduced it to a simple propositional statement, go back and find three or four things in the passage that support it. 'Why is that true?' 'What will happen if I do?' 'What are the consequences if I don't?' 'Is there any help?' Every sermon must answer the grand 'So what? How does that apply to me? What are you trying to get me to do?' If you can't answer that, you're not ready to start the sermon. Determine the central idea, support it in three or four ways from the text, and then write your outline."[322]

George E. Sweazey

"The Bible is still the basic handbook for evangelistic preaching; prayer is the primary method in sermon preparation; a loving study of people is the best source of ideas."[323]

Hershel Hobbs

"As for specific preparation of a sermon, I employ the following procedure. First, I select the passage of Scripture. Using commentaries and the Hebrew and Greek text, I exegete the passage. In presenting the sermon, I do not start out with exegesis. I treat this as I move through the passage in the sermon. Next, I decide on the title of the sermon. It must be short, designed to attract attention, and easily remembered. After deciding the introduction and proposition, I choose the major points for development....Then I choose illustrations to be used at given points in the sermon. Finally, I work out the conclusion, designed both to summarize the message and to lead into the invitation."[324]

---

[321] Bisagno, *Letters to Timothy*, 154–155.
[322] Ibid., 157.
[323] Sweazey, *Effective Evangelism*, 171.
[324] Bodey, *Inside the Sermon*, 129.

Samples

James Stewart

"Every Sunday morning when it comes ought to find you awed and thrilled by the reflection—*God is to be in action today, through me, for these people; this day may be crucial, this service decisive, for someone now ripe for the vision of Jesus.* Remember that every soul before you has its own story of need and that if the Gospel of Christ does not meet such need, nothing on earth can. Aim at results. Expect mighty works to happen. Realize that, although your congregation may be small, every soul is infinitely precious. Never forget that Christ Himself, according to His promise, is in the midst, making the plainest and most ordinary church building into the house of God and gate to Heaven. Hear His voice saying, 'This day is the Scripture fulfilled in your ears. This day is salvation come to this house.' Then preaching, which might otherwise be a dead formality and a barren routine, an implicit denial of its own high claim, will become a power and a passion; and the note of strong, decisive reality, like a trumpet, will awaken the souls of men."[325]

"'Great sermons,' declared Henry Ward Beecher, 'are nuisances. Show sermons are the temptation of the Devil. Life and death issues are in your mouth when you preach the Gospel of Christ, and it is simply tragic trifling to make the sermon a declamatory firework show or a garish display of the flowers of rhetoric.'"[326]

Francis W. Dixon

"They 'SO' preached that a great number believed (Acts 14:1). What does that little word 'so' tell us? It tells us that there was something about their preaching which the Holy Spirit quickly honored, and therefore great results followed. You see, they not only preached; they 'so' preached. There was something special about their preaching. What was it? I suggest

---

[325] Stewart, *Heralds of God*, 47–48.
[326] Ibid., 40.

103

to you that it was plain so that all could understand it; it was full of authority, being based upon the inspired Word of God; they preached the Gospel, as we learn from verse 7: 'And there they preached the gospel'—the good news of God's love in Jesus Christ and of His willingness to save all who believe. Their preaching was bold and courageous and earnest, as we learn from verse 3, 'speaking boldly in the Lord'; their preaching was full of entreaty and compassion—and let me tell you something else, the preachers were mightily anointed with the Holy Spirit. They preached 'in demonstration of the Spirit and with power.' What need there is for such preaching today and for this kind of preacher! How solemn this is! It is possible so to speak, to preach, that many people are converted; and it is also possible to speak or to preach so that no one is converted. The lesson we have to learn is, first, that the message has to be right, and, second, that the messenger has to be right."[327]
John R. Rice

"So, preacher, start with the Scripture. Find the theme, the real subject itself, in the Scripture. Find the outline in the Scripture; or if the outline itself is just logically deduced, then find Scriptures to back up every statement and quote them. Use many Scriptures to make clear the point and use Bible illustrations wherever possible....The Scripture itself brings conviction to people who are not convicted, brings light to people in darkness, brings salvation to those who are lost. We need Bible preaching."[328]

Rice would prepare his sermon outline or rework it prior to every sermon to keep it freshly burning in his mind and heart. He would use old sermons but always, right before the service, outline the message again.[329]

---

[327] Dixon, "Flashback to Iconium," 9–10.
[328] John Rice, "Preaching We Need."
[329] Hyles, *Teaching on Preaching,* Chapter two.

Samples

Warren Wiersbe

"I mull over the text. I pray. I meditate and exegete. I talk to my Bible and ask questions of the text. I take notes. I think. I sweat. And then God gives me what He wants me to have. Often while I'm preaching, I say things spontaneously that amaze me and everybody else. It's not direct inspiration, obviously; it's more like illumination, and the light comes on brighter."[330]

Johnny Hunt

"I am a Bible expositor. I normally commit myself to a book that I preach through....I found that preaching through books, I don't have to look for a text for the next week. I just have to be prepared to study that passage. I normally read it several times, then begin to see the theme, which becomes my title. I always write out my introduction in detail. And then I begin to lay out the major points and the subpoints underneath....I do thank God for the wonderful commentaries that give me a better understanding of the structure of the text in the original language, as well as the words and their meanings."[331]

J. I. Packer

"My method is, so to speak, first to walk round my text, or whatever I suspect will be my text (for at first, I am not always sure about that), looking at it in its larger context (i.e., as part of the book from which it comes and of the Bible as a whole) and scribbling possible schemes of points to teach, angles of interaction with life and its problems to pursue, and personal applications to develop. I find that I need to start this process several days before the message has to be produced, for getting an outline that seems right—that is, one that expresses my heart and that I see how to use in searching the hearts of others—often takes me some time."[332] Packer stated that it is

---

[330] Bailey and Wiersbe, *Black and White*, 88.
[331] Johnny Hunt, Personal Correspondence, 9 Dec 2008.
[332] Bodey, *Inside the Sermon*, 191.

only after this process is completed that he then turns to expository commentaries and homiletical materials to assist in the sermon's continued development. As with Sidlow Baxter, Packer finds expositional help in Matthew Henry's commentary more useful than that in modern expositions.[333]

Andrew Murray

"I may preach or write or think or meditate and delight in being occupied with the things in God's Book and in God's Kingdom, and yet the power of the Holy Ghost may be markedly absent. I fear that if you take the preaching throughout the Church of Christ and ask why there is, alas! so little converting power in the preaching of the Word, why there is so much work and often so little result for eternity, why the Word has so little power to build up believers in holiness and consecration, the answer will come: It is the absence of the power of the Holy Ghost."[334]

J. C. Ryle

First, "have a clear view of the subject upon which you are going to preach." Second, "try to use in all your sermons, as far as you can, simple words." Third, "take care to aim at a simple style of composition." Fourth, "use a direct style [i.e. using 'I' and 'you' and not 'we']." Fifth, "use plenty of anecdotes and illustrations."[335]

G. Campbell Morgan

"The supreme work of the Christian minister is the work of preaching. This is a day in which one of our great perils is that of doing a thousand little things to the neglect of the one thing, which is preaching."[336] Harold Murray said of G. Campbell Morgan, "He believes in having a text and defining his theme. He thinks that if a man quotes a text at the beginning of his

---

[333] Ibid.
[334] Murray, *Absolute Surrender*, 87.
[335] Holloway, "J. C. Ryle."
[336] Fabarez, *Preaching That Changes Lives*, 84.

sermon and then wanders miles away from it, he is not preaching; he is just talking."[337]

David Brainerd

"I never got away from Jesus and Him crucified in my preaching. I found that once these people were gripped by the great evangelical meaning of Christ's sacrifice on our behalf, I did not have to give them many instructions about changing their behavior."[338]

Junior Hill

"John the Baptist was not afraid of what he said. John the Baptist never had any courses on how to win friends and influence people. He didn't have any more sense than just to address the issues of the day....Have we so soon forgotten that Jesus said, "If they hated me, they will hate you"? Ladies and gentlemen, we're not in a popularity contest to try to appease the pagan world. We're the servants of the high God who called us to declare the truth of the Bible. I'm glad some of you are like John the Baptist. You're not afraid to say what you need to say. I don't think there is any virtue in being harsh and judgmental and meanspirited, and I'm not saying that at all. I don't want to be that kind of preacher. But I want to be a preacher that, when I stand up, I'm not afraid to say what God puts on my heart....

"One of my pastor friends said to one of our mutual friends, 'I wish you would recommend me to another church.' And the pastor said, 'You've got a good church. Why would you want to be recommended for somewhere else?' Listen to what he said. He said, 'Because I deserve better.' You don't deserve the breath you breathe. If God has honored you by choosing you to be a preacher, how dare you tell God that the place where He has put you is not important?

---

[337] "Gospel Attitudes."
[338] P. L. Tan, *7700 Illustrations*, No. 657.

"Some of you pastors are serving in churches that the world calls small. Some of you pastors are in a difficult church way out there somewhere. You're not seen. Nobody brags on you. I want to tell you something, sir. You are somebody. I get so tired, so weary, of hearing pastors belittle the small churches and pastors who are doing their best for God. Do you know who my heroes are? Most of you are going to be out there in the wilderness. Nobody's going to brag on you. You're going to die, and not many folks are going to remember where you served. I've got news for you. You guys are the real heroes of the faith. I have friends who spent all of their ministries never pastoring a church that ran more than fifty, and they did it gladly where God put them."[339]

Oswald Smith

"The world does not need sermons; it needs a message. You can go to seminary and learn how to preach sermons, but you will have to go to God to get messages."[340]

Billy Graham

"When I stand up to preach the Gospel...I no longer worry about whether anybody is going to respond or anybody is going to find Christ. I know that in every audience I talk to there are some people whose hearts God has prepared if I am faithful in presenting the message of Christ. I may not see any visible results....We are not to count. We are to be faithful and vindicate the righteousness of God by presenting His Word."[341]

John Piper

"How do you preach so that the preaching is a demonstration of God's power and not your own? I am trying to learn the answer to that question in my own life and preaching. I have a long way to go before I could ever be satisfied with my preaching....So for me to say, 'Here is how you preach in the power

---

[339] Hill, "The Greatest Preacher."
[340] Oswald Smith, Sermon Illustrations.
[341] Graham, *Life Wisdom*, 54.

of the Holy Spirit' is a very risky thing. Yet I can describe where I am in the quest for this precious, indispensable experience. There are five steps that I follow in seeking to preach not in my own strength but in the strength that God supplies. (1) I *admit* to the Lord my utter helplessness without him. (2) Therefore, I *pray* for help. I beg for insight, power, humility, love, memory and freedom I need to preach this message for the glory of God's name, the gladness of his people, and the ingathering of the elect. (3) I *trust*. (4) I *act* in the confidence that God will fulfill his Word. (5) I *thank* God. At the end of the message I express gratitude that he has sustained me and that the truth of his Word and the purchase of his cross have been preached in some measure in the power of his Spirit to the glory of his name."[342] Piper states that he almost always takes these steps before entering the pulpit to preach.

John H. Jowett

"What manner of man must the preacher be when he enters his workshop, and what kind of work shall he do? A little while ago I was reading the life of a very distinguished English judge, Lord Bowen, and in an illuminating statement of the powers and qualities required for success at the bar he used these words: 'Cases are won in chambers.' That is to say, so far as the barrister is concerned, his critical arena is not the public court but his own private room. He will not win triumph by extemporary wit, but by hard work. Cases are not won by jaunty 'sorties' of flashing appeal, but by well-marshalled facts and disciplined arguments marching solidly together in invincible strength. 'Cases are won in chambers.' And if a barrister is practically to conquer his jury before he meets them, by the victorious strength and sway of his preparations, shall it be otherwise with a preacher before he seeks the verdict of his congregation? With us, too, 'cases are won in chambers.'"[343]

---

[342] Piper, *Supremacy of God*, 44–46.
[343] Jowett, *The Preacher*, 113.

L. R. Scarborough

"A lazy preacher deadens the pulpit."[344]

F.B. Meyer

"The highest point of sermon utterance is when a preacher is 'possessed,' and certainly, in the judgment of the writer, such possession comes oftenest and easiest to a man who has lived, slept, walked and eaten in fellowship with a passage for the best part of a week."[345]

Martin Luther

Luther advised young preachers, "Stand up straight, speak out boldly, and sit down quickly."[346]

A.W. Tozer

"The fish that goes along with the current hasn't any trouble with the current, but as soon as he starts the other way, the current gets sore at him. Just as long as you go the way the wind blows, everybody will say you're very fine and commend you for being deeply religious. If you decide to go God's way instead of the way the wind blows, they'll say that your roof leaks or that something has happened to you and you're a fanatic. You can go along with the times, or you can be like Zacharias and Elisabeth and refuse to go along with the times. Personally I've decided that a long time ago. They say that if you don't conform to the times and find a common ground for getting along with everybody, nobody will listen to you. The more I'm nonconformist, the more people want to hear me....

"I've been told that I've missed the boat, but I reply that I wasn't trying to catch that boat. That boat and a lot of others like it can go on without me, and I'll be quite happy. We can conform to the religion of our times if we want to. I weigh 145 pounds dripping wet, but I stand here to tell you that I'm a noncomformist, twice born, and a rebel; and I will not conform to

[344] Tim Rogers, "Franchising McChurch."
[345] Knott, *Prepare an Expository Sermon,* 101.
[346] Luther, Preacherscorner.

the times. Up to now I've been able to get a hearing and refused to conform to the times. But if a day ever comes when to conform to the times is the price you have to pay to be heard, then I'll go out and start where I started before on the street corner and preach there. But I won't conform to the times. They say you are supposed to do it. They say, 'Don't you know we have the same message but it's just different times we're living in?' I know the voice of the serpent when I hear it. The hiss of the serpent is in that, and I recognize that. So we can either conform, or we can withdraw from the whole business; and Paul says, 'From such turn away.'"[347]

Evangelistic Sermon Examples
Gipsy Smith (Evangelist); "Are You Still Unsaved?"[348]

Jeremiah 8:20

I wish to speak to you about the two last words in this verse. Think of some of the things they suggest. Whatever you or I may think, there are only two classes of people—the saved and the unsaved.

I. There Are Some Saved by God's Grace

The people who have passed from death unto life; those who are described by the words of the apostle: "There is therefore no condemnation to them which are in Christ Jesus"; those described by that wonderful word, "Beloved, now are we the sons of God, and it doth not yet appear what we shall be: but we know that, when he shall appear, we shall be like him; for we shall see him as he is"; those who are born again and have the witness within that they are accepted in the Beloved can say with the poet:

---

[347] Tozer, *Worship and Entertainment,* 136–137.
[348] Gyspy Smith, "Still Unsaved?"

Amazing grace, 'tis Heaven below
  To feel His blood applied
And Jesus, only Jesus know,
  My Jesus crucified.

They can say with Charles Wesley:

No condemnation now I dread;
  Jesus, and all in Him, is mine!
Alive in Him, my living Head,
  And clothed in righteousness divine,
Bold I approach the eternal throne
And claim the crown through Christ my own.

Those hidden in Him by faith can say with the apostle: "For the law of the Spirit of life in Christ Jesus hath made me free from the law of sin and death. For what the law could not do, in that it was weak through the flesh, God sending his own Son in the likeness of sinful flesh, and for sin, condemned sin in the flesh: That the righteousness of the law might be fulfilled in us, who walk not after the flesh, but after the Spirit" (Romans 8:2–4). For the law in Christ Jesus "hath made us free" (Galatians 5:1).

There are many among you who know what that experience is. You have come to Calvary by faith; you have bathed His feet with your tears and wiped them with the hair of your head. You have heard Him say just as truly as He said it to the man with the palsy, "Thy sins are forgiven thee"; and you came from the cross singing, "I love Him because He first loved me."

There are those among you—I say it on the authority of the Word of God—who have passed from death unto life, who know Jesus saved you. You have handed yourself over to be

Christ's. You have sealed the contract; you are God's property. And you can say, "Not my own, but saved by Jesus, I am His. My life is His and must flow along His channels, my words must be spoken as in His presence, and my all must be done as for eternity." You know you are saved. You are saved by grace. It is all of free grace, perfect love working on behalf of those who are perfectly worthless. It is not by works of righteousness which we have done, but according to His mercy. No work of our own would accomplish this; we are not saved *by* works, but saved *for* works.

You cannot be saved by your works. You cannot build a house without materials, and you cannot live a new life with an old heart. You must know Christ in your own heart before you can claim those mighty words—SAVED BY GRACE.

II. There Are Multitudes Not Saved

My heart saddens as I think of the multitudes who are not saved. God knows who those are. He sees the innermost heart. "Behold, thou desirest truth in the inward parts," says the psalmist. God can turn the light on in the dingiest corner of every heart and life. Though there may be the profession and the cloak of religion and the outward garb—going to church, hymn singing, Bible reading and all these things—yet the heart itself may be like a cage of unclean birds. Though the outward platter be clean, there may be rottenness and corruption within. That was the charge our Lord brought against the people who thought themselves saved and who rejected the Light when it came.

Some of you are in the same state; indeed, you are angry with me for telling you the truth. You would rather be left alone. You don't thank me or anybody else for telling you the truth. The Devil within you cries out, as he did to the Son of God, "What have I to do with thee, Jesus, thou Son of God most high? I beseech thee, torment me not." And that is the sad part of it to me. Here in the twentieth century—with light, education, respectability, churchgoing and a sort of sentimental concern for all these things—on your poor, scarred conscience, on your poor, worthless and wasted and even churchgoing respectable life, there is written, as by the finger of God, those two words: "not saved." The ink in which they are written was distilled by your own iniquity, which makes it all the blacker.

Many from godly homes are lost. Yet it need not have been so; you might have been saved. Some of you come from the best homes; you have the best training possible. Love—yes, the tenderness of a mother's love and all that that means, a father's love and all that that means! The sweetest and most beautiful surroundings were yours. You were born, cradled and nurtured in a home filled with goodness. There is the moral momentum, the result of a godly ancestry. In your veins—in some of you— there flows the blood of saints and martyrs; yet you are not saved. Think of your opportunities, of your Sunday school days and your church days. You have been lifted to the gates of gold with the superior weight of advanced opportunity. You cannot plead ignorance at the bar of God; the very angels would cry out against you: "We flew to that man on errands of mercy." The sun, moon and stars would cry out; the rocks, the streams, and all nature would join in the chorus: "Away with him," or, "He knew better."

If you had been born in a gypsy tent, as I was, where there was no Bible, I could pity you. But you come from homes where a Bible was in every room, where you were just saturated with a mother's influence. It might have been and ought to have been different, for you had the light—light enough to save a nation.

How much God has done to save you! God help us to think! Think of all that has been lavished on you, all the hopes that have been centered and focused upon you. Think of all that God has done for you, the trouble He has taken and the patience with which He has borne with you. Think of the mercy He has shown you and all the life given to you. Remember, He has spared you for one purpose—to save you. But somehow you have managed to thwart and frustrate His designs until today. "Not saved"—and salvation cost so much, was purchased so dearly.

If you want to know how dearly, go a long way back. Sin is old, but the blood is older. God had a Lamb slain before the foundation of the world. And if you want to know how much it cost God to save you, go back to the beginning, away back over the mighty sea of time. And if that is too far, go to Calvary, to Bethlehem, to Nazareth, to Gethsemane.

Did you ever think of it? It was no sudden sorrow that overtook Him, but a long-looked-for and anticipated agony. When He worked on that carpenter's bench and took hold of that piece of timber, He must have thought of the piece that would be a cross upon which He would hang. When He took up that hammer, don't you suppose He thought of another hammer that would one day be used to drive nails through His hands and feet? When He handled those nails, don't you think there were other nails in His thoughts that would fasten Him to the cross? When He took the knots out of that timber, don't you think they would remind Him of the thorns that would pierce His lovely brow?

Ah, He knew it all yet faced it all. He did not turn to the right nor to the left. When His loved ones tried to prevent His going to that bloody tree, He set them back and set His face toward Calvary. He was born in another man's stable and buried in another man's grave. His first pillow was straw; His last, a crown of thorns. His first companions were cattle; His last, thieves. His first resting place was somebody else's manger; His last, somebody else's cross. And it was for me, for you! Have you ever thanked Him? Have you ever gone on your knees to show your gratefulness? You have cursed Him, taken His name in vain, rejected Him and spurned Him and His followers. You have ridiculed or criticized unmercifully, but you have never thanked Jesus! That is the damning sin—ingratitude. My brother, there is nothing that has cost God so much as this, yet there is nothing which you have treated with such contempt.

Don't be afraid of the cross. I know it is your humiliation, but it is also your salvation. I know it shows up your darkness and your sin, but it is the key which unlocks the gates of gold and invites everybody to come in and share the bounties of God's love. I would rather be Gipsy Smith this side of the cross than Adam on the other side. If we sin, we have an Advocate with the Father. They used to go to the cross to die; now they go to live. It used to be the place of death; now it is the place of life. I hear words—words sweeter than any music the world has ever listened to—flashing out from that cross with its outstretched arms inviting the world, crying: "Him that cometh to me I will in no wise cast out." God help you to come!

Missing the most important thing in the world! Think of it in this light: "Not saved," yet salvation is so important. If your sin was base and black enough, cruel enough to tear Jesus from the throne and nail Him to the accursed tree—and He was obedient even unto death—what will your sin do with you if you do not get rid of it? It will have no mercy. Unless you are saved according to God's plan, you are lost. There is no other name, no other way, no other salvation; and if you miss this, you miss all.

Your salvation depends upon that cross; your emancipation depends upon that surrender; your hopes for this life and for the life to come hang on that cross. Pull that down, and you are doomed. The world has absolutely nothing instead to offer you. Turn your back on this, and you are lost forever!

Opportunity passing away and you still neglect! Think of it in this light—not saved, and your chances of being saved going, passing away. Some of you have less chance now than you ever had in your life; and if you miss this opportunity, you may never have another. You can never tell how near death may be; and if you let this chance go by, God help you, for it may be your last on earth.

My brother, my sister, be saved now. Jesus calls and wants to save you, but even He cannot save you against your will. He has seen your heart moved and made tender, yet you have gone away unsaved. He has had to say, "Ye will not come to me, that ye might have life." If I could save you, I would. If my arms were strong enough and long enough, I would bear you all to Jesus. If one word of mine could do it, I would speak it. If there were anything I could do that would bring the unsaved gathering to my Lord, how gladly would I work a miracle! But it is beyond me. And there are some things Jesus cannot do. One is that He cannot save a soul against its will. And unless some of you make haste, He will have to tell you someday that He would have saved you, but you thwarted Him. He longed to do it, but you would not have it. You resisted to the bitter end.

When my father was a young man, a band of our people, the gypsies, fifty or more, had been picking a field of hops on a farm near Tunbridge [England]. Some of you may be old enough to remember it, for it is a matter of history; and if you ever have occasion to visit Tunbridge, ask to see the monument they erected to my people.

These gypsies had finished one field and were crossing to another field on the other side of the Medway. They mounted the wagon—men, women and children—and away the horses started. With jokes, songs and laughter they made merry music to the other toilers in the fields as they passed. As they turned a bend in the lane, they saw the old, rotten, wooden bridge over which they hoped to pass safely. The water was in flood and flowing over the roadway. When the women saw it, they were frightened. Some of them screamed; gypsy women are only like other women. Before the drivers could stop the horses, startled by the screams, they ran away, crashing into the sides of the old structure. Instantly all were thrown into the flowing river current.

A brave young gypsy seized one of the horses drifting down while watching for one who was dearer to him than anyone

117

else in the world—his mother. (The gypsy boy loves his mother.) Presently he saw her. After many struggles, he reached her. But she seized him in such a way that he could not manage to save her. At last she sank. When the day of the funeral came, there were thirty-nine gypsies buried. People gathered from all the countryside to show their sympathy with these poor people. Forgetting the crowd and the clergyman, the poor lad crept down into the trench which contained the coffins, and, kneeling beside his mother's, he cried, "Mother! Mother! I tried to save you! I did all a man could do to save you, but you would not let me!" And if some of you don't turn, Gipsy Smith will have to cry at the Bar of God, "I did all a man could do to save you, but you would not let me!" And Christ will have to say, "I did all a God could do to save you, but you would not let Me."

Oh, be saved, His grace is free;

Oh, be saved, He died for thee.

Dr. W. A. Criswell (Pastor); "The Way Made Plain"[349]
Acts 8:35

So once again we are your debtors, choir, instrumentalists, and the thousands of you who are listening to this hour on the Radio of the Southwest, KRLD, and on the radio of our Bible institute, KCBI. You are listening to the service of the First Baptist Church in Dallas. And you are listening to the pastor of the church bringing a message, one of sixteen favorite sermons; and it is entitled "The Way Made Plain."

We want you to open your Bibles with us in this great auditorium and read out loud from the eighth chapter of the Book of Acts; Acts chapter 8, beginning at verse 35 and reading to verse 39, almost to the end of the chapter—35 through 39.

---

[349] Criswell, "Way Made Plain"

Now, all of us, let's read it out loud together—Acts, chapter 8, beginning at verse 35, reading through verse 39 together:

Then Philip opened his mouth and began at the same Scripture and preached unto him Jesus.

And as they went on their way they came unto a certain water. And the eunuch said, "See, here is water; what doth hinder me to be baptized?"

And Philip said, "If thou believest with all thine heart, thou mayest." And he answered and said, "I believe that Jesus Christ is the Son of God."

And he commanded the chariot to stand still. And they went down, both, into the water—both Philip and the eunuch—and he baptized him.

And when they were come up out of the water, the Spirit of the Lord caught away Philip, that the eunuch saw him no more. And he went on his way rejoicing.

This is one of the most poignant of all of the conversions that are described in the Bible.

One of the attendant eagles of the oriental harem was the ever present eunuch. And this man was a victim of that terrible institution. He was an emasculated man. He was a withered branch. He was a dry stick. He was without hope of issue or posterity or family. But he must have been a most gifted man. Because even though he was a eunuch, he was the treasurer. We would call him the Secretary of the Treasury. In England he would be called the Chancellor of the Exchequer. He was the treasurer of the great ancient nation of Ethiopia under Candace, the queen.

He must have had a wonderful conversion to the truth. Somehow, he was a convert to the one and only God. And coming to Jerusalem for to worship, he had found there a scroll of the prophet Isaiah. And as he returned in his chariot to the capital of Ethiopia, he was reading aloud the fifty-third chapter of Isaiah.

119

The Lord was merciful to that man. He had sent Philip the evangelist down into the desert to stand by the roadside that goes through Gaza. And when the chariot came by with the attendant driving those horses and that treasurer sitting in the chariot, reading out loud the fifty-third chapter of Isaiah, the Holy Spirit said to the evangelist, "Join thyself to the chariot."

And when the Ethiopian eunuch invited Philip to come and sit with him, he was reading that passage that describes the blessed Jesus. "All we like sheep have gone astray. We turned everyone to his own way. And the Lord hath laid on Him the iniquity of us all. He was cut off. And who shall declare His generation?"

And the eunuch turned to the evangelist and said, "Of whom is the prophet speaking? Is he talking about himself or of some other man?" And beginning at the same Scripture, the fifty-third chapter of Isaiah, he preached unto him Jesus. So there are some mighty and wonderful things revealed to us in that simple avowal, "And he preached unto him Jesus."

First, the gospel message is the simple story of Jesus. That's what it is. In the fifteenth chapter of the First Corinthian letter, Paul describes, he delineates, what the Gospel is. He says, "Brethren, I declare unto you, I make known unto you the gospel wherein ye stand, wherein ye are saved." What is it? "How that Christ died for our sins according to the Scriptures, He was buried, and the third day He rose again, according to the Scriptures."

The Gospel is the simple story of Jesus. If we send a missionary across the sea and he preaches the Gospel, what does he preach? He preaches about Jesus. If a man stands in the pulpit, and after the service is over you go out the door and you say, "That preacher preaches the Gospel," what do you mean? You mean he preaches Jesus.

The Gospel is the story of the Lord Jesus: Jesus born of a virgin; Jesus going about in His ministry doing good; Jesus dying on the cross for our sins; Jesus buried in the tomb; the third day, Jesus raised from among the dead; forty days later, Jesus ascending up into Heaven; Jesus at the right hand of God; and, some triumphant, golden tomorrow, Jesus coming again. That's what you preach when you preach the Gospel. You preach Jesus. "And beginning at the same Scripture, he preached unto him Jesus."

I heard one time of a city preacher, learned, gifted, taught, educated, an academician. And Sunday by Sunday he brought messages to his congregation, fashionable and rich, concerning all of the things of academia: things about literature, things about economics, things about philosophy, things about science, speaking to his people each Sunday about all of these things up there in the high intellectual world in which he lived.

Upon a day, a little girl came to his office at the church and said her mother had sent for him. Her mother was sick and dying and would he come and tell her how to die? He demurred, for he found that the child lived in a slum area, in a tenement area in the great city. But the little child was so insistent that her mother had sent her, that finally, acquiescing, he followed the child down into the slums of the city in a certain tenement building, up all of those stairways into a dark room. And there on a bed lay a dying woman. He took his place by her side and said, "You have sent for me. What can I do?"

And the mother replied, "I cannot live. I am dying, and I'm not ready. Would you tell me how to die? Would you tell me how to meet God? Would you tell me how I can be saved?" That fashionable preacher, who for the years had been in that pulpit speaking of all of these philosophies and all of these high intellectual speculations, began to speak to her in the terms and in the language and in the thought by which he had been preaching all through the years. The poor woman, with deepening disappointment, could not even understand the nomenclature that he used, much less what he was talking about. The preacher bowed his head and cried, "O God, help me. Help me."

And when he prayed, there came back to his heart the memories of his godly mother and how she had taught him the simple story of Jesus as a little child. And that preacher, by the side of that dying woman, began to tell her about Jesus—how we were lost and He came down from Heaven to teach us the way, and how He died for our sins, and how He was raised and ascended back to glory, and how He is waiting there for those who put their trust in Him. And when he began to talk about Jesus and the simple story of the Lord and how, if we trust in Him, He will save us and how He is waiting now to receive us, she began to nod her head, "Oh, yes," she said. "Oh, yes," she said, "I can trust a Savior like that."

You know what happened? The next Lord's Day he stood up in his fashionable pulpit, and, before all of those people in the city, he described to them what had happened the week before. And he ended it with this sentence: "My dear people, I want you to know, I got that woman into the Kingdom of Heaven this day. And what is more, I got in myself."

That is the Gospel. And however we may explain it or exegete it, however we may expound it or preach about it, the heart and the core and the center of the gospel message is always the simple story of Jesus. "And he preached unto him Jesus."

Not only is the gospel message the simple story of Jesus, but the way of salvation is that plain and simple way of trusting Jesus. One time I went through that whole Bible, and I underscored wherever in the Bible God tells a man how to be saved. Then when I had finished going through the Bible, I looked at all of the passages I had marked. And I looked and was astonished to behold a certain thing. It was this: Wherever in the Bible God tells a man how to be saved, He always does it in one simple, monosyllabic sentence—never two sentences, never. Not even two sentences! When God tells a man how to be saved, He will always do it in one, simple sentence.

For example, in the first chapter of John, verse 11 it says, "He came unto his own, and his own received him not." Then verse 12 says, "But to as many as received Him, to them gave He the right to become the children of God, even to them that trust in His name"—one simple sentence. Or again, in the third chapter of John, verses 14 and 15, "As Moses lifted up the serpent in the wilderness, even so must the Son of Man be lifted up, that whosoever believeth in Him should not perish, but have eternal life"—one simple sentence.

And the next sentence telling us how to be saved is the most famous sentence in the world in human literature, the most preciously meaningful—John 3:16. Say it with me together, one simple sentence. Say it out loud with me together. "For God so loved the world that he gave his only begotten Son that whosoever believeth in him should not perish but have everlasting life"—one simple sentence.

John 5:24, "Verily, verily, I say unto you, he that heareth My word and believeth on Him that sent Me hath everlasting life, and shall not come into condemnation, but is passed from death into life"—one simple sentence. Or Romans, chapter 10, verses 9 and 10, "If thou shalt confess with thy mouth Jesus is Lord and believe in thine heart that He liveth, that God raised Him from the dead, thou shalt be saved, for with the heart one believeth to a God-kind of righteousness, and with the mouth confession is made unto salvation"—one simple sentence.

When a man comes down that aisle and openly confesses his faith in the Lord Jesus, he is saved—one simple sentence. There is no exception to that. Wherever God tells us how to be saved, He will always do it in one simple sentence.

I have a dear preacher friend. Somebody sent him word that there was a 13-year-old boy in the hospital who was dying and asked, "Would you go tell him how to be saved?" And the pastor went to the hospital and such-and-such room. There that boy was in an oxygen tent. And he asked the nurse if he could speak to the boy. And the nurse kindly said, "Yes." And so he put his head under the oxygen tent with the boy, and he said, "Son, they tell me that you know that you are not going to live." And the boy said, "That's right. I'm going to die." And the pastor said, "Son, they tell me you're not a Christian and you're not saved." And the boy said, "That's right. I've never been saved." And the pastor said, "Son, I want to tell you how to be saved. I want to tell you how to die. I want to tell you how to meet God."

And he read to him those simple passages that we have just quoted on how to be saved. And the boy broke in, and, looking into the face of the pastor in astonishment, he said, "But, Sir, is it that easy? Is it that easy?" And the pastor replied, "Son, easy for you, but not for Him, not for Him. You see, He took our sins and bore them in His own body on the tree. He suffered in our stead. By His stripes we are healed." Easy for us, because He won that battle for us! He took our sins for us. He paid the penalty for us. He died for us that we might never die but have everlasting life in Him. How to be saved is simply trusting Jesus. "And he preached unto him Jesus."

Number three, not only is the gospel message a simple message (it's Jesus), and not only is the way to be saved a simple way (it's Jesus), but, third, the great mighty act of conversion is always a simple act, committing your life to the Lord Jesus.

One time I got on my knees and I said, "Dear God, You say in Your Word, 'Believe on the Lord Jesus Christ and thou shalt be saved.' Believe on the Lord Jesus. Lord, what is it to believe? What is saving faith? What is saving trust? 'Believe on the Lord Jesus Christ and thou shalt be saved.' Lord, what does it mean to believe?" And the Lord spoke to my heart with this passage: II Timothy 1:12, "For I know whom I have believed"—there is my word—"for I know whom I have believed. I am persuaded He is able to keep that which I have committed unto Him against that final and ultimate day."

God's answer—what is saving faith, what is it to trust in Jesus unto salvation? It is that simple thing of committing your life to the Lord Jesus—this day, this evening, tomorrow's day, to old age, in death and forever. I commit my life, my soul, my destiny, my every tomorrow, every hope I have, Lord, I commit it unto Thee. I place it in Thy dear, nail-pierced hands. That's what it is. The great act of conversion is the committal of your life to the Lord Jesus, that plain and simple thing. From now on it belongs to Him—my heart, my destiny, my every tomorrow.

I grew up, as you know, out in West Texas and Oklahoma. And in the days of the missionary preaching to the "blanket Indians," the Plains Indians, there was one of these gospel men who had a tent and in western Oklahoma had pitched it on those high prairies. And he was preaching the Gospel to an Indian tribe, a "blanket Indian" tribe, the Plains Indians. And as the meeting progressed and as he was preaching the Gospel to those Indians, in one of his services the Indian chief stood up and came down there and stood in front of the missionary. And looking up into his face, he said, "Missionary, Indian chief give his tomahawk to Jesus." And he laid it at the missionary's feet. The missionary paid no attention to him, just kept on preaching about Jesus.

The Indian chief arose a second time, walked down to the front and looking up into the face of the missionary, said, "Missionary, Indian chief give his blanket to Jesus." And he laid his blanket at the feet of the missionary. The missionary paid no attention to him at all, just kept on preaching about the Lord Jesus.

He arose again, went outside of the tent, tied his pony to a stake of the tent, walked back in and looked up at the missionary and said, "Missionary, Indian chief give his pony to Jesus." That's the last thing that he had. Missionary paid no attention to him at all, just kept on preaching about Jesus. The chief arose one other time, came down to the front—only this time he knelt, and, looking up into the face of the missionary, he said, "Missionary, Indian chief give himself to Jesus."

That's what it is to be saved. We don't buy our way into the Kingdom of Heaven. We don't bribe our way into the Kingdom of Heaven. We just give ourselves in faith and in trust and in committal to the Lord Jesus, and He saves us. He writes our name in the Lamb's book of life. He numbers them, He numbers us, among God's redeemed. The great act of conversion is the committal of your life to Jesus. "And he preached unto him Jesus."

Will you notice in the fourth place, the entrance into the church, the family of God, is an obedience to the great commandment, the great commission of the Lord Jesus. We are to go and to make disciples of all of the people, baptizing them in the name of the Father and of the Son and of the Holy Spirit. In I Corinthians 12:13, "By one Spirit are we all baptized into the body of Christ."

There are two kinds of baptism. There is the Spirit baptism, when God adds us to the body of the Lord. We become a member of the household of faith. It is a baptismal work of the Holy Spirit. Then there is an outward sign of it, water baptism— baptized into the body, baptized into the family of Christ.

"And as they went on their way, they came unto a certain water, and the eunuch said, See here is water. What doth hinder me to be baptized? I want to be baptized. Philip answered and said, If thou believest with all thine heart, thou mayest. And he answered and said, I do believe. I take Jesus as my Savior. I believe He is the Son of God. And they commanded the chariot to stand still, and they went down both into the water, both Philip and the eunuch. And he baptized him. And when they were come up out of the water, the Lord took away Philip, and that eunuch treasurer went on his way."

Hallelujah! Glory to God! Happy in the Lord—our entrance into the church, into the body of Christ, is in our baptism, a simple, humble, obedience to the Great Commission and the great commandment of Jesus. And that's the first thing that will come into the heart of somebody who trusts in the Lord as

Savior. "Pastor, I want to be baptized just as Jesus was, just as He commanded, and just as all of the saved of God have been. See, here is water. I want to be baptized."

Fifth, and last, and our assignment now and forever is praising the blessed Lord Jesus. He's everything. He's all in all. Loving Him, serving Him, dedicating heart and life and tomorrow to Him, just loving the Lord, praising God forever—is not that the sign and the image and the revelation of Heaven itself? "Unto him"—I'm quoting now the redeemed of all of the ages, revealed to us in the Apocalypse—"Unto Him who loved us and washed us from our sins in His own blood, unto Him be glory and dominion and power forever and forever!" That is the paean of praise. That's the text of the anthem that we shall sing in Heaven and in earth—just praising Jesus, our all in all.

I entered once a home of care,
And penury and want were there,
  But joy and peace withal.
I asked the aged mother whence
Her helpless widowhood's defense.
  She answered, "Christ is all."

I saw the martyr at the stake—
The flames could not his courage shake,
  Nor death his soul appall.
I asked him whence his strength was given;
He looked triumphantly to heaven
  And answered, "Christ is all."

I stood beside the dying bed,
Where lay a child with aching head,
  Waiting Jesus' call.

I saw him smile—'twas sweet as May—
And as his spirit passed away,
  He whispered, "Christ is all."

I dreamed that hoary time had fled;
The earth and sea gave up their dead;
  A fire dissolved this ball.
I saw the church's ransomed throng;
I caught the burden of their song—
  'Twas this, that Christ is all in all in all.

["Christ Is All," W. A. Williams]

A people waiting for the Lord, loving the Lord, serving the Lord, committing heart and life to the blessed Jesus—"And he preached unto him Jesus."

And that is our prayerful and humble and precious invitation to you tonight, to give your heart and life and every tomorrow in faith and trust, in love, in committal to the blessed Lord Jesus—a boy, a girl, a father and mother, a whole family, a couple, just one somebody, you. In a moment we shall stand and sing our hymn of appeal. And the pastor will be there at the front, praying and waiting for you. And if the Spirit of God invites you to the Lord Jesus, would you answer with your life? "I'm coming tonight. I want to accept Jesus as my Savior," or, "I want to be baptized just as the Lord commanded us in His blessed Book," or, "We want to place our life and letter here in this dear church," or answering some other call of the Spirit of God in your heart.

Make the decision now. And in a moment when we stand to sing, stand coming down that aisle, coming down that stairway, on the first note of the first stanza. When you stand up, stand up coming. May God bless you; may the angels attend you.

May the Lord give you that faith to commit time and eternity in His blessed hands. Come now. Take the Lord now. Follow Him in faith now. Do it, on the first note of this first stanza, while we stand and while we sing.

"Preparing to preach is not the same as preparing a sermon. Preparing the sermon is only part of the preparation. A man must prepare himself."[350]—W. E. Sangster

"Preaching is the art of making a sermon and delivering it? Why, no, that is not preaching. Preaching is the art of making a preacher and delivering that....Preaching is the outrush of the soul in speech. Therefore, the elemental business of preaching is not with the preaching but with the preacher! It is no trouble to preach, but a vast trouble to construct a preacher....What then, in light of this, is the task of the preacher? Plainly this, the amassing of a great soul so as to have something worthwhile to give....The sermon is the preacher up to date."[351]—William Quayle

"A prepared messenger is more important than a prepared message."[352]—Robert Munger

"There is no greater need for the preacher than that he should know God. I care not about his lack of eloquence and artistry, about his ill-constructed discourse or his poorly enunciated message, if only it is evident that God is a reality to him and that he has learned to abide in Christ. The preparation of the heart is of far greater importance than the preparation of the sermon."[353]—John Stott

"The more a man allows his mind to grow slack and lazy and flabby, the less the Holy Spirit can say to him. True preaching comes when the loving heart and the disciplined mind are laid at the disposal of the Holy Spirit."[354]—William Barclay

"Only what I live can I impart to others."[355]—Augustine

---

[350] Sangster, *Craft of Sermon Construction*, 203.
[351] Quayle, *The Pastor-Preacher*, 27, 32.
[352] Munger, "Sermon Illustrations."
[353] Stott, *Preacher's Portrait*, 68.
[354] Barclay, *Promise of the Spirit,* 96.
[355] Sorenson, "Pulpit and the Pew."

6
Soul

Evangelistic preaching involves more than just preparing a sermon. In order to be effective in evangelistic preaching, the preacher himself must be prepared.

Requirements for a Prepared Preacher

The Preacher Must Be Converted

C. H. Spurgeon declared, "God will not use dead tools for working living miracles."[356] Adrian Rogers said, "The preacher's conversion is vital because you cannot dispense what you do not know any more than you can come from where you have not been....People coming to faith through the Word of God does not mean that God has blessed the work of the unregenerated preacher. Such an act by God means God has blessed His Word and demonstrated mercy upon the individual."[357]

John Wesley was awakened by the Holy Spirit that he was an unsaved preacher. In his autobiography, Wesley gives this account of his conversion: "Wednesday, May 24. In the evening I went very unwillingly to a society in Aldersgate Street, where one was reading Luther's preface to the Epistle to the Romans. About a quarter before nine, while he was describing the change which God works in the heart through faith in Christ, I felt my heart strangely warmed. I felt I did trust in Christ, Christ alone, for salvation; and an assurance was given me that he had taken away *my* sins, even *mine*, and saved *me* from the law of sin and death....Thursday, May 25th. The moment I awaked, 'Jesus, Master' was in my heart and in my mouth; and I found all my strength lay in keeping my eye fixed upon Him and my soul waiting on him continually."[358] Wesley had to overcome an unsound biblical belief about salvation,

---

[356] Harrison, *How to win Souls,* 11.
[357] Rogers and Patterson, *Love Worth Finding,* 169.
[358] Wesley, *Representative Collection,* 66–67.

ministry performance, position and pride to get the "real thing." Other preachers testify of this same experience.

The Preacher Must Be Called

Saddened we are at the exodus from the ministry by some 1,600 pastors monthly across denominational lines. Brooks Faulkner, a former SBC LeaderCare counselor, estimates that of this number, one hundred are from the Southern Baptist Convention.[359] Additionally only fifty percent of those who enter the ministry will be in the ministry five years later, and of these, only ten percent will remain in the ministry until retirement.[360] This departure sadly is due to moral, health, family, financial, or 'burnout' reasons for some; but I fear many may be attributable to a question of the genuineness of the call. The Bible is silent as to why John Mark left the ministry (Acts 13:13), but it may be attributable to a lack of a call. In Acts 13:2, Scripture teaches that the Holy Spirit separated (called out) two (Barnabas and Paul) for the missionary assignment, but a third went (John Mark).

It is absolutely imperative that a man know with all certainty he is called by sovereign God to preach, lest he be discontent and ineffective in ministry or quit when discouraged and criticized. The abiding confidence of having been divinely called has been personally the "rope" I have hung onto in stormy seas in the pastorate and evangelism. It is a rope that is sure and steadfast. J. H. Jowett underscores the importance of a man's being divinely chosen to preach in stating, "Now I hold with profound conviction that before a man selects the Christian ministry as his vocation, he must have the assurance that the selection has been imperatively constrained by the eternal God. The call of the eternal must ring through the rooms of his soul as clearly as the sound of the morning bell rings through the valley of Switzerland, calling the peasants to early prayer and praise. The candidate for the ministry must move like a

---

[359] John Mark Ministries, "Pastor Dropout Rate."
[360] Pastoral Care, Inc., "Statistics."

man in secret bonds. 'Necessity is laid' upon him. His choice is not a preference among alternatives. Ultimately he has no alternative; all other possibilities become dumb; there is only one clear call sounding forth as the imperative summons of the eternal God."[361]

Adam Clarke, in a letter to a preacher, stated: "No man should engage in the work in which you are engaged, unless he verily feel that he is inwardly moved by the Holy Ghost to take upon him this office. He must not presume that he is thus moved because he has been educated for the ministry; in cases of this kind, man may propose but God must dispose."[362] Oswald Chambers said, "If a man is called to preach the Gospel, God will crush him till the light of the eye, the power of the life, the ambition of the heart, is all riveted on Himself. That is not done easily. It is not a question of saintliness; it has to do with the call of God."[363]

Vance Havner wrote an article entitled "The Making of a Minister" in which he stated, "Ministers used to believe that they had received a divine call. Today many enter the ministry as a profession just as they would law or medicine. But preaching is a calling, and whatever other reasons young Samuel may have, he should hear the Unmistakable Voice."[364] Have you clearly heard that "Unmistakable Voice" with regard to ministry? The voice of *The Baptist Hour* (eighteen years), Hershel Hobbs, advised, "God calls all Christians to serve Him. But in a special way he calls some into distinctively Christian vocations. A preacher should not choose the ministry but should be chosen for it. Yet so deeply personal and spiritual is this call that no preacher can explain his call to another. But a preacher knows he is called. Otherwise he should not try to fill this

---

[361] Jowett, *The Preacher*, 12.
[362] Clarke, *Letter to a Preacher*, 11.
[363] Robert Morgan, *Stories, Illustration, and Quotes,* 107.
[364] Sorenson, "Pulpit and the Pew."

role."[365] Many men have seen "GPC" etched in burning letters in the sky, understanding this to be a word from God saying, "Go Preach Christ." In reality it was God saying, "Go Plow Corn." Someone said that if you are called to ministry, don't let the armies of the world stop you; if you are not, you had best stop yourself.

The Preacher Must Be Clean

L. R. Scarborough said, "Those who handle the vessels of the Lord must have pure hearts and clean hands. 'Holiness unto the Lord' must be on the skirts of God's spiritual priests today."[366] The apostle Paul, though clean in deed and motive in his own eyes, before the Lord found it imperative to *persuade* the Corinthians of his integrity—not simply to vindicate himself but so the Gospel he proclaimed would be received freely (II Corinthians 5:11). William Barclay comments, "A man's message will always be heard in the context of his character. That is why the preacher and the teacher must be beyond suspicion. We have to avoid, not only evil, but the very appearance of evil, lest anything make others think less, not of us, but of the message which we bring."[367]

It has been said, "Never do anything that makes God look bad." This is especially true for the preacher. Stephen Olford, in a lecture series at NOBTS, said, "Beloved, if you stand behind this holy desk and your life isn't pure, if your life isn't absolutely holy as far as you know it, if you are not walking under an unclouded sky with the ungrieved, unquenched Holy Spirit in your life, then, my friend, you've absolutely blocked the message from any authority whatsoever."[368]

Ralph Conners tells the story of two rival Canadian football teams. On one of these teams was a player named Cameron who was quick and agile. He was the hope of his team, and his

---

[365] Bodey, *Inside the Sermon*, 125–126.
[366] Scarborough, *With Christ*, 12–13.
[367] Barclay, *Letters to the Corinthians*, 208.
[368] Doy Cave, "Preaching Is Much More"

playing assured it of victory. However, the night before the big game he broke training rules and got drunk. In the game, instead of being their help, he was their hurt. That game went down in the annals of that university as a game they had every right to win but lost because Cameron was unfit. Preachers, I wonder how many dynamic evangelistic sermons we preach ineffectively, without fruit, because we are spiritually unfit. One may become very proficient in preaching, but it will prove insufficient to win souls if his heart is not fully consecrated to God.

George Whitefield liked always to have his preaching attire scrupulously clean. He would say, "These are not trifles; a minister must be without spot, even in his garments, if he can." Spurgeon to this declared, "Purity cannot be carried too far in a minister."[369] John MacArthur, commenting on I Timothy 6:11, stated, "A man of God is a lifelong fugitive, fleeing those things that would destroy him and his ministry....He not only does right but also thinks right; he not only behaves properly but also is properly motivated. He is a man that serves God with reverence and awe (Hebrews 12:28)."[370]

The apostle Paul is an exemplary pattern for the preacher in regard to holiness of conduct in that no man could accuse him of unethical or immoral conduct privately or publicly (Acts 20:18). Psalm 24:3–5 should ring in the minister's ear as he prepares to preach to the unsaved, "Who shall ascend into the hill of the LORD? or who shall stand in his holy place? He that hath clean hands, and a pure heart; who hath not lifted up his soul unto vanity, nor sworn deceitfully. He shall receive the blessing from the LORD, and righteousness from the God of his salvation." Clean hands and a pure heart in the minister are a must to communicate God's Word of salvation effectively. Phillips Brooks said, "It does not take great men to do great

---

[369] Spurgeon, *Lectures to My Students,* 197.
[370] Rosscup, *How to Preach Biblically,* 64, 67.

things; it only takes consecrated men."[371] Spurgeon cautioned, "Take care, dear reader, that you do not forsake the path of duty by leaving your occupation, and take care you do not dishonor your profession while in it. Think little of yourselves, but do not think too little of your callings."[372]

The Preacher Must Be Close

Constant communion with the Lord is indispensable to the preacher. In the front of W. A. Criswell's preaching Bible are found these words:

He stands best who kneels most.

He stands strongest who kneels weakest.

He stands longest who kneels longest.[373]

Faris Whitesell underscores this essential, "The preacher must be a man of prayer....He should pray for his messages... soak them in prayer...pray as he goes into the pulpit, pray as he preaches insofar as possible, and follow up his sermons with prayer."[374] "Vales of trouble are separated from mountains of triumph by a few moments of prayer."[375]

Following an awesome sermon by Alexander Whyte, a listener commented, "Dr. Whyte, you preached today like you had just emerged from the throne chamber of the Almighty." Whyte replied, "In point of fact, I have."[376] C. H. Spurgeon stated, "The call of Christ's servants comes from above. Jesus stands on the mountain, evermore above the world in holiness, earnestness, love and power. Those whom He calls must go up the mountain to Him; they must seek to rise to His level by living in constant communion with Him. They may not be able to mount to classic honors or attain scholastic eminence, but they must, like Moses, go up into the mount of God and have famil-

---

[371] Criswell, *Criswell's Guidebook for Pastors,* 235.
[372] Spurgeon, *Morning and Evening,* June 27.
[373] Criswell, *Criswell's Guidebook for Pastors,* 31.
[374] Rosscup, *How to Preach Biblically,* 57.
[375] Yates, *Preaching from the Prophets,* 31.
[376] Rosscup, *How to Preach Biblically,* 55.

iar intercourse with the unseen God, or they will never be fitted to proclaim the Gospel of peace."[377]

Based upon Spurgeon's statement likening his prayer to talking to a bank clerk, he seldom prayed more than five minutes at a time.[378] But it is said that he never went five minutes without praying, maintaining continual connection with the Lord. In light of this fact it is no wonder God used him mightily in and out of the pulpit. This great London pastor again said, "Get you close to Christ, and carry the remembrance of Him about you from day to day, and you will do right royal deeds. Come, let us slay sin, for Christ was slain. Come, let us bury all our pride, for Christ was buried. Come, let us rise to newness of life, for Christ has risen. Let us be united with our crucified Lord in His one great object—let us live and die with Him, and then every action of our lives will be very beautiful."[379]

A glowing, vibrant consistent devotional life is imperative to maintain closeness to the Savior and prepare the heart for preaching. Billy Graham stated, "I take time each day in the morning and evening to read passages of Scripture and ask the Lord to speak to me through them—apart from any preparations of sermon material."[380] Andrew Bonar said of Robert Murray M'Cheyne, "From the first he fed others by what he himself was feeding upon. His preaching was in a manner the development of his soul's experience. It was a giving out of the inward life."[381]

Wiersbe comments, "If God isn't speaking to me, how can He speak through me to others? We aren't reservoirs that pump out sermons; we're channels through whom the water of life

[377] Spurgeon, *Morning and Evening,* September 10.
[378] Piper, "Preaching Through Adversity."
[379] Spurgeon, "To Lovers of Jesus."
[380] Graham, *Life Wisdom,* 113.
[381] Wiersbe, *Dynamics of Preaching,* 113.

can flow."[382] "If we could live every moment of every day under the eye of God," says Leonard Ravenhill, "if we did every act in the light of the judgment seat, if we sold every article in the light of the judgment seat, if we prayed every prayer in light of the judgment seat, if we tithed all our possessions in light of the judgment seat, if we preachers prepared every sermon with one eye on damned humanity and the other on the judgment seat, then we would have a Holy Ghost revival that would shake this earth and that, in no time at all, would liberate millions of precious souls."[383]

Writing of Phillips Brooks, Dan Green stated, "Perhaps the greatest hallmark of Brooks' preaching was the intimate tie between his personal life and his power in the pulpit. As he explained during one of his lectures: 'Nothing but fire kindles fire. To know in one's whole nature what it is to live by Christ; to be His and not our own; to be so occupied by gratitude for what He did for us and for what He continually is to us that His will and His glory shall be the sole desires of our life…that is the first necessity of the preacher.'"[384]

John H. Jowett remarked, "I am profoundly convinced that one of the greatest perils which besets ministers is a restless scattering of our energies over an amazing multiplicity of activities which leaves little time for absorbing communion with God."[385] Dr. Wallace Rogers, a former college religion professor of mine, used to say, "If you are too busy to prepare to preach, you are too busy." The same is true with regard to devotional time with the Lord. "Never neglect your spiritual meals, or you will lack stamina, and your spirits will sink. Live on the substantial doctrines of grace, and you will outlive and outwork those who delight in the pastry and syllabubs of 'mod-

---

[382] Ibid.
[383] Ravenhill, *Why Revival Tarries*, 57.
[384] Koessler, *Moody Handbook on Preaching*, 109.
[385] Knight, *Knight's Illustrations for Today*, 247.

ern thought.'"[386] William Gurnall wrote, "To the minister, into your hand this sword of the Lord is given in an especial manner....Tremble at the charge which is deposited. Oh, how shall the people grow if the minister does not? How shall he grow if he does not daily drink in more than he pours forth?"[387]

The Preacher Must Be Consumed

D. L. Moody testified of the difference the fullness of the Holy Spirit makes in a preacher's life, "One day in New York—what a day! I can't describe it! I seldom refer to it! It is almost too sacred to name! I can only say God revealed Himself to me! I had such an experience of love that I had to ask Him to stay His hand! I went to preaching again. The sermons were no different. I did not present any new truth, yet hundreds were converted. I would not be back where I was before that blessed experience."[388]

The need of every preacher is to make the discovery of the Spirit-filled life as Moody did; not only his heart will "catch fire," but his sermons will too. The secret of Holy Spirit's infilling is simply a thirsting for His control that is unquenchable, the emptying out of sin in self through repentance thoroughly, the crying out in prayer for His fullness incessantly, and the surrendering of self totally. "If a son shall ask bread of any of you that is a father, will he give him a stone? or if *he ask* a fish, will he for a fish give him a serpent? Or if he shall ask an egg, will he offer him a scorpion? If ye then, being evil, know how to give good gifts unto your children: how much more shall *your* heavenly Father give the Holy Spirit to them that ask him?" (Luke 11:11–13).

A. J. Gordon remarked, "It costs much to obtain power of the Spirit. It costs self-surrender and humiliation and a yielding up of our most precious things to God. It costs the perseverance of long waiting and the faith of strong trusts. But when we are

---

[386] Spurgeon, *Lectures to My Students*, 310.
[387] Gurnall, *Christian in Complete Armour*, Vol. 2, 282.
[388] Tan, *Encyclopedia of 7700 Illustrations*, No. 2230.

really in that power, we shall find the difference, that whereas before it was hard for us to do the easiest things, now it is easy for us to do the hard things."[389] D. L. Moody was once told by another that he would give the world to possess the same power Moody did. Moody replied, "That's exactly what it will cost."

Stott comments, "On what conditions may preachers hope to be vehicles of divine power? We must be faithful in handling the Word of God, expounding the Scriptures, and preaching the cross, for there is power in God's Word and in Christ's cross. But how can we become channels for the power of the Holy Spirit? How can the promise of John be fulfilled, that from our innermost being the 'rivers of living water' will flow into the lives of others (Jn. 4:14)? I believe there are two essential conditions: holiness and humility."[390]

"Words spoken, prayers uttered, acts done in the energy of self alone, have no power of spiritual germination....Except the Spirit speak through us, there will be no *quickening* in those about us. The sermon delivered in pride of intellect or rush of mere human eloquence may excite the intellect, arouse admiration, or stir emotion, but it cannot *transmit life*. And naught but life begets life, for 'it is THE SPIRIT THAT QUICKENETH.' 'I do not often have to reproach myself for failure to serve; but I do often, for *serving without anointing*,' said a noted Christian worker. Ministry without the Spirit, of what value is it? The answer is the same—'the flesh profiteth nothing'—and proves how solemn is our responsibility to live the abiding life, the life of constant distrust of self and constant dependence upon and drawing from the indwelling Spirit."[391]

Leonard Ravenhill pointedly says, "Preacher, if your soul is barren, if tears are absent from your eyes, if converts are absent from your altar, then take no comfort in popularity; refuse the

---

[389] Walden, *Sword Scrapbook*, 222.
[390] Stott, *The Preacher's Portrait*, 107.
[391] McConkey, *Three-Fold Secret*, 102–103.

consolation of your degrees or of the books you have written! Sincerely but passionately invite the Holy Ghost to plague your heart with grief because you are spiritually unable to bring to birth. Oh, the reproach of barren altars! Has the Holy Ghost delight in our electric organs, carpeted aisles, and new decorations if the crib is empty? Never! Oh, that the deathlike stillness of the sanctuary could be shattered by the blessed cry of newborn babes!"[392]

The London pastor C. H. Spurgeon, preaching on Matthew 28:18, made the preacher's need of the omnipotence of God in preaching clear when he said, "I scarcely ever come into this pulpit without bemoaning myself that ever I should be called to a task for which I seem more unfit than any other man that ever was born. Woe is me that I should have to preach a Gospel which so overmasters me, and which I feel that I am so unfit to preach! Yet I could not give it up, for it were a far greater woe to me not to preach the Gospel of Jesus Christ. Unless the Holy Ghost blesses the Word, we who preach the Gospel are of all men most miserable, for we have attempted a task that is impossible; we have entered upon a sphere where nothing but the supernatural will ever avail. If the Holy Spirit does not renew the hearts of our hearers, we cannot do it. If the Holy Ghost does not regenerate, them we cannot. If He does not send the truth home into their souls, we might as well speak into the ear of a corpse. All that we have to do is quite beyond our unaided power; we must have our Master with us, or we can do nothing. We deeply feel our need of this great truth; we not merely say it, but we are driven every day by our own deep sense of need to rejoice that our Lord has declared, 'All power is given unto me in heaven and in earth,' for we need all power. Every kind of power that there is in Heaven and in earth we shall need before we can fully discharge this ministry. Before the nations shall all be brought to hear the Gospel of Christ, before testimony to Him shall be borne in every land,

---

[392] Ravenhill, *Why Revival Tarries*, 135.

we shall need the whole omnipotence of God; we shall want every forge in Heaven and earth ere this is done. Thank God that this power is all laid by ready for our use; the strength that is equal to such a stupendous task as this is already provided."[393]

W. A. Criswell observed, "So God's messenger may say today, 'I wasn't wrapped in my own academic robes on the Lord's Day. I wasn't hiding behind all the degrees that I have tried to win on the Lord's Day. I wasn't trying to say what man would say on the Lord's Day. I was in the Spirit on the Lord's Day. When I walked into the pulpit, it might have been "pore" English, faulty construction, and homiletically unsound; but when I stood there, such as I was and what I could do, that did I say and preach in the power of the Holy Spirit. I was in the Spirit on the Lord's Day. Then, as I tried to speak and to preach and to shepherd my people, I did it in the unction and power and baptism of the Holy Spirit, so help me God.'"[394] L. R. Scarborough did not mince his words in saying, "Many a minister is on a treadmill, marking time, drying up, not earning his salt, because he has no passion for souls and no power for effective service."[395] If Scarborough's words identify your life, then repent and yield to the total control of the Holy Spirit. Resolve not to enter the pulpit again until you are endued from on high with the power of the Holy Spirit.

The Preacher Must Be Concerned

A burden for the unsaved must grip the preacher's very soul. Adam Clarke, in his excellent challenge to a young preacher, advised, "You preach, not merely to explain God's Word, but to save souls; whenever you forget this, you go astray."[396] The preacher in preparing to preach must grasp the real condition of the sinner as revealed in Scripture and muse over it until his

---

[393] Spurgeon, "Our Omnipotent Leader."
[394] Sorenson, "The Pulpit and the Pew."
[395] Scarborough , *With Christ,* 30.
[396] Clarke, *Letter to a Young Preacher,* 20.

heart is inflamed for souls. According to Luke 19:10, he is lost; according to John 3:16, he is perishing; according to Ephesians 2:1, he is dead in trespasses and sins; and according to John 3:18, he is condemned. Burn in your heart the reality of man's condition—his restlessness, emptiness, meaninglessness, insignificance, loneliness, hurting, and his being just a heartbeat away from Hell, until you can't wait to stand in the pulpit and declare to him the way to salvation. Feed this flame in your heart constantly, and it will be manifested clearly in preaching and reaping.

"The initial expression of pastoral care by an evangelist is the projection of his sincerity and identification with his pronouncements. If his auditors do not behold the 'authentic sign' of genuineness in the evangelist, they will hardly believe that he could care for them."[397] R. A. Torrey declared, "I would rather win souls than be the greatest king or emperor on earth; I would rather win souls than be the greatest general that ever commanded an army; I would rather win souls than be the greatest poet or novelist or literary man who ever walked this earth. My one ambition in life is to win as many as possible. Oh, it is the only thing worth doing, to save souls and men and women—we can all do it!"[398]

Preachers on Soul Preparation

John MacArthur

"Behind the content of his message is the character of the expositor. He must be set apart from mundane matters, lifted above worldly aims and ambitions, and devoted singularly to God's service."[399]

Adrian Rogers

"The preacher's own personal integrity is imperative to his authority, for I do not believe it is possible to separate the man

---

[397] Morris, "Pastoral Care."
[398] Martin, *Apostle of Certainty,* 189.
[399] Rosscup, *How to Preach Biblically,* 63.

143

from his message. If the preacher is to experience real authority in the ministry, then he must be the embodiment of the message he proclaims....I believe that a preacher of the Gospel of Jesus Christ ought to aspire to be as pure as driven snow."[400] Rogers, speaking at a Criswell College luncheon, stated that he is often asked by young pastors for advice regarding ministry. "I've thought about this, and I've boiled it down to one word—integrity; if you are faithful in that which is small, you will be faithful in that which is much."[401]

Kyle M. Yates

"The highest form of obedience is to continue to remain at our post of duty when we cannot see why we are kept there."[402]

John Bunyan

Bunyan describes the preacher in this manner, "His back to the world, his face toward Heaven, and a Book in his hand."[403]

Alexander Whyte

Whyte, at a young man's ordination to the ministry, advised, "Be up earlier than usual to meditate and pray over it. Steep every sentence of it in the Spirit....And pray after it."[404] Whyte's biographer stated that the "master notes of his preaching" were discipline, prayer, inner motive, humility before God and men, and purity acquired through suffering."[405] Speaking to a group of theological students, Whyte stated, "A congregation is awaiting you, to be made by you, after you are made by God."[406]

---

[400] Rogers and Patterson, *Love Worth Finding*, 173.
[401] Norm Miller, "Warren on Criswell."
[402] Yates, *Preaching from the Prophets,* 30.
[403] Sorenson, "The Pulpit and the Pew."
[404] Mayhue and Thomas, *Master's Perspective,* 168.
[405] Rosscup, *How to Preach Biblically*, 55.
[406] Sorenson, "The Pulpit and the Pew."

C. H. Spurgeon

"There is something in the very tone of the man who has been with Jesus which has more power to touch the heart than the most perfect oratory; remember this and maintain an unbroken walk with God. You will need much night work in secret if you are to gather many of your Lord's lost sheep. Only by prayer and fasting can you gain power to cast out the worst of devils. Let men say what they will about the sovereignty, God connects special success with special states of heart, and if these be lacking, He will not do mighty works.[407]

"Those who serve God must serve Him in His own way, and in His strength, or He will never accept their service. That which man doth, unaided by divine strength, God can never own. The mere fruits of the earth He casteth away; He will reap only that corn, the seed of which was sown from Heaven, watered by grace and ripened by the sun of divine love. God will empty out all that thou hast before He will put His own into thee; He will first clean out thy granaries before He will fill them with the finest of the wheat. God will have no strength used in his battles but the strength which He Himself imparts. Are you mourning over your own weakness? Take courage, for there must be a consciousness of weakness before the Lord will give thee victory. Your emptiness is but the preparation for your being filled, and your casting down is but the making ready for your lifting up."[408]

Frank Pollard

"Well, what must a preacher be? How does one prepare oneself to communicate God's Word effectively? Some of the solution is found in answer to these questions: 'Have you bought into what you're selling?'; 'Can you do without it?'; 'Is the main thing the main thing?'; 'Are you real?'; and 'Who is in

---

[407] Spurgeon, *Lectures to My Students*, 345.
[408] Spurgeon, *Morning and Evening*, November 4.

charge of your career?'[409] I summarize this excellent message in this manner.

1. Have you bought into what you're selling? Are you saved, 'fessed up, and cleaned up? "The hand that makes another clean cannot itself be dirty."

2. Can you do without it? Is preaching something you want to do or have to do? If you can do without preaching, get out of the ministry.

3. Is the main thing the main thing? The central theme of the preacher's preaching must be the person and work of Jesus Christ. John Wesley writes in his journal, "I came to town and offered them Christ." This should be the preacher's priority in preaching.

4. Are you real? Integrity is essential. Honesty with oneself is imperative. Humility must replace arrogance; and reliance upon the Holy Spirit, cleverness.

5. Who is in charge of your career? "I am doing what I am doing because God called me to do it. I am doing it where I'm doing it because He put me here."

Michael Fabarez

"The personal life of the preacher is the foundation upon which his every sermon stands. He certainly cannot expect to be used of God to change lives if his own life is stagnant....If you are to preach life-changing sermons, you must be able to say with I Corinthians 11:1, 'Imitate me, just as I also imitate Christ.' That is why Paul tells the young preacher to 'watch your life and doctrine closely' (I Timothy 4:16 NIV)....If God is to speak through human personality, then let us remember the urgent need for that human vessel to be clean."[410]

---

[409] Duduit, *Handbook on Contemporary Preaching*, 135–136.
[410] Fabarez, *Preaching that Changes Lives*, 28.

Warren Wiersbe

"The preacher must cultivate his own personal walk with the Lord. The pulpit is no place for borrowed blessings. They must flow out of the minister's fellowship with God in order to be fresh and exciting. In other words, the preacher as well as the sermon must be prepared. The two go together. In every part of his being—physical, mental, emotional, spiritual—the preacher must be a prepared vessel to contain, and then to share, the message of life."[411]

John Newton

In a letter to a young preacher, Newton wrote, "Your borrowing help from others may arise from a diffidence of yourself, which is not blameable; but it may arise, in part, likewise from a diffidence of the Lord, which is hurtful. I wish you may get encouragement from that word, Exodus 4:11, 12. It was a great encouragement to me. While I would press you to diligence in every rational means for the improvement of your stock in knowledge and your ability of utterance, I would have you remember that *preaching is a gift*. It cannot be learned by industry and imitation only, as a man may learn to make a chair or a table; it comes from above, and if you patiently wait upon God, He will bestow this gift upon you and increase it in you. It will grow by exercise. 'To him that hath shall be given, and he shall have more abundantly.' And be chiefly solicitous to obtain an unction upon what you do say. Perhaps those sermons in which you feel yourself most deficient may be made most useful to others. I hope you will endeavor likewise to be plain and familiar in your language and manner, though not low or vulgar, so as to suit yourself as much as possible to the apprehensions of the most ignorant people. There are in all congregations some persons exceedingly ignorant; yet they

---

[411] Wiersbe, *Elements of Preaching.*

have precious souls, and the Lord often calls such. I pray the Lord to make you wise to win souls. I hope He will."[412]

Faris Whitesell

"It [the Bible] cannot do its saving work rightly apart from certain presuppositions on the part of the messenger. The first such presupposition is that he is living the life taught in the Scriptures. He must be an embodiment of Christian salvation and Christian graces. His life must be a demonstration of faith, prayer, humility, kindness, love, patience, self-sacrifice, joy, optimism, goodness. The second presupposition is that he must know the Bible and be able to show its relevancy to the plight of man today."[413]

Billy Graham

"Any preacher who preaches beyond that which he has experienced is incapable of preaching with conviction."[414]

E.M. Bounds

"We have emphasized sermon preparation until we have lost sight of the important thing to be prepared—the heart. A prepared heart is much better than a prepared sermon. A prepared heart will make a prepared sermon....Life-giving preaching costs the preacher much—death to self, crucifixion to the world, the travail of his own soul. Only crucified preaching can give life. Crucified preaching can only come from a crucified man."[415]

Adam Clarke

"Go from your knees to the chapel. Get a renewal of your commission each time you preach, in a renewed sense of the favor of God. Carry your authority to declare the Word of God not in your hand but in your heart....You must walk as in the presence of God. Extremes beget extremes. Take heed then that

[412] Newton, "Gift of Preaching."
[413] Whitesell, *Basic New Testament Evangelism,* 83–84.
[414] Graham, "Experience Before Preaching."
[415] Bounds, *Power through Prayer,* 81–82.

while you avoid levity on one hand, you fall not into sour god-liness on the other."[416]

Chuck Swindoll

"If you think the gathering of biblical facts and standing up with a Bible in your hand will automatically equip you to communicate well, you are deeply mistaken. It will not. You must work at being interesting. Boredom is a gross violation, being dull is a grave offense, and irrelevance is a disgrace to the Gospel. Too often these three crimes go unpunished, and we preachers are the criminals....preaching is not as simple as dumping a half-ton load of religious whine and a hodgepodge of verbs, nouns, and adjectives, but preparing the heart, sharpening the mind, delivering the goods with care, sensitivity, timing, and clarity. It's the difference between slopping hogs and feeding sheep....[Therefore] study hard, pray like mad, think it through, tell the truth, then stand tall. But while you're on your feet, don't clothe the riches of Christ in rags. Say it well."[417]

Curtis Hutson

"It helps you to be intense if you live the sermon that's to be preached. If you are going to preach on Hell, read as many sermons as you can find on the subject. See men lost and going to Hell—see it so real that you could weep over it."[418]

Robert Murray M'Cheyne

"Get your texts from God—your thoughts, your words, from God....It is not great talents God blesses so much as great likeness to Jesus. A holy minister is an awful weapon in the hand of God. A word spoken by you when your conscience is clear and your heart full of God's Spirit is worth ten thousand words spoken in unbelief and sin."[419]

---

[416] Clarke, *Letter to a Young Preacher*, 34, 58.
[417] Evangelical Church of Fullerton Newsletter.
[418] Hutson, "Evangelistic Preaching."
[419] M'Cheyne, *Sermons*, Back Cover.

John Bisagno

"Dear pastor, your preaching is your priority. Your time with God, your sermon preparation, the credibility of your life, your personal study, all that you do moves toward that focal point of your public preaching ministry....In a sense we are preparing to preach all day long."[420]

Phillips Brooks

He counseled young preachers, "Never allow yourself to feel equal to your work. If you ever find that spirit growing on you, be afraid."[421]

Andrew Murray

"We ministers of the Gospel, how we are in danger of getting into a condition of *work, work, work!* And we pray over it, but the freshness and buoyancy and joy of the heavenly life are not always present. Let us seek to understand that the life of the branch is a life of much fruit because it is a life rooted in Christ, the living, heavenly Vine....What has the branch to do? You know that precious, inexhaustible word that Christ used: Abide. Your life is to be an abiding life. And how is the abiding to be? It is to be just like the branch in the vine, abiding every minute of the day. There are the branches, in close communion, in unbroken communion, with the vine from January to December. And cannot I live every day—cannot I live in abiding communion with the heavenly Vine?"[422]

---

[420] Bisagno, *Letters to Timothy*, 154.
[421] Piper, *Supremacy of God*, 38.
[422] Murray, *Absolute Surrender*, 120–121.

"Evangelistic preaching is the most important of all preaching when we consider what it seeks to do. Evangelistic preaching must expose sin, exalt Christ, explain the way of salvation, persuade men to repent and believe."[423]—Faris Whitesell

"A prophet enters the Holy of Holies and comes out speaking what he hears; a scribe goes into his study and comes out telling what he has read."[424]—A.W. Tozer

"Any gospel preaching that does not rebuke sin, does not arouse conviction, does not show what God's Word says about His wrath upon sin and the eternal punishment of unrepentant sinners, will not be successful preaching to the unsaved."[425]—John R. Rice

"Always inconvenience yourself rather than your audience: your Master would have done so."[426]—C. H. Spurgeon

"I wish that I knew how to preach. I have tried to do so for thirty years or so, but I am only beginning to learn the art...I rejoice that Jesus forgives the sins of my sermons."[427]—C. H. Spurgeon

[423] Whitesell, *Basic New Testament Evangelism*, 104.
[424] Sorenson, "The Pulpit and the Pew."
[425] John Rice, *The Evangelist*, 183.
[426] Allen, *Exploring the Mind*, M-533.
[427] Ibid.

7
Suggestions

Practical hints for evangelistic preaching:

1. Verify the wireless microphone has fresh batteries and is working properly. Double-check operation procedure.

2. Proper placement of the microphone on the coat lapel or shirt is imperative for best sound quality.

3. Leave the cell phone in your car or the pastor's study. The habit of carrying a cell phone continuously poses the danger of inadvertent failure to turn it off prior to preaching.

4. Relieve nervousness or gain composure by taking several slow deep breaths prior to rising to preach.

5. Change idiosyncrasies of speech that hinder message receptivity. John Wesley said, "Take care of anything awkward or affected either in your gesture, phrase or pronunciation."[428] Prior to John McCain's nomination acceptance speech at the Republican National Convention in August 2008, a talk show host was asked if he had any suggestions for McCain's delivery. This radio personality responded, "Not to say 'My friend' a thousand times." Phrases like "Now listen" and "Stay with me" must not be overused. In the political arena one hears much about a candidate's body language. Experts in such a field are queried about a candidate's speech and mannerisms to ascertain his true feelings. Even so, eye movement, hand gestures, and facial expressions in evangelistic preaching either undergird the sermon or undermine it.

6. Develop a sermon seed file for evangelistic messages. In study for a sermon, it's not unusual to come across ideas for other messages. Jot these ideas down on a piece of paper and place them in a file folder for later reference. Additionally, daily devotions and dialogue with other preachers will provide "seed" for this file.

---

[428] Spurgeon, *Lectures to My Students,* 113.

7. Don't turn toward the choir in preaching, breaking eye contact with the primary audience, the unsaved seated in front of you.

8. Drink a bottle of water (room temperature) prior to preaching. "Water lubricates the lungs, larynx, esophagus, throat, mouth, tongue, and lips—all the bodily parts involved in generating and projecting speech. Our vocal cords are surrounded by a mucous membrane that needs to stay wet and fluid if our voices are going to work properly."[429] The travel time for water to get to the stomach, through the digestive system and make the return trip to hydrate the voice is four hours.

9. Be reluctant to change the sermon, but remain open to do so if the Holy Spirit directs.

10. Resist lengthy introductions and long sermons. Typically the sermon should be no longer than twenty five minutes. Keep in mind the audience you are seeking to reach are not spiritually minded people, but are "deaf, dumb and dead" spiritually, inapt to digest too much too fast.

11. Preach to the lone lost man. Refuse to lay aside the evangelistic message simply because there is only one lost soul known to be present; it may be a divinely appointed opportunity to capture his soul for Jesus.

12. "Start low. Aim high. Catch fire as you go." This is great advice for the preacher in preaching. Avoid starting high and remaining there for the entire sermon. Vary the rate of delivery speed. Spurgeon's stenographer stated the London preacher averaged 140 words a minute but never maintained the same speed in two main sections of a sermon. In driving his "team of horses" (sermon) he varied the rate of speed, slowing down from time to time. Francis L. Patton, former President at Princeton University, stated, "No one but a dunce would proceed at the same rate all through the sermon. Begin at a moderate pace, and later at times trip along lightly. When you come

---

[429] Robert Morgan, ed., *Annual Preacher's SourceBook,* 382.

to something you wish the hearer to remember, be sure to say it slowly."[430] Do diligence not to sound winded, gasping for air in preaching.

13. Take preventative measures against possible distractions. Provide child care for children five years old and younger; ask for cell phones to be turned off; print the invitational hymn in the bulletin or project it onto a screen; know in advance how you will deal with the "invitational repeaters" (who simply come for prayer), so that you remain available to the lost; confirm that the music leader and you are on the same page; never assume guest musicians know they have a time limitation. Nearly every minister has been in services, as I was recently, in which a guest soloist sang five selections, talking prior to each! I finally got the pulpit at 7:45 P.M. (7 P.M. start). Guest musicians must clearly understand they have only five to six minutes on the program, time for two selections.

We love babies, but their cries can hinder the effect of the evangelistic sermon. Prevention is the key, as already stated. But how do you handle the problem tactfully once the service has begun? First, pray for the baby to hush or for the parent to remove him or her from the service prior to your rising to preach. Second, once in the pulpit, pray publicly for an atmosphere of quietude, one free from disturbance where lost men can consider the claims of Christ. This approach has saved numerous services over the years from grave interruption without embarrassment or offense to anyone, since baby crying is never addressed directly.

14. Let your time consciousness be unconscious to others. Discreetly place your watch in a place where only you can see it.

15. In working with another pastor in an evangelistic service, alert him as to how he will know you are finished with the invitational appeal so he does not interrupt. I simply tell pastors

---

[430] Blackwood, *Preparation of Sermons*, 212.

that when my appeal is completed I will kneel at the altar in prayer. In the event the host pastor (in revival or crusade) starts gesturing with his hands and talking during the invitation while you are still extending it, do not try to wrestle it back, but ease down to the altar, yielding to him.

16. The invitational hymn selection must be evangelistic. This hymn must serve as a hammer to drive the nail of the message home to the congregation. Its selection requires prayer and preacher input; its performance requires prayer and choir rehearsal. It must be a familiar hymn.

17. Never be offended or make scolding comments when people leave the service in the midst of a sermon.

18. At times lengthy testimonials or excessive music will put you in the pulpit late. In such occasions, it is best just to preach without referring to either. The congregation is aware of what transpired prior to your rising to preach.

19. Accept constructive criticism; ask for it. Don't be over-sensitive to criticism of preaching evangelistically—the sermon, style or summons. Allow the Holy Spirit to sift the criticism received so that only what is beneficial remains. Spurgeon, during his first years preaching in London, would weekly receive a letter from an unknown critic who listed his faults. Years later, after having corrected those faults, Spurgeon thanked God for those anonymous criticisms with regret that he could not thank the person who helped him in this regard.[431] C. H. Spurgeon, again remarking on criticism the preacher receives, stated, "Hard words wound some delicate minds very keenly. Many of the best ministers, from the very spirituality of their character, are exceedingly sensitive—too sensitive for such a world as this. 'A kick that scarce would move a horse would kill a sound divine.'"[432] Vance Havner stated, "It is not our business to make the message acceptable,

---

[431] Ibid., 215.
[432] Spurgeon, *Lectures to My Students*, 161.

but to make it available. We are not to see that they like it, but that they get it."[433]

20. Rest is essential to be at your best physically, mentally and spiritually in the pulpit. Retire early the night before preaching, and when preaching at night plan rest during the day. At Amsterdam '83, Stephen Olford told evangelists, "Organize your afternoon for rest. As and when possible, it is important to build up physical and nervous energy for the main event of the day—the evening crusade rally or church service; so use your afternoons for this purpose."[434] During this same Amsterdam conference, in a Q and A session I attended, Billy Graham was asked how he prepared to preach. In part he answered that he felt it a must to get to bed early the night prior to preaching the next morning.

21. Problems with a hoarse or irritated throat? According to Dr. Joseph C. Stemple, professor in the Division of Communication Sciences and Disorders at the University of Kentucky, "The best remedy for this is to stay well-hydrated with non-caffeinated liquids. Dry vocal folds do not vibrate well." The use of things containing citric acid, like lemons for example, promotes dehydration and should be avoided. Some literature suggests that Slippery Elm lozenges may be helpful.[435]

22. Do not refer to people by name (members and guests) in the sermon unless in a positive manner, and that without any possible embarrassment.

23. Avoid complimenting singers in one service and not in the next. Stay sensitive to the feelings of all who provide musical numbers. A good rule is compliment privately, not publicly.

24. Attire is important. It is hard to beat a coat and tie when preaching to adult or mixed audiences in a church or crusade setting. W. A. Criswell stated, "I like for a preacher to look like

---

[433] Havner, "Acceptability of Preaching."
[434] Douglas, *Work of the Evangelist*, 774.
[435] Stemple, "Personal Correspondence."

a preacher, not like a bum. I would expect the head of a state or an ambassador from a mighty nation to look the part. The preacher is ambassador plenipotentiary from the greatest court in the universe, even from the throne of Heaven itself. He ought to reflect the garments of glory in his own manner of dress....Be wise and cautious in the selection of your clothing. Avoid extremes and unusual dress. Darker colors seem to carry more of a command for respect than lighter ones. Accessories matching the suit can be most impressive....Do not stuff your pocket full of things. Never let them bulge. Your shirt collar ought to be large enough to give you proper room in which to speak and deliver your message....Wear your best clothing with a big, sincere, glowing smile. The world needs it."[436]

People judge you by your appearance, talk, conduct and companions. Since few will have the opportunity hear you talk or view your walk or observe your associates, they base opinions of you strictly on your looks. First Samuel 16:7 cautions, "Man looketh on the outward appearance." Curtis Hutson states, "Some good people (and I add preachers) have two strikes against them before they ever say a word because of a poor personal appearance. Before they say or do anything, an incorrect judgment has already been formed based solely on appearance."[437]

25. Don't apologize for being sick (as is apt to be the case from time to time); just preach.

26. Bounce sermon thoughts off pastors or evangelists. "The more your sermon is field-tested, the more you will grow in its truth—and how to communicate it."[438]

27. In revivals, instruct the host pastor to keep lodging accommodations private. I heard a pastor at the conclusion of an evangelistic service state to his people that the preacher was staying at a certain motel, and he urged them to call him if so

---

[436] Criswell, *Guidebook for Pastors*, 38.
[437] Hutson, *Things I Have Learned*, 80.
[438] Bodey, *Inside the Sermon*, 60.

desired. This was wrong in every respect, considering the culture of the day and the mindset of some who would like to demean the man and his office.

28. Advise the music leader not to stand behind the pulpit or use hand movement during the singing of the invitation. He should remain motionless to one side or the other on the platform.

29. The format of the evangelistic service must pulsate with an evangelistic theme from opening song to invitational hymn. Nonessentials to the service, all that would not be supportive to an evangelistic thrust, must be omitted (even sacred cows like the reading of the announcements). There is a flow to the evangelistic service that is more easily recognized than described, caught than taught, imitated than dictated. With it, the evangelistic sermon is strengthened; without it, the sermon is weakened. Learn how to program the evangelistic service by reading instructional books and observation.

30. Receive people during the invitation with a firm forearm extended. Preventive measures must be taken to insure those responding do not drape their bodies upon you.

31. Commend and defend preachers who are better evangelistic preachers than you. L. R. Scarborough cautions, "The envious or jealous preacher can have neither favor with men nor power from God. Jealousy is a trait of little spirits."[439]

32. Keep your word with regard to statements made during the invitation ("This will be the last stanza we will sing," for example).

33. In cold weather, when greeting people following preaching, avoid doing so at a door that opens into the chilling night air, as a preventative measure from getting sick.

34. Give forethought as to how to handle someone who interrupts the sermon by taking the floor and talking. The manner in which this is dealt with can either kill the service or

---

[439] Scarborough, *With Christ,* 80.

enable at least a portion of it to be salvaged. Sooner or later this will be experienced by most every preacher.

35. Whenever possible give the evangelistic sermon time to "seethe" before preaching. J. Henry Jowett cautions, "The weakness of smaller preachers is that their time is 'always ready'; the mighty preachers have long seasons when they know their time 'is not yet come.' They have the strength to go slowly and even to 'stand.' They do not 'rush into print,' or into speech, with 'unproportioned thought.' They can keep the message back, sometimes for years, until some day there is a soul in it, and a movement about it, which tells them 'the hour is come.' Beware of the facility which, if given a day's notice, is ready to preach on anything! Let us cultivate the strength of leisureliness, the long, strong processes of meditation, the self-control that refuses to be premature, the discipline that can patiently await maturity....It may be that a word will lay hold of you so imperatively as to make you feel that its proclamation is urgent and that its hour has come. But I think it frequently happens that we go into the pulpit with truth that is undigested and with messages that are immature. Our minds have not done their work thoroughly, and when we present our work to the public, there is a good deal of floating sediment in our thought and a consequent cloudiness about our words. Now it is a good thing to put a subject away to mature and clarify. When my grandmother was making cider, she used to let it stand for long seasons in the sunlight 'to give it a soul!' And I think that many of our sermons, when the preliminary work has been done, should be laid aside for a while before they are offered to our congregations. There are subconscious powers in the life that seem to continue the ripening process when our active judgments are engaged elsewhere."[440] This truth I have learned not from books but personal experience. "Unripe" sermons produce far less fruit for the Lord than those given the time to develop fully.

---

[440] Jowett, *The Preacher*, 132, 130.

36. In ministering in revivals, endeavor to keep the people informed as to which nights an evangelistic sermon will be proclaimed. Sad it is for the saints to gather in their lost friends on a night the preacher speaks on stewardship!

37. Don't allow the pulpit to hinder proclamation. C. H. Spurgeon said in regard to preaching, "It is the truth of God mediated through a man's voice, life, heart, mind, in fact, his whole being."[441] W. A. Criswell, commenting on this statement, remarked, "That is why Spurgeon preached from behind a rail, not a pulpit desk. He felt that since a man preaches with his whole body, it should not be hidden from view."[442] Spurgeon detested pulpits, stating, "What horrible inventions they are! If we could once abolish them, we might say concerning them as Joshua did concerning Jericho, 'Cursed be he that buildeth this Jericho,' for the old-fashioned pulpit has been a greater curse to the churches than is at first sight evident. No barrister would ever enter a pulpit to plead a case at the bar. How could he hope to succeed while buried almost up to his shoulders?…Ministers cannot be blamed for ungainly postures and attitudes when only a very small part of their bodies can be seen during a discourse."[443] Harvey Springer declared, "Most preachers hide three-fourths of their personality behind a BIG pulpit."[444] John Bisagno commented, "To be hidden behind a large pulpit robs the preacher of much of his effectiveness in the delivery of an evangelistic sermon."[445]

38. Inasmuch as possible, avoid taking pain medications the day you will preach, for they can impair mental sharpness.

39. Keep a breath mint in your pocket for use during the invitation.

---

[441] Wallace, "Illustrations on Preaching."

[442] Ibid.

[443] Spurgeon, *Lectures to My Students,* 276–277.

[444] Bill Rice, Part 2, 6.

[445] Bisagno, *Power of Positive Evangelism,* 9.

40. C. H. Spurgeon stated, "Those who criticize statistics usually have none to report."[446] But we must be careful in sharing decisions to do so accurately and not for self-praise.

41. Mark potential evangelistic sermon texts in the Bible with the abbreviation "ET."

42. To prepare the soil for the seed you are about to plant and the invitation that will be issued, it is good to arrive early to the church, assembly, crusade tent or classroom to mingle with those gathering. In doing this you have already established rapport with most of the people before you ever stand to speak.

43. "We must in these times say a great deal in a few words, but not too much, nor with too much amplification. One thought fixed on the mind will be better than fifty thoughts made to flit across the ear."[447]

44. Keep a spare shaving kit complete with razor, shaving cream, aftershave lotion, toothbrush and toothpaste in the trunk of the car for those motel stays in which you forget the primary shaving kit. Wherein possible include in this spare kit a battery-operated microshaver.

45. R. G. Lee gives counsel about his last action before entering the pulpit to preach. Two young seminarians went to hear him preach. Later they talked with him in his study, and one said, "Dr. Lee, what is the very last thing you do before walking to the platform when the service begins?" The famous preacher said, "The last thing I do is to look into a mirror to be sure my hair is combed, my tie is straight, and my zipper is fastened." Somewhat surprised and astounded, the young seminarian said, "It seems to me that the last thing a preacher ought to do is kneel and pray before entering the pulpit." Dr. Lee replied, "Young man, if you haven't already been praying, it's too late when it's time for the service to begin."[448]

---

[446] Wiersbe, *Bible Exposition Commentary,* Vol. 1, 722.
[447] Spurgeon, *Lectures to My Students,* 77.
[448] Bill Rice, Part 1, 10

46. Unless absolutely necessary, avoid drinking water in the pulpit. A man remarked after seeing a preacher drink water while preaching, "That was the first time I ever saw a windmill run on water." Obviously it can be a distraction.

47. In revival meetings, refuse to meet with individuals of the church without the pastor's sanction.

48. Know your audience's level of comprehension so as not to "shoot over their heads."

49. Regarding pulpit prayer, George Whitfield stated of one preacher, "He prayed me into a good frame of mind, and if he had stopped there, it would have been very well; but he prayed me out of it again by keeping on."[449] Spurgeon advises regarding the prayer before the sermon, "Do not let your prayer be long."[450]

50. Write "turn mic on" inside the worship program prior to the service as a reminder.

51. Inform the evangelistic preacher of the number of unsaved recognized in the service prior to his rising to preach.

52. Check the sound monitors on the platform prior to service, or else you may be blasted with your own sermon.

53. I have discovered the prime potential for an evangelistic sermon is the Sunday morning service.

54. To keep the sermon "fresh," wait until the time is near for its proclamation to develop the preaching outline. I generally write out a sermon in manuscript form but wait until the service is nigh at hand to "fasten it like a nail" in my heart and soul by writing out the preaching outline.

55. Initially read an evangelistic sermon at least once a week for illumination in its preparation, inspiration for its declaration, instruction in its presentation, and direction in its invitation.

---

[449] Ibid., 61.
[450] Ibid., 60.

56. Do not unduly promote the speaker for the evangelistic service. A pastor built a minister friend up as a pulpit giant prior to his speaking engagement in a church. Following the service, a man approached him and said, "You're no giant!" It is proper and profitable to promote the evangelistic speaker but with due caution not to do so in excess. "He must increase, but I must decrease" (John 3:30).

57. Keep your shoes shined. Criswell suggests it is best to wear dark socks in preaching, matching the sock color with the shoe color.[451]

58. Know what the invitational selection is prior to rising to preach so that you can bridge your sermon with it.

59. Endeavor not to allow the presence of a preacher, professor or dignitary to impact your preaching. D. L. Moody was leading a crusade in England when a worker came upon the platform to inform him that a very important nobleman had come into the hall. Moody responded, "May the meeting be a blessing to him," and he preached just as before.[452]

60. Watch the sweets. Sugar (and milk) has a tendency to form mucus, which can cause problems with your speaking voice.[453]

61. Lloyd Perry suggests the auditorium temperature should be 65 degrees, allowing the body heat to raise it to 68–70 degrees.[454]

62. "In a sermon, Greek and Hebrew are like underwear: they add a lot of support, but you don't want to let them show."[455]

63. In preaching, only seven per cent gets across with our words (vocabulary, outline, and illustrations), thirty-eight per

---

[451] Criswell, *Guidebook for Pastors*, 39.

[452] Wiersbe, *Bible Exposition Commentary*. Vol. 1, 685.

[453] Vines and Shaddix, *Power in the Pulpit*, 80.

[454] Gugliotto, *Hand-Book for Bible Study,* 143.

[455] Green, *Illustrations for Biblical Preaching,* 286.

cent with our tone of voice (diction, resonance, and inflection), and nearly fifty-five per cent hits home with our body language (stance, gestures, and expression).[456]

64. Get to the pulpit within thirty minutes of the service's starting time to avoid a sense of rush in preaching.

65. Always talk *to* people, not *at* them.

66. Simplicity in sermon content and delivery is essential. J. C. Ryle comments, "Of course the first object of a minister should be to preach the truth, the whole truth, and nothing but 'the truth as it is in Jesus.' But the next thing he ought to aim at is that his sermon may be understood, and it will not be understood by most of his hearers if it is not simple."[457]

67. Keep a back-up microphone handy in case the need arises while preaching. During the time that I was writing this book, I preached at a Christian camp chapel service using a lapel microphone and needed to switch out to a hand-held microphone for greater volume due to the loud sound of rain upon the metal roof. The transition went without a hitch.

68. Do not announce the main divisions of the sermon at the outset of preaching. "It gives everything away. It holds no surprises in reserve. It may, indeed, if used on rare occasions prove effective enough. But, on the whole, it is apt to be destructive of interest if people know in advance exactly where you intend to lead them."[458]

69. Let the end be the end. Upon the conclusion of the invitation have the benediction and go home.

70. Never fail to make plain the need and means of salvation, even in non-evangelistic messages. Had I been an unsaved person seeking peace with God at the church I attended recently, I would have left clueless!

---

[456] Gugliotto, *Hand-Book for Bible Study,* 142.
[457] Ryle, "Simplicity in Preaching."
[458] Stewart, *Heralds of God,* 134.

71. Make much of the salvation decisions made in the service. Scripture reveals there is rejoicing in the presence of the angels when a person gets saved; how much more this celebration should be among those who know what it is like to be saved out of darkness into His marvelous light. Make this a big deal, because it *is* a big deal! Nothing sparks the fire of revival in a saint's life like knowing someone has been saved in the service, so share these decisions with the congregation prior to dismissal.

72. Avoid clearing the throat, for it is detrimental to the vocal chords.

73. Is it difficult to look the congregation in the face while you are preaching? Prior to rising to preach, select two people who are seated midway in the sanctuary (opposite sides) and initially look at them as you preach; once you are comfortable, look to others. It will be helpful to meet these two people prior to the start of the service or during the greeting time within the service.

74. In being commended for sermons preached, follow Corrie Ten Boom's example. Gather the compliments with humility (don't refuse them) as one would gather flowers, and at the end of the day, present them to Him to whom they belong as a bouquet of praise and thanksgiving.

75. Don't waste the church bulletin. Prior to rising to preach, jot a quick note of gratitude on the church bulletin or order of service to someone who faithfully stands with you in the ministry and put it in the mail the next day. This one- or two-line note will mean volumes to its recipient, especially in their knowing it was written just prior to your rising to preach.

76. Don't lock yourself into certain sermons to preach in a revival by promoting them in advance. John Bisagno said, "I would never announce six or eight sermons ahead of time.

There may be reasons why you will need to change, and we must be sensitive to the Holy Spirit as we preach."[459]

77. On selection of reference works, Charles Ryrie advises, "If one is building a library, especially on limited funds, my advice is to buy timeless books (including reference material) and borrow timely books that, though significant for a time, will not be particularly useful after a few years."[460]

78. It should be understood that once the hymn of invitation has begun it is not to be changed without direction from the preacher. It is advisable to have three back-up invitation songs selected, numbered one, two, and three. The preacher discreetly raises one, two or three fingers to the music leader at the moment he wants to make a transition to another hymn.[461]

79. The preacher's spirit during a revival meeting will be remembered far longer than his sermons will.

80. I find it best on the last night of an evangelistic meeting not to express appreciation for support and hospitality until the conclusion of the invitation. Expressing gratitude prior to preaching on the last night seems to give a note of conclusion and finality to the service psychologically, and this certainly is the last thing you want to happen.

81. Sit with the congregation as a worshipper prior to preaching. This has been my practice for many years. Warren Wiersbe cites its value, "In the church we attend, all we have on the platform is the worship team, the musicians, and the instruments. The pastor sits with the congregation on the right-hand side in the third row. We know he's there. When visitors come in, they wonder who is going to preach. Then he gets up and preaches. They like that. The older folks had to get used to this. The pastor took all the chairs off the platform, and now nobody sits in Moses' seat....In other words, not only is the

---

[459] Bisagno, *Power of Positive Evangelism*, 11.
[460] Ryrie, *Practical Guide*, 76.
[461] Bisagno, *Power of Positive Evangelism*, 19.

pulpit out of the way, but the platform is out of the way *(so as not to hinder the proclamation of the Word).*"[462]

82. Criswell's advice on your place of study: "Without doubt, and I cannot emphasize the conviction too much, the best place for the pastor's study and library is in a separated room in his home. The preacher who has his study at the church uses his finest morning hours to shave, bathe, comb his hair, tie his shoes, start his car, drive to the church, unlock his door, and look nice for any stranger who may wander in. I do not need my mind to be fresh and rested to comb my hair and tie my shoes. I can do those things when I have studied myself stupid."[463]

83. Never become too "big" to lead a revival in a "small church." Junior Hill is a good example of a noted evangelist who accepts invitations from all sizes of congregation.

84. Be courteous to your brothers in ministry by responding to their e-mails, letters and phone calls.

85. At times it will be "impossible" to break away from a train of thought in the study to eat a meal or answer the phone when summoned by your wife. It is expedient therefore to help her understand something of the art of sermon study so she will understand when these times occur.

86. Never doubt the power of the preached Word to bring sinners to Christ beyond the hour it is proclaimed. R. A. Torrey tells of a man who was converted at age ninety-six when he recalled a sermon on I Corinthians 16:22 he had heard John Farrel preach eighty-six years earlier.[464]

87. At Amsterdam '83, I heard Josh McDowell state evangelists should not drive home the last night of revival (out of

---

[462] Bailey and Wiersbe, *Black and White*, 96. (words in italics added for clarification).
[463] Criswell, *Guidebook for Pastors*, 68.
[464] Hutson, *Great Preaching on Hell,* 202.

town meetings) but stay overnight so as to return to wife and children fresh and not exhausted.

88. Should you preach from texts requested by others? Spurgeon states, "My answer would be, as a rule, *never;* and if there must be exceptions, let them be few....When a friend suggests a topic, think it over and consider whether it be appropriate and see whether it comes to you with power. Receive the request courteously,...but if the Lord whom you serve does not cast His light upon the text, do not preach from it, let who may persuade you."[465]

89. I was asked by a young pastor if he should talk to the host pastor of a church that annually conducted evangelistic meetings about having him preach one year. I emphatically answered, "No." The evangelist/pastor must rely upon the Holy Spirit to open doors of ministry. The moment a minister begins integrating the human element into the equation of ministry— church size, revival budget, status of church or pastor—and pushing himself on a pastor, the invitation, if extended, is contaminated with self. Preach the Word, do the work of an evangelist, pray earnestly, stay faithful, remain open to preach in revivals, and the Lord will open such doors of His choosing in His time.

90. I was approached by a man in a revival who seventeen years earlier had heard me preach in a crusade. He remembered the sermon, but also the fact that I had not sung with the congregation. He noted that I had sung vibrantly in this revival and was wondering why I hadn't sung in the crusade. I could only speculate (hoarseness, throat irritation, fatigue), but let this serve as a reminder that saints in the pew are watching the man in the pulpit prior to his rising to preach. Therefore, be mindful of worship participation with the people: stand when they stand, sing when they sing, shake hands when they shake hands, and practice silence when they are silent (no conversations on the platform). Personal mannerisms prior to preaching

---

[465] Spurgeon, *Lectures to My Students,* 96.

will either help build a bridge to the people in preaching or undermine it.

"I cannot say that I have had dry seasons when sermon ideas were scarce. My problem is time to preach the sermons I want to preach or else deciding when to preach a given sermon."[466]—Hershel Hobbs

"Don't hold back because you cannot preach in St. Paul's; be content to talk to one or two in a cottage. Very good wheat grows in little fields. You may cook in small pots as well as in big ones. Little pigeons can carry great messages. Even a little dog can bark at a thief, wake up the master, and save the house. A spark is fire. A sentence of truth has Heaven in it. Do what you do right thoroughly, pray over it heartily, and leave the result to God."[467]—C. H. Spurgeon

---

[466] Bodey, *Inside the Sermon,* 127.
[467] Robert Morgan, *Stories, Illustrations and Quotes,* 798.

8
Seeds

A cartoon depicts a discouraged preacher with elbows on a large desk and face in his hands. Behind this preacher are bookshelves filled with hundreds of books that reach to the ceiling. The caption reads, "I can't think of anything to preach."[468] The lesson of the cartoon is that there is much to preach if the minister is disciplined to mine it out of the gold-mine of God's Word. C. H. Spurgeon said that he got flour and milk and currants and raisins and sugar and salt and other ingredients from many sources, but he made his own cakes.[469] Jerry Vines remarked, "I milk a lot of cows, but I try to make my own butter."[470] Francis Bacon stated, "Some students never study but, like the spider, spin everything out from within, beautiful webs that never last. Some are like ants that steal whatever they find, store it away, and use it later. But the bee sets the example for us all. He takes from the many flowers, but he makes his own honey."[471]

Gathering Seeds

Where does the minister gather *ingredients* (seeds) for evangelistic messages? Hershel Hobbs stated such seeds may come from "reading a book, a conversation, recognition of a need, or current events. There are ideas everywhere if one is alert to grasp them. But most of my ideas come from devotional reading and exegetical studying of the Scriptures. During these times, sermon ideas jump from the Scriptures like trout in the lake."[472] Sidlow Baxter's sermon seeds in largest part came from the continual reading of the Bible, not in search for such, but in sheer pleasure for edification or relaxation. Baxter said that in such reading, "sermons will leap out of their hiding

---

[468] McDill, *12 Essential Skills.*
[469] Bodey, *Inside the Sermon*, 13.
[470] Vines, *Exploring,* Preface.
[471] Green, *Illustrations for Biblical Preaching*, 283.
[472] Bodey, *Inside the Sermon*, 127.

places and pounce upon us like glorious panthers which we simply cannot shake off."[473] Additionally Baxter maintains that Matthew Henry's Commentary among all whole commentaries on the Bible provides the most in fertile sermon suggestions for the evangelical preacher.[474]

J. I. Packer gathers sermon suggestions from the known needs of congregations and his own experience of being taught and disciplined by God. Calvin's *Institutes* has suggested to Packer many messages over the years.[475] C. H. Spurgeon said of William Gurnall (1616–1679), "I have found his work the best thought-breeder in all our library. I should think more discourses have been suggested by it than by any other. I have often resorted to it when my own fire has been burning low."[476]

Early in my ministry I developed a sermon seed file in which I deposit material from various sources that strike me as possessing sermonic value (illustrations, sermon outlines, insights gleaned from devotionals and Bible study).

Evangelistic Sermon Material
Ten Evangelistic Sermon Topics
1. Good but Lost (Matthew 19:16–22)
2. The Healing of the Gadarene Demoniac (Mark 5:1–20)
3. The Man Healed at the Gate Beautiful (Acts 3:2–13)
4. The Prodigal Son (Luke 15:11–32)
5. The Value of a Soul (Matthew 16:26)
6. The Harvest Is Past and We Are Not Saved (Jeremiah 8:20)
7. Why Be a Christian? (Hebrews 13:8)
8. Who Are Christians? (Psalm 95)
9. How Shall You Escape If You Neglect This Great Salvation? (Hebrews 2:3)
10. Almost but Lost (Acts 26:28)

---

[473] Ibid., 12.
[474] Ibid.
[475] Ibid., 191.
[476] Earle, *The Gospel of Luke,* Foreword.

Ten New Testament Evangelistic Sermon Texts
1. John 3:16
2. John 10:9
3. Acts 16:30–31
4. Matthew 7:13–14
5. Matthew 7:21–23
6. Matthew 11:28–30
7. Matthew 18:11
8. Matthew 24:36–42
9. Mark 1:40–42
10. Matthew 10:28

Ten Old Testament Evangelistic Texts

Robert Coleman, referring to preaching evangelistically in the Old Testament, stated, "Typology offers another method, moving from a type in an Old Testament passage to the anti-type in Christ. Or one can go the way of analogy, showing the relationship between God's message for Israel and Christ's message for the church. The longitudinal method traces a theme of the Old Testament to Christ in the New Testament."[477] Faris Whitesell said, "The inexhaustible possibilities of the Old Testament for evangelistic preaching are relatively unrealized and consequently too infrequently utilized....It is full of flaming evangelistic material. God will use its truths to bring conviction and salvation to the lost. It will produce that 'law-work' so foundational to 'grace-work.'...Again, Christ is in the Old Testament, and when we find Him there and preach Him as the answer to human need, we are evangelistic."[478]
1. Proverbs 14:12
2. Proverbs 27:1
3. Joel 3:14–17
4. Numbers 21:4–9
5. Proverbs 29:1
6. Isaiah 45:22

---

[477] Gibson, ed., *Preaching the Old Testament*, 187.
[478] Whitesell, *Evangelistic Preaching*, 13, 21.

7. Amos 7:7–9
8. Jeremiah 8:20
9. Joshua 24:15
10. Amos 4:12

Ten Evangelistic Sermon Texts on Doctrines

Faris Whitesell writes, "Doctrinal preaching is evangelistic preaching of the highest order. Every Bible doctrine measures man and finds him falling short of God's requirements. Every doctrine calls him to higher ground and larger service. All Bible doctrines are practical if carried through to their logical conclusion, and particularly do they show the unsaved man his need of salvation."[479]

1. Luke 16:19–31 (Hell)
2. John 14:1–6 (Heaven)
3. Revelation 20:11–15 (Judgment)
4. Hebrews 9:27 (Death and Judgment)
5. Matthew 24:37 (Second Coming)
6. Acts 17:30–31 (Repentance)
7. Matthew 28:6 (Resurrection of Christ)
8. John 19:4 (Deity of Christ)
9. John 20:30–31 (Deity of Christ)
10. II Timothy 3:15–17 (Bible)

Ten Evangelistic Sermon Questions in the New Testament

1. "What must I do to be saved?" (Acts 16: 30)

2. "How shall we escape if we neglect so great a salvation?" (Hebrews 2:3)

3. "For what is a man profited if he shall gain the whole world and lose his own soul?" (Matthew 16:26a)

4. "What shall a man give in exchange for his soul?" (Matthew 16:26b)

5. "But whom say ye that I am?" (Mark 8:29)

6. "What think ye of Christ, whose son is He?" (Matthew 22:42)

---

[479] Ibid., 101.

7. "Good Master, what shall I do, that I may inherit eternal life?" (Mark 10:17)

8. "What shall be the sign of thy coming and of the end of the world?" (Matthew 24:3)

9. "What shall I do then with Jesus which is called the Christ?" (Matthew 27:22)

10. "How can a man be born when he is old?" (John 3:4)

Ten Evangelistic Sermon Questions in the Old Testament
1. "Who may abide the day of His coming?" (Malachi 3:2)
2. "Art thou in health, my brother?" (II Samuel 20:9)
3. "Where art thou?" (Genesis 3:9)
4. "Watchman, what of the night?" (Isaiah 21:11)
5. "What profit shall we have, if we pray unto him?" (Job 21:15)
6. "Why art thou cast down, O my soul?" (Psalm 42:11)
7. "Is it well with thee? is it well with thy husband? is it well with the child?" (II Kings 4:26)
8. "Who is on the Lord's side?" (Exodus 32:26)
9. "Is the young man Absalom safe?" (II Samuel 18:32)
10. "If a man die, shall he live again?" (Job 14:14)

Ten New Testament Conversions for Evangelistic Sermons
1. Nicodemus (John 3:1–16)
2. Cornelius (Acts 10:1–48)
3. Saul of Tarsus (Acts 9:1–20)
4. Philippian Jailer (Acts 16:16–34)
5. Ethiopian Eunuch (Acts 8:26–39)
6. Woman at Jacob's Well (John 4:6–30)
7. Zacchaeus (Luke 19:1–10)
8. Thief on the Cross (Luke 23:32–45)
9. Lydia of Thyatira (Acts 16:1–15)
10. A Sinful Woman (Luke 7:36–50)

Old Testament Conversions for Evangelistic Sermons
1. Nebuchadnezzar (Daniel 4:28–37)
2. Naaman (II Kings 5:1–15)
3. Darius (Daniel 6:25–27)

177

4. Manasseh (II Chronicles 33:10–13; 18–19)

5. King of Nineveh (Jonah 3:5–9)

6. Rahab (Joshua 6:25)

Old Testament Types of Salvation

1. Brazen Serpent (Numbers 21:4–9)

2. Scapegoat (Leviticus 16:20–22)

3. Noah's Ark (Genesis 7:6)

4. Gate to Tabernacle—Only One Gate (Exodus 25:8)

5. Lot's Escape from Sodom (Genesis 19:17)

6. Naaman (II Kings 5:1–14)

7. Israel's Deliverance from Egypt (Exodus 3:10–15)

8. When I See the Blood (Exodus 12:13)

Ten Evangelistic Sermon Titles and Texts of Great Preachers

1. T. Dewitt Talmage: "A Fool's Last Night on Earth" (Luke 12:20)

2. W. B. Riley: "One Man's Chance to Be Saved" (John 5:1–9)

3. L. R. Scarborough: "Lost!" (Luke 19:10)

4. E. J. Daniels: "The High Cost of Being Lost" (Luke 14:25–33)

5. C. H. Spurgeon: "Escape For Thy Life!" (Genesis 19:17)

6. Bailey Smith: "Wheat or Tares" (Matthew 13:24–30)

7. Robert Murray M'Cheyne: "Eternal Punishment" (Mark 9:44)

8. Billy Graham: "The Narrow Gate" (Matthew 7:13–14)

9. R. A. Torrey: "God's Blockades on the Road to Hell" (II Peter 3:9; John 3:16)

10. George W. Truett: "The Doom of Delay" (Genesis 19:16)

Evangelistic Preaching to Children

Spurgeon, in *Come Ye Children,* stated, "As soon as a child is capable of being lost, it is capable of being saved. As soon as a child can sin, that child can, if God's grace assist it, believe and receive the Word of God....Believe that children can be saved just as much as yourselves. I do most firmly believe in the salvation of children. When you see the young heart brought to the Savior, do not stand by and speak harshly, mistrusting everything."[480] Effective evangelistic preaching to children hinges upon confidence (they can be saved); communication (clarity of need and way to be saved); conciseness (ten—fifteen minutes) and conservation (once they are saved).

Ten Evangelistic Sermon Outlines for Children

God blessed each of these sermons to the salvation of children.

1. John 3:16 Sent Me, (Story teaching that John 3:16 can get a cold boy warm, hungry boy fed, dirty boy clean, and a lost boy found), John 3:16

2. A Handful of Theology, (God, man, sin, salvation, eternity), Psalm 34:11

3. The Knocking Savior, (knocking person, knocking purpose, knocking place and knocking promise), Revelation 3:20

4. Who Is a Christian? (saved, secure, satisfied, separated, servant), Acts 11:24

5. Unsafe Lifeboats, (churchgoing, baptism, goodness, Christian home, deeds; only Safe Lifeboat is Jesus), Acts 27:30–33

6. The Colors of Salvation, (black, red, white, green, gold), Acts 20:21

7. The Ten Commandments, (a mirror showing our sin and need of a Savior), Exodus 20:3–17

8. Tagging the Bases, (salvation, baptism/church, service and eternity), Colossians 3:4

9. What Salvation Is Like, (Opening a door to let someone enter, receiving a gift, accepting an invitation, taking a bath, and choosing a path to follow), Romans 6:23b

10. The Key to Heaven's Door, (only one key; not key of church attendance, being good, Lord's Supper, baptism, doing good deeds), John 10:10

---

[480] Spurgeon, *Come Ye Children*, 101, 103.

What to tell a child? Spurgeon suggests, "Tell him he must be born again. Don't bolster him up with the fancy of his own innocence, but show him his sin. Mention the childish sins to which he is prone and pray the Holy Spirit to work conviction in his heart and conscience. Deal with the young in much the same way as you would with the old. Be thorough and honest with them. These boys and girls need pardon through the precious blood as surely as any of us. Do not hesitate to tell the child his ruin; he will not else desire the remedy. Tell him also of the punishment of sin, and warn him of its terror. Be tender, but be true. Do not hide from the youthful sinner the truth, however terrible it may be. Now that he has come to years of responsibility, if he believes not in Christ, it will go ill with him at the last great day. Set before him the judgment seat, and remind him that he will have to give an account of things done in the body. Labor to arouse the conscience, and pray God the Holy Spirit to work by you till the heart becomes tender and the mind perceives the need of the great salvation."[481]

Twelve Evangelistic Sermon Outlines

Hyman Appelman: What Will You Do with Jesus?[482]

Matthew 17: 22

Introduction

    1. It is a direct question.

    2. It is a disturbing question.

    3. It is an imperative question.

    4. It is a present question.

    5. It is a pressing question.

  I. Much Depends upon Doing the Right Thing with Christ

    A. Our acceptance or condemnation before God

      (John 3:1)

    B. Our peace of conscience (Rom. 5:1; 8:1)

---

[481] Ibid., 72–73.

[482] Appelman, *Sermon Outlines and Illustrations,* 54–55.

C. Eternal life (John 5:24; 3:36; I John 5:11–12)

D. Our becoming sons of God (John 1:12)

E. True joy (I Pet. 1:8; "Whom having not seen…")

II. What We Must Do with Him

A. Accept Him or reject Him (John 12:44–48)

B. Let Him in or shut Him out (Rev. 3:20)

C. Confess Him or deny Him (Matt. 10:32–33)

D. Be for Him or against Him (Matt. 12:30)

III. Consider Who He Was

A. "Him hath God exalted…to be a Prince and a Savior"

B. A divinely appointed King (Acts 2:36; 5:31)

C. The Son of God (Mark 1:11)

D. Your Savior (Isa. 53:5–6)

IV. Think What He Has Done

A. Came from Heaven for you (Luke 19:10)

B. Brought you the love and life of God (John 10:10)

C. Died for your sins on the cross (Rom. 5:8; I John 2:2)

V. What Will You Do With Jesus Now?

A. What will you do with Him in your personal life?

B. What will you do with Him in your home?

C. What will you do with Him in your work?

D. What will you do with Him in the church?

Hyman Appelman: Four Rights and One Wrong[483]
Mark 10:17–22

Introduction

The thing he lacked was that he needed an experience of grace with the Lord Jesus Christ. The thing that he lacked was the salvation of his soul. Let us analyze this boy's experience. This story containing the statement of this young man's attitude toward Jesus Christ is a vivid, true-to-everyday-life, portrait-sized description of almost every sinner with whom I have ever talked, especially the Gentile sinner.

1. He came to the Right Person. "Jesus"

2. He came in the Right Spirit. "Kneeling"

3. He came with the Right Question. "What must I do to inherit eternal life?"

4. He received the Right Answer. "Come, take up the cross and follow me."

5. He did the Wrong Thing. "He turned his back on the Lord Jesus Christ."

Conclusion

You also have come to the right Person. You also have come in the right attitude. You also have asked the right question. You also have received the right answer. Now, now, now, do the right thing. Take up the cross of repentance. Exercise your God-given faith. Follow the Lord Jesus Christ. The end is salvation, safely, surety, and satisfaction.

---

[483] Appelman, "Four Rights."

Jerome O. Williams: The Plan of Salvation[484]
II Corinthians 5:19

Introduction

The five fundamental facts connected with the plan of salvation.

1. Redeemer

"God was in Christ." Here we have incarnation. "The Word was made flesh and dwelt among us." It was essential for the Christ to come to earth in the flesh.

2. Redemption

"Reconciling the world unto Himself." Here we see the atonement, the eternal purpose of the death of Christ on the cross. There can be no redemption without the shedding of blood.

3. Revelation

"Hath committed unto us the word of reconciliation." The Lord has revealed unto us His everlasting purpose through the Word. How essential it is to winning the lost people of the world to accept the plan of salvation.

4. Regeneration

"We pray you in Christ's stead, be ye reconciled to God." "Ye must be born again." No person will be able to enter the kingdom without the new life in Christ.

5. Righteousness

"That we might be made the righteousness of God in him." Right in heart and life with God and man—this is the need to be attained in salvation.

---

[484] Williams, *Sermons in Outline,* 171–172.

C. H. Spurgeon: An Urgent Problem[485]
Psalm 95:7–8

Introduction

Let us at once come to the text. The simple plan of our speaking this morning shall at once be laid before you....There is a sad tendency in man to harden his heart even when God speaks, therefore saith the Holy Ghost to us, "Harden not your heart, as in the provocation."

I. The Time Specified. "Today if ye will hear his voice."

This is the uniform time and sense of the Holy Ghost's exhortations. He saith nothing about tomorrow, except to forbid our boasting of it, since we know not what a day shall bring forth. All His instructions are set to the time and tune of "today, today, today."

A. Today is the time of obligation.

Every man...having rebelled against his God...is under law to repent of sin today.

B. Today is the time of opportunity.

There is set before us an open door of approach to God. It is the day of grace, today, a day of gospel preaching, a day of an open Bible, a day of promises, a day in which the Spirit of God comes to work with men, a day in which Jesus Christ is set forth evidently crucified among you, a day in which the mercy seat is approachable, a day in which justice is God's strange work but in which mercy is His joyful occupation....You cannot have a better time for coming to Christ than the season prescribed in the text; namely, "today."

C. It is a time limited.

Today will not last forever; a day is but a day.

---

[485] Spurgeon, *12 Sermons on Decision,* 69–81.

D. A time of promise.

For when God saith to a man, Come to Me at such a time, He by that very word makes an engagement to meet him.

II. The Voice to Be Regarded. "Today if ye will hear his voice."

Place the emphasis upon the word "his."

A. The voice of God is the voice of authority.

B. It is the voice of love.

How wooing are its tones! The Lord in Holy Scripture speaks of mercy and of pardon bought with blood of His dear Son.

C. This is the voice of power.

This is a sweet thought for those of you who are without strength. You will perhaps say, "I cannot turn unto God"; but He can turn you.

D. It is a pleading voice.

God, by calling you, pledges Himself that He will hear you if you come.

E. The voice of God is easy to hear.

What deafness must sin have caused to man that he cannot hear the voice of God!...I fear that some of you are so very busy that you will not reserve your ear for God even for half an hour....If you lose your soul, you have lost all.

III. The Evil to Be Dreaded. "Harden not your hearts."

"Harden not your hearts"; you cannot soften them, but you can harden them.

A. It will be a serious evil if you do so.

It is a greater sin in some than in others.

B. This dreadful sin can be committed in a great many ways.

Only one thing can soften the heart, and that is the blood of Christ applied by the Holy Spirit; but fifty things can harden the heart.

1. Some by a resolution not to feel.

2. Many harden their hearts by delay.

3. Hundreds harden their hearts by pretended doubts.

This sin will bring with it the most fearful consequences. You wish to rest at last; you long to rest even now. But it cannot be till you yield to God. You are not at peace now, and you never will be if you harden your hearts.

Conclusion

God is gently drawing some of you this morning; I can feel that he is doing so. I have deep sympathy with you; I know how you are feeling. You want to get alone and fall down on your knees to pray. Pray now! Cry, "God be merciful to me a sinner" in the pew at once. You need not wait to get home.... Escape for thy life! Today if thou wilt hear His voice, harden not your heart.

Frank Shivers: The Knocking Savior
Revelation 3:20

Introduction

The text before us is spoken to the lukewarm church, but according to Alexander Maclaren it has universal truth and application. Maclaren states, "The 'any man' which follows is wide enough to warrant our stretching out the representation as far as the bounds of humanity extend and believing that wherever there is a closed heart there is a knocking Christ and that all men are lightened by the Light which came into the world."[486]

Holman Hunt has painted a beautiful picture he titled "The Light of the World." It shows Jesus knocking on a huge door with lantern in hand. The door is locked from the inside. No one comes to open the door. This painting was based upon Revelation 3:20. Consider with me several truths concerning this knocking at your heart's door.

    I. The Knocking Person—Who is knocking at your heart door seeking entrance?

It is Jesus ("I stand at the door") who is knocking on your heart door. Who is Jesus? "I, who left Heaven to come to earth to die upon a cross and be raised from the dead just for you, *stand* at your heart's door and knock." "I, who made and sustain you and have all authority over you, solicit you to open the door." "I, who love you with an everlasting love, knock upon your heart's door." "I Stand" speaks of continual action. "*I Stand*," not a preacher or messenger. This word "knock" refers to a strong and powerful knock, though gracious and tender.

    II. The Knocking Purpose—Why does Jesus seek an entrance into your heart?

"That I may come in..." It is that you may have Pardon (II Corinthians 5:20), Peace (Romans 5:1), Plan (Romans 12:1–2), and Paradise (Heaven, John 14:1–6).

    III. The Knocking Place—Where does Jesus knock seeking entrance?

"I stand at the door and knock." This depicts Jesus in close proximity to you right now. How far can one be from a door and knock upon it? The distance of an outstretched arm. Picture your heart as a castle with many doors of entrance on which Jesus may knock seeking entrance.

---

[486] Maclaren, *Expositions of Holy Scripture,* Vol. 17, 303.

    A. The Door of the Scripture (Romans 10:17;
       Psalm 119:130)

    B. The Door of the Saint (example of others)

    C. The Door of Sermons (I Corinthians 1:18)

    D. The Door of Sorrow and Suffering (Psalm 119:71)

    E. The Door of the Soul Winner (Acts 8:35)

    F. The Door of Success (Romans 2:4)

    G. The Door of Sense (common sense, conscience;
       I Timothy 4:2).

  IV. The Knocking Promise—What does Jesus promise
      when you open the door?

"If any man hear my voice, and open the door." Jesus promises that if you open the door He will "enter" regardless of the sin committed or how unworthy you may count yourself. This is a promise of Him who cannot lie. He will do what is promised. He did this for me and millions of others when we opened the door. He will do the same for you.

Conclusion

How can you open the door to Jesus? The Bible makes clear this door swings open on the hinges of faith and repentance (Acts 20:21). Right now open the door by acknowledging sorrow for your sin against a Holy God and receive Jesus Christ into your life as Lord and Savior. Jesus will not put His shoulder to the door and force it open nor in anywise push it down. You must open the door willingly and freely to His gracious offer of reconciliation to God and life eternal. The Lord opened the locked door of Lydia's heart by His persuasion, illumination, and revelation of need, and He is seeking to do the same for you (Acts 16:14).

Seeds

Frank Shivers: Hell

Luke 16:19–31

Why preach on Hell? To *preach* the Book (whole counsel of God), to *plead* with the unsaved to become a Christian, and to *pump* saints to witness. The narrative of the rich man and Lazarus told by Jesus reveals Hell's sordid nature. (Luke 16:19–31)

1. Hell is a *place of Pain* (V. 23–24). Physical and mental torment unimaginable will be experienced in Hell. Scripture makes clear that there will be varying degrees of punishment inflicted in Hell (Matthew 10:15; 11:22, 24; Mark 6:11; Hebrews 10:29).

2. Hell is a *place of Passion* (V. 24). Insatiable appetites and desires plague the inhabitants of Hell forever and ever.

3. Hell is a *place of Parting* (V. 26). The unsaved are forever separated from the redeemed.

4. Hell is a *place of Prayer* (V. 27). The eternally damned will come to see the need of God but woefully too late. Hell is a domain in which man with weeping, wailing, and gnashing of teeth cry out to God for salvation, but in vain.

5. Hell is a *place of Permeating Darkness.* Jude describes Hell as "the blackness of darkness forever" (Jude 13). Utter blackness makes relationships impossible in Hell. C. S. Lewis declared Hell is a place of "nothing but yourself for all eternity!" The inhabitants of Hell know only isolation and utter loneliness; there are no friendships or fellowship.

6. Hell is a *place of Permanence* (V. 26). Hell hath no "Exits." There is no way out of Hell, so there is no hope for its inhabitants. This is one of the worst things about Hell. It is a place where you will be absolutely without hope, for not even God can grant deliverance. One can purchase a shirt in the country store in Hell, Michigan, that states, "I've been to Hell and back"; but a person cannot purchase such a shirt in Satan's domain of eternal darkness.

189

Conclusion

However, the worst part of Hell is that it is a place where God is not! God does not desire any person to go to Hell (II Peter 3:9). A great blockade has been erected in your pathway to Hell, the cross of Jesus Christ. To go to Hell, you must walk around the cross in rejection of Jesus Christ. You ask, "How can a loving God send someone to Hell?" It is man's doing. Hell was made for the devil and his demons, not man. Man goes to Hell by personal choice. If you die and end up in Hell, you will go there over the warnings of God, the prayers of the saints, the preaching of the minister, the wooing of the Holy Spirit, and the Holy Bible. God has done all He can to keep you out of Hell. You must choose not to go there by repenting of sin and following Christ as Lord and Savior. It is a solemn thought, but you could be in Hell by midnight, as was the case of the rich man in Scripture.

George W. Truett: Preparation for Meeting God [487]
Amos 4:12

Introduction

I shall not now stop to discuss these five words in their setting but shall begin my message by asking you, one by one, this all-important question: Are you prepared for your meeting with God? Meet Him you must. Your relations to Him are inescapable: "We must all appear before the judgment seat of Christ." It is more serious than that: "So then every one of us shall give an account of himself to God." Are you prepared for your inevitable meeting with God? These five little words suggest for us three infinitely important questions.

1. "Prepare to meet thy God?"—why?

2. "Prepare to meet thy God?"—how?

3. "Prepare to meet thy God?"—when?

---

[487] Truett, *Quest For Souls,* 88–103.

Conclusion

Are there men and women in this gathering tonight who could not in conscience lift their hands, thus witnessing that they are on Christ's side? Are there men and women listening to me who say, "Oh, sir, I am wrong with God and know it. I could not lift my hand. I am wrong with God and know it." Oh, that tonight you would end your delay! Listen to Jesus: "Him that cometh to me I will in no wise cast out." Listen again: "Boast not thyself of tomorrow, for thou knowest not what a day may bring forth." And again: "Today, if ye hear His voice, harden not your heart."

Martyn Lloyd–Jones: Jairus—Complete Salvation[488]

Mark 5:22

I. How is Jesus Christ to be approached?

We have said that salvation is entirely in Him and of Him from the beginning right on to the end. How, then, is He to be approached? What a vital question this is! One has only to read the New Testament in a very superficial manner to see this most clearly. Observe the different people that approach our Lord. How different is the treatment which they received! Jairus is received, his request is granted, and he is blessed. He clearly approached the Lord in the right way, in the only way which leads to blessing. What is that way?

II. What happens to those who so approach Him?

What remarkable discoveries Jairus made that day and especially about the person of Jesus Christ! He had certain ideas about him before he left his own home. And on the basis of such ideas, he had approached Him. But his experience that day taught him that Jesus Christ has to be known personally before He can be properly known. You will never really know Jesus until you submit to Him. When you approach Jesus,

---

[488] Lloyd-Jones, *Evangelistic Sermons at Aberavon*, 241–257.

A. You find that He is ready to receive you and prepared to respond to your humble cry.
B. You learn about His solicitude and watchful care over you.
C. You become conscious of His power.
D. He answers all your doubts and questionings and fears.
E. He purifies and sanctifies you.

He fights a battle within you. Follow Him and trust yourself to Him, and nothing shall be able to withstand you or thwart you or hinder you. Follow Him, and He will make you more than a conqueror over the world, the flesh, and the devil. As He cast out those people from the room of Jairus' house, so He will cast out and cast down every enemy of your soul. Yes, and He will continue to do so until He brings the work to a triumphant conclusion.

Conclusion

In your need, in your desperate position, face to face with God and his law, come to Jesus Christ confessing your sins and believing that He died for you. Yield yourself to Him and follow Him, singing with us as you do so: "All the way my Savior leads me…"

J. Harold Smith: God's Three Deadlines[489]
Matthew 12:32–33

(Note: It is estimated that Smith preached over 70,000 sermons, but this one was the most powerful.)

Introduction

In this message, I have but one desire, and that is to awaken some to their awful fate and doom. May this be a message of warning not to take that final and last step over "GOD'S DEADLINE." One more step, and some will be beyond the

---

[489] J. Harold Smith, *God's Three Deadlines*, 7.

point of redemption. There will be no hope left: STOP! STOP AND THINK! Only lost souls can cross deadlines one and two; a saint cannot cross those. The third deadline can only be crossed by a member of the family of God, a true born-again believer.

1. Blaspheming the Holy Ghost or committing the unpardonable sin (Matthew 12:31–32; Luke 12:10; Numbers 16:29–34). All that Jesus did, He did by the power of the Holy Spirit. When Jesus healed a man, it was by the power of the Holy Spirit. When the Pharisees said Jesus healed by the power of Satan, they blasphemed and denied the power of the Holy Spirit. Murder is forgivable, mass murder is forgivable, insane murder is forgivable, but blaspheming the Holy Spirit is not forgivable. This is denying the powerful activity of the Holy Spirit among men.

2. Sinning away your day of grace (Proverbs 29:1; Genesis 6:3; John 12:38–40; 6:44). These are those who are friends of the pastor, they attend church, they know their Bible, but they are not saved. These are those in powerful churches who do not know Christ. These are greatly evidenced by a lack of appetite for the things of God and the Word of God. These are those who refuse to accept the invitation of the Holy Spirit of God when it is given.

3. The sin unto death (I John 5:16; Amos 4:6–12; Ephesians 4:30; I Corinthians 5:5). God knows everything about each and every one of us. If there is a little, hidden pet sin in your heart, God sees it, and we cannot hide it. If you are a born-again believer and God sees that sin, it grieves Him. We ought never to grieve the Holy Spirit. Born-again Christians are saved forever, but if sin gets in our heart and we refuse to confess it, God's says to Satan, "Take him."

L. R. Scarborough: The Perils of Postponement[490]
Acts 24:24

This man (Felix) put off the call of God. He postponed the most important matter that ever comes to the decision of men. God called him; his conscience stirred; he was shaken in his boots. And yet he put it off and postponed it. I want to tell you tonight, my friends, this is one of the shrewdest tricks that the devil has ever played....Now, my friends, I want you to listen to me a little while tonight as I speak to you about the perils of postponing the most vital matter in the Kingdom of God, the awful risk you make in putting off this matter of salvation and your coming back to God.

I. The Peril of the Wrath of God

God is not only a God of love; He is a God of wrath....And every hour you put off the matter of your salvation or your coming back to God, you run the awful risk of coming under the wrath of God.

II. The Peril of the Mercy of God

God says, "My spirit will not always strive with men." He has been merciful to you. He has called on you for your salvation, and you have put Him off....Sometime His mercy will be turned into wrath, and that Divine Spirit will knock at the door of your heart no more.

III. The Peril of Death

Every grave in the cemetery is a sermon; every tombstone by the roadside is a sermon; and every sickness in your body, every pain, and every ache you have is a call of the Almighty God for you to get on God's side and be saved from your sins. Oh, my friend, I wish you would not run the risk of not being saved another day or another night.

---

[490] Scarborough, *Prepare to Meet God,* 110–122.

IV. The Peril of the Hardening of the Heart

There is not anything more damnable and mean and iniquitous that sin does to us than that it hardens our hearts against the call of God!...God help you to know that every time you go through a meeting like this, you just that much harden your heart against God, and there is a peril and a danger that is awful.

V. The Peril of Feelings

The old Devil is a sly old coon about it. He will tell you that you ought not to seek Jesus Christ until you feel like it. I believe in experimental religion. I believe that when a soul is saved, he can know that he is saved....But I want you to understand about these feelings. You do not have to feel good before you trust Jesus Christ.

Conclusion

If your judgment tells you that you are a sinner, God help you to start to God and open the door of your heart and let Jesus come in. The Devil says, "Wait, wait for a more convenient season." He says, "Just put it off. It will be better tomorrow night." There are trainloads of men going to Hell tonight all because they are waiting for a more convenient season. God help you to take advantage of the opportunity that is given you and seek the Lord Jesus Christ as your Savior....I plead with you, do not put it off. God is here tonight; salvation is a present salvation. Jesus Christ is able and willing to save. Thank God, he is ready to save; and tonight if you will turn your heart longingly to him...desiring to give up your sins, he will save you where you are now. God help you not to put off any longer this matter of salvation.

Curtis Hutson: The Danger of Delay [491]
Genesis 19:14–16

Let me give you several reasons why it is dangerous to delay. The man who knows he is a sinner, knows there is a real Heaven, knows Jesus died for sinners, knows that he can be saved, and yet delays, faces

I. The Danger of a Hardened Heart

The truth is, every time the Holy Spirit speaks to your heart and you say no to accepting Christ, your heart becomes harder and harder, until, after a while, when God speaks you don't even hear His voice.

II. The Danger of Losing His Soul

Man is a living soul, and Jesus said, "For what shall it profit a man if he shall gain the whole world, and lose his own soul" (Mark 8:36).

III. The Danger of Going to Hell

You may not like to hear about it, but there is a real, literal, burning Hell; and when man dies without Christ, he goes there (Luke 16:22, 23).

IV. The Danger of Missing Heaven

If you are a sinner and delay getting saved, you face the danger of missing Heaven.

V. The Danger of Not Participating in the Rapture

The man who knows the Gospel, who has heard how to be saved, who has had an opportunity to be saved—if that man dies without Jesus Christ or if Jesus Christ comes while that man is still alive, his opportunity for salvation will be closed.

VI. The Danger of Sudden Death

Nobody knows when he is going to die....There is the danger of sudden death; you don't know when you will die.

---

[491] Hutson, "The Danger of Delay."

Conclusion

To continue to wait is the worst kind of sin that you can commit. The only sin that will send you to Hell is unbelief. Unbelief is the one sin for which Jesus did not die. If He died for unbelief, everybody would be saved, because the only folks going to Hell are the ones who won't believe on the Lord Jesus Christ. You can be saved. Don't put it off any longer.

Curtis Hutson: What Does God Really Count?[492]

Titus 3:5

God does not count Wednesday nights. As a matter of fact, He doesn't even count Sunday mornings or Sunday nights. He doesn't count tithing. He doesn't even count baptism. When it comes to going to Heaven, God counts only one thing, and that is Jesus and what He did on the cross two thousand years ago.

I. God Does Not Count Good Works (Ephesians 2: 8–9)

There is not one verse in all the Bible that says anything about working to go to Heaven.

II. God Does Not Count Our Righteousness

If a man went to Heaven on his own righteousness, he would have to be as holy and as righteous as God Himself. And no man except Jesus Christ has ever been righteous.

III. God Does Not Count Baptism

Those who think that God requires water baptism as an entrance into Heaven teach that the water washes away sins. The only thing that remits sins is the blood of Christ (Hebrews 9:22).

IV. What Does God Really Count?

God does not count Wednesday nights. He doesn't count Sunday mornings or Sunday nights or any other nights. God does not count our own righteousness. He does not count our

---

[492] Hutson, *Salvation Crystal Clear II,* 183–193.

good works. He does not count baptism or any other ceremony or ritual. He only counts one thing: the death of His Son Jesus Christ. And the Scripture plainly says in Isaiah 53:11 that He was satisfied with the sacrifice His Son made for our sins. If Jesus Christ said it was finished and God Himself said He was satisfied, then why can't we be satisfied with Christ's death and not add anything to it?

Conclusion

The only way to show that you are satisfied with Christ's death for your sins is to trust Him and Him alone for salvation....If you are counting on anything other than Jesus Christ to take you to Heaven, then you are counting on something that God doesn't count. Won't you trust Christ today?

"The gift of the evangelist is a distinct gift which few men possess in superlative degree, but when it is found, it is the third of all the gifts of the Holy Spirit, preceded only by the gifts of apostleship and prophecy....We need them desperately. May God grant that the gift with increased frequency and meaning may fall upon our preachers today."[493]—W. A. Criswell

"An evangelist usually itinerates from place to place. He is uniquely gifted by God for this ministry, the chief end of which is leading lost people to faith in Jesus."[494]—Roy Fish

"These two men (Jonathan Edwards and John Wesley) model a truth that we need scholarly evangelists and evangelistic scholars. My plea is if you have an evangelist gift, don't give up on the study; and if you have ability to do scholarly work, don't give up on evangelism."[495]—Haddon Robinson

---

[493] Fordham, *Heart of God,* 12.
[494] Ibid., 14.
[495] Robinson, "Scholarly Evangelists."

9
Specialists

George E. Sweazey calls the vocational evangelist "The Specialist," stating that while almost every preacher can study to be effective in evangelism, the evangelist has a rare genius for it. Sweazey continues, "Specialists develop skills which God can greatly use....The scarcity of such leaders is one of the most serious weaknesses of our time. The appearance of a new generation of them will be one of the surest signs of a revival in the church."[496] Faris Whitesell adds, "Specialization is one of the marked trends of the times. One man can no longer do everything; life is too intricate, mechanized, and departmentalized. This tendency to specialize carries over into Christian work to some extent. Surely there is need for specialists in the work of evangelism. This most important aspect of Christian activity deserves the attention of specialists."[497]

There is a dearth in the land with regard to such specialists who have the gift of being harvest men. If ever there was a day to "pray the Lord of the harvest that He would send forth laborers into His harvest" (Matthew 9:38), it is this day, for the "harvest truly *is* plenteous, but the laborers *are* few" (Matthew 9:37). This chapter primarily deals with the preaching evangelist, though it applies to all in vocational evangelism.

The Scriptural Office of the Evangelist

Christ instituted the office of evangelist at the same time He instituted the pastoral office (Ephesians 4:11). It is startling and heartrending that Christians in many churches do not have any idea of the specific call and function of the evangelist within the body of Christ. In fact, if a hundred Christians were asked about the office or role of the vocational evangelist, there would be a hundred different answers. It is time for believers to engage in a Biblical study of the vocational evangelist to

---

[496] Sweazey, *Effective Evangelism*, 166.
[497] Whitesell, *Basic New Testament Evangelism*, 123.

expose erroneous assumptions and embrace Jesus' view and assigned role regarding them (Ephesians 4:11–12). The misunderstanding and neglect of the office of *pastor* by Christians would undermine God's purpose for the church; likewise does the ignorance or blatant neglect of that of the *evangelist*. Billy Graham, commenting on the confusion that exists concerning the work of the evangelist, said, "And yet we cannot risk confusion if we are to make the impact on our generation that God expects of us."[498] The evangelist is clearly as distinct a gift to the church by Christ as the pastor.

Regarding the office of pastor and evangelist, C. H. Spurgeon commented, "If the ministry should become weak and feeble among us, the church richly deserves it, for this, the most important part of her whole organization, has been more neglected than anything else."[499] The word *evangelist* means "to announce the Good News, to proclaim the Gospel of Christ." An evangelist is a traveling preacher who is divinely set aside and gifted by God to proclaim the message of the cross to the unsaved. "Evangelists are a gift of Christ to the churches and are not to be despised, rejected, neglected, or unjustly criticized. Their work is just as important in its relationship to the whole program of Christ as the work of other gifts mentioned."[500]

Pastors and evangelists support the work of each other. Primarily, evangelists are *obstetricians* and pastors are *pediatricians*.[501] Evangelists are harvest men given to the church. They are gifted in the spiritual birthing of the unsaved, while pastors nurture the newborn, edifying the body of Christ (I Corinthians 3:4–9). Wayne Barber stated, "So you have your evangelists, then you have your pastor/teachers. These are the Master's men. Instead of gifts bestowed upon men, we have got gifted

---

[498] Douglas, *Work of the Evangelist*, 5.
[499] Spurgeon, "Ascension of Christ."
[500] Whitesell, *Basic New Testament Evangelism*, 117.
[501] Stedman, "Building and Maintenance."

men bestowed upon the church. This is so the church can begin to grow and come into the stature of the fullness of Christ. It is required to be equipped, so He gives the equippers to the church."[502]

C. H. Spurgeon remarked, "There remain rich gifts among us still, which I fear we do not sufficiently prize. Among men, God's richest gifts are men of high vocation, separated for the ministry of the Gospel. From our ascended Lord come all true *evangelists;* these are they who preach the Gospel in divers places and find it the power of God unto salvation. They are founders of churches, breakers of new soil, men of a missionary spirit who build not on other men's foundations, but dig out for themselves. We need many such deliverers of the good news where as yet the message has not been heard. I scarcely know of any greater blessing to the church than the sending forth of earnest, indefatigable, anointed men of God, taught of the Lord to be winners of souls."[503]

The biblical evangelist is set apart by Christ for the building up of the church numerically. One serves in this capacity not because he is second rate, unable to make it as a pastor, but because it is a divine call. Unlike that of the pastoral office, the evangelist ministry is not restricted to one church but to the church of Christ at large. The evangelist's livelihood (means of financial support) is dissimilar to that of a pastor and is to be provided by the churches, camps, and conferences he serves and Christians at large. The evangelist lives and serves by faith in a full-time capacity, believing God will, through His people, sustain both his family and ministry. The evangelist lives an uncommon life. He moves about constantly from city to city, is *often* separated from family and friends, sleeps in various places at various times, eats irregularly, lives with uncertainty about how bills and living needs will be supplied, and serves people who at times are critical; yet he is all the while excited

---

[502] Wayne Barber, "Unity of the Spirit."
[503] Spurgeon, "Ascension of Christ."

and grateful to do what he does for Christ. Pray that "the Lord of the harvest" will raise up more evangelists, that He will open "doors of utterance" for the evangelist, and that the needs of the evangelist will be supplied "according to the riches of God in Christ Jesus."

A picture of the biblical evangelist is Phillip (Acts 21:8; 8:26–40). The *motive* of the evangelist is the divine call placed upon his life (8:26; Ephesians 4:11). The evangelist has no discretionary power to alter this call; he must simply obey it. He is one *thrust* into the work of evangelism by the Holy Spirit and is passionate about doing it.

The *message* of the evangelist is "Jesus Christ and Him crucified" (8:35). Prior to a Billy Graham crusade in Osaka, Japan, the governor asked Billy Graham, "Why is it that the church in Japan is about the same as it was in the 17th century?" Answering his own question, he said, "I believe it is because the Gospel has not been made clear to the Japanese people. I hope that you will make it clear."[504] The evangelist's task is to make the presentation of the Gospel crystal clear in America and regions beyond so all can understand.

The *method* of the evangelist is simply readiness to go and tell the gospel story compassionately to all, regardless of place, people, or price (8:27, 40). The evangelist knows how to present Christ to the unsaved tactfully but also is gifted by God to draw the net bringing the lost to a decision, whether privately or in public services (8:37). Revivals are the primary service evangelists render, and with these in decline, the church must utilize the evangelist for other ministries and embrace him financially. Failure to do so, I fear, will eventually force gifted evangelists out of the ministry. Churches at large and Christians in general should consider supporting an evangelist financially and prayerfully (Matthew 10:10).

---

[504] Douglas, *Work of the Evangelist*, 7.

The *office of evangelist* was established by our ascending Lord to plant churches, partner with churches in evangelism, pursue souls, preach the Gospel, and perfect ("equip") the saint. This office has not been deleted, and the evangelist's call has not been rescinded by Christ. It will not be "till we all come in the unity of the faith, and of the knowledge of the Son of God, unto a perfect man, unto the measure of the stature of the fullness of Christ" (Ephesians 4:13). Its recognition and utilization are needed more now than ever.

In preaching on the subject of "Ethics in Evangelism," Don Womack stated, "It is a sin of commission to reject the divine office of the evangelist, a sin of omission to ignore the office, and a sin of transgression to abuse the office."[505] Billy Graham stated, "The calling of evangelist is one of the great gifts that God has given to the church and is as important as the seminary professor or church pastor....A great need in the church today is to recognize and dignify the gift of the evangelist."[506] Faris Whitesell said, "We conclude, then, that Christ still grants the evangelistic gift to chosen men. Churches should recognize and use evangelists. If so-called evangelists have been unworthy of the title, that does not mean that evangelists as a class have been discredited."[507]

Set Apart as a Vocational Evangelist

Regarding the call to vocational evangelism, it is important to realize the matter has already been decided and set in stone by God. "And He gave some...evangelists" (Ephesians 4:11). It is a divine appointment, not a matter of personal preference. Man cannot educate and equip himself to do what God alone authorizes. The degree of "giftedness" in evangelism is measured out according to God's plan. The preacher's role in the call to evangelism is to operate within its framework submissively, joyfully, humbly, passionately, selflessly, studiously,

---

[505] Trent, *Evangelists in Action,* 14.
[506] Adler, *Ask Billy Graham,* 43.
[507] Whitesell, *Basic New Testament Evangelism,* 123.

with all integrity, morally, and spiritually, ever "sharpening" it to its fullest potential.

How can one know if God has set him apart for the office of evangelist, specifically as a preaching evangelist?

The Appeal of the Soul (I Timothy 3:1)

C. H. Spurgeon identifies the first sign of the heavenly calling as "an intense, all-absorbing desire for the work. In order to [have] a true call to the ministry, there must be an irresistible, overwhelming craving and raging thirst for telling to others what God has done to our own souls."[508] Although this remark is addressed regarding the office of pastor, these words certainly pertain to him called to the office of evangelist—even more. The divinely called evangelist longs and yearns to preach Christ to the salvation of souls in every venue, regardless of cost or consequence. With Paul, the evangelist cries, "For necessity is laid upon me. Woe unto me if I preach not the gospel" (I Corinthians 9:16). In the call to the office of evangelist, God puts a "fire in the bones" to evangelize that neither time, trouble, nor tribunal can quench.

As a seminary student, I was cautioned not to tell God what I didn't want to do, for that could be the very thing He would call me to do. Later I learned the fallacy of that thinking, that God actually gives a person the gift of a burning desire (as that of an evangelist) for the assignment commissioned. If one can live without being an evangelist, then God has not called him to this work. John R. Rice, an evangelist himself, commented, "Would you really like to be an evangelist? Do you have a burden in your heart for this work? That may be, then, evidence of the call of God."[509]

The Affirmation of Saints (Proverbs 11:14)

God uses His people to endorse those whom He calls to this work. When I was a sophomore in college, classmates were

---

[508] Spurgeon, *Lectures to My Students*, 26.
[509] John Rice, *The Evangelist*, 217.

used of God to reveal and confirm my call into evangelism. "Yet this appeal," says Spurgeon, "is not final nor infallible and is only to be estimated in proportion to the intelligence and piety of those consulted."[510] Consult with those who are deeply spiritual, possess great discernment, and who will be candid in their advisement. Especially with regard to a call to the office of evangelist, seek counsel from pastors and evangelists. "Considerable weight," says Spurgeon, "is to be given to the judgment of men and women who live near to God, and in most instances their verdict will not be a mistaken one."[511]

The minister or person who is so consulted resides in a most definitive place, for should he voice the wrong opinion, an unfit man may pursue evangelism or a fit man walk away from it. He must with grave discernment look beyond the present image cast by the counselee to ascertain the true call. The counselor must heed the words of the apostle Paul, "Be in no hurry to lay hands on anyone in dedication to the Lord's service," lest he partakes in the sin of hasty ordination. Paul cautions that approving one for a ministerial office who is not qualified makes him culpable for the man's sin of serving as an unqualified minister and, thus, misleading people (I Timothy 5:22, GNT). John MacArthur continues with his commentary of this text, "Some versions translate 'pure' as 'free from sin.' Paul wanted Timothy, by not participating in the recognition of unqualified elders, to remain untainted by others' sins. The church desperately needed qualified spiritual leaders, but the selection had to be carefully executed."[512] Clearly the need of more evangelists does not justify their hasty recruitment and rash endorsement.

The Attestation of Service

Though not an iron-clad indicator of a call to evangelism, one's soul-winning fruitfulness in preaching and in private

---

[510] Spurgeon, *Lectures to My Students*, 30.
[511] Ibid.
[512] MacArthur, *MacArthur Study Bible.*

speaks strongly to its possibility, as its absence speaks against it.

The Approval of Spouse

The call to evangelism involves not just the man but his wife, should he be married. It is essential therefore that she be totally supportive regarding it. Every evangelist attests to the fact that his work would not be possible were it not for a wife which backed him to the hilt. Mary, my wife, has made the far greater sacrifice than I in evangelism by staying home, rearing our children, and keeping the home fires burning in my absence. Not once in thirty-six years of evangelism has she ever sought to hinder my continuance in this work, despite its difficulties financially and my time away from home. The degree of what success I have experienced in evangelism is attributable to the Lord, first, and to Mary, second. This is shared to cite how important it is that the man of God and his wife are on the same page with regard to the work of an evangelist. It is advisable that every potential "first lady" to an evangelist consult the wife of an evangelist about the role of an evangelist's wife prior to granting approval.

The Assertion of Scripture

The nearest thing we have in Scripture that reveals traits of a person called into evangelism is the example of the evangelist Phillip (Acts 8). A review of these traits will help in ascertaining God's will with regard to a call to evangelism. Faris Whitesell said, "Phillip therefore seems to exhibit several essential qualities which should be found in the life of every evangelist: character above reproach, fullness of the Spirit, zeal for the lost, ability to evangelize both publicly and privately, success in facing and overcoming obstacles, implicit obedience to the guidance of the Lord, and grace to live the Christian life at home."[513]

---

[513] Whitesell, *Basic New Testament Evangelism,* 122.

The Aptitude of Self

An honest evaluation of one's personal aptitude to preach winsomely, to lead others to Christ privately, to motivate and equip the church in soul winning and strengthen the hands of the pastor in evangelism speaks loudly with regard to a call to evangelism. C. H. Spurgeon, in referring to a call to preach in general (but which is relevant with the specific call to evangelism) stated, "Still, a man must not consider that he is called to preach until he has proved that he can speak....If a man be called to preach, he will be endowed with a degree of speaking ability, which he will cultivate and increase."[514] In the call to evangelism as with the pastorate, God gifts the man with the ability for the task. These gifts, though they may be developed to be more effective, cannot be self-acquired.

The Assurance of Sufficiency (Philippians 4:11–13, 19)

He whom the Lord calls to the work of an itinerant evangelist is granted faith for the journey. The uncertainty of tomorrow regarding financial support, opportunity of service, criticism and trial requires surefootedness in solid, confident faith that God is in control. Evangelism is not the place for the minister who likes everything to be black and white in a ledger book. It entails a call to live by faith believing that God will sustain. The evangelist claims, and thus is sustained by, God's promise that "unto every one of us is given grace according to the measure of the gift of Christ" (Ephesians 4:7). This sure anchor of enabling, equipping, emboldening, and empowering grace will hold the evangelist's vessel steady through the storms of poverty, persecution, peril, and persistent attack by Satan.

The Agony of Separation

The evangelist, by virtue of his call, will be often away from home. This separation from wife and children, though necessary, is grievous. John R. Rice stated, "An evangelist knows

---

[514] Spurgeon, *Lectures to My Students*, 28.

what it is to be a stranger to his own children! An evangelist knows what it is to leave a lonely wife bearing burdens that no young wife ought to have to carry without a husband....For that reason it is that Jesus said, 'If any man come to me, and hate not his father, and mother, and wife, and children, and brethren, and sisters, yea, and his own life also, he cannot be my disciple'" (Luke 14: 26).[515] Indeed, this is the greatest difficulty of the work of the evangelist! The man called to be an evangelist must count this grave cost prior to entering the work. A homebody certainly cannot be an evangelist (unless his "home" travels with him).

The Authorization of the Spirit

Taking all that has been stated into serious consideration, ultimately, in the final analysis, what constitutes a call into evangelism is the seal of the Spirit, His stamp of approval. Paul declares that "it is His Spirit that beareth witness to our spirit that we have passed from death unto life" (Romans 8:16). It is this same Spirit that will bear witness in equal measure with one's spirit that he is called to the work of the evangelist. It is He that will speak the word of confirmation or not to the open and waiting heart. Spurgeon, referring to the ascending Christ's gifts to the church of pastor, evangelist and teacher, frankly declared, "He alone can give them; any that come without Him are imposters."[516]

J. H. Jowett on the Call to Christian Ministry

"And so we cannot tell how the call will come to us, what will be the manner of its coming. It may be that the divine constraint will be as soft and gentle as a glance: 'I will guide thee with Mine eye.' It may be that we can scarcely describe the guidance, it is so shy and quiet and unobtrusive. Or it may be that the constraint will seize us as with a strong and invisible grip, as though we were in the custody of an iron hand from

---

[515] John Rice, *The Evangelist*, 210–211.
[516] Spurgeon, "Ascension of Christ."

which we cannot escape. That, I think, is the significance of the strangely violent figure used by the Prophet Isaiah: 'The Lord said unto me *with a strong hand.*' The divine calling laid hold of the young prophet as though with a 'strong hand' that imprisoned him like a vice! He felt he had no alternative! He was carried along by divine coercion! 'Necessity was laid' upon him! He was 'in bonds' and he must obey.

"And I think this feeling of the 'strong hand,' this sense of mysterious coercion, is sometimes a dumb constraint which offers but little illumination to the judgment. What I mean is this: a man may realize his call to the ministry in the powerful imperative of a dumb grip for which he can offer no adequate reason. He is sure of the constraint. It is as manifest as gravity. But when he seeks for explanations to justify himself, he feels he is moving in the twilight or in the deeper mystery of the night. He knows the 'feel' of the 'strong hand' that moves him, but he cannot give a satisfactory interpretation of the movement....

"And so it is that the manner of one man's 'call' may be very different to the manner of another man's 'call,' but in the essential matter, they are one and the same. I would affirm my own conviction that in all genuine callings to the ministry there is a sense of the divine initiative, a solemn communication of the divine will, a mysterious feeling of commission, which leaves a man no alternative, but which sets him in the road of this vocation bearing the ambassage of a servant and instrument of the eternal God."[517]

Billy Graham's View of the Call to Be an Evangelist

Upon President Richard Nixon's offer to Billy Graham for a job in his administration, Graham replied, "You could not offer me a job as ambassador or a cabinet post that I would give a

---

[517] Jowett, *The Preacher,* 16–18.

second thought to. When God called me to preach, it was for life."[518]

What about You?

The church desperately needs more God gifted evangelists. Concerning God's question in Isaiah 6:8, "Whom shall I send? And who will go for me?" John Wesley wrote George Whitefield asking, "What, Mr. Whitefield, if thou art that man?"[519] Whitefield shook a continent for God. I ask that same question: "What if thou art that man?" What if God is calling to vocational evangelism? Stand ready to respond with Isaiah, Whitefield, Graham, Moody, and others, "Here am I. Send me; send me."

Alert young preacher boys in whom signs of this call seem to be evident to give serious consideration to its possibility. Veteran evangelists must embrace and invest in young evangelists, allowing the mighty rivers of their spiritual knowledge and experience to flow into them and then through them. The church at large must pray the Lord of the harvest to raise up more men for the work of the preaching evangelist. John R. Rice said, "The Lord Jesus said distinctly in Matthew 9:35–38, and again in Luke 10:2, that 'the harvest truly is plenteous [or great], but the laborers are few'; and He said that we should 'pray...therefore the Lord of the harvest, that he would send forth laborers into his harvest.' Then surely fathers and mothers should pray that God will call their sons to be great soul winners. Would it not be proper for them to pray that God would raise them up as mighty, Spirit-filled evangelists? And would it not be proper for young men to pray that God would send them into the harvest as evangelists? I think so."[520]

Spurgeon sounds a similar note, "Yet since thou hast not great personal gifts, serve the church by praying the Lord who has ascended to give us more evangelists, pastors, and teachers.

---

[518] Graham, *Life Wisdom,* 62.
[519] Hurst, *John Wesley,* 90.
[520] John Rice, *The Evangelist,* 217.

There is a petition which Christ has commanded us to offer, and yet I very seldom hear it. It is this one. 'Pray ye therefore the Lord of the harvest, that he will send forth laborers into his harvest.' We greatly lack evangelists and pastors. I do not mean that we lack muffs who occupy the pulpits and empty the pews. I believe the market has for many years been sufficiently supplied therewith; but we lack men who can stir the heart, arouse the conscience, and build up the church."[521]

Pray, brother and sister, pray for the raising up of gifted harvest evangelists, for they are swiftly disappearing from the land. The church of my generation sorely misses E. J. Daniels, J. Harold Smith, Hyman Appelman, and Eddie Martin. Powerful evangelists like Junior Hill, Bailey Smith, Bill Stafford, Freddie Gage, Luis Palau will not forever be among us. Who stands in line to take their baton and carry it to the finish line? Who? It is time to pray for anointed successors to be raised up.

Additionally, bold initiatives must be taken in the denomination and church to undergird financially the evangelist and his work.

---

[521] Spurgeon, "Ascension of Christ."

"Lord, let me not live to be useless!"[522]—John Wesley

"Think yourself empty, read yourself full, write yourself clear, pray yourself clean, get in the pulpit, and let yourself go!"[523]—W. H. Griffith Thomas

"But supremely, an evangelistic approach to the Bible looks for ways to make one 'wise for salvation through faith in Jesus Christ.'"[524]—Robert E. Coleman

"If no one gets saved through this discourse, I cannot carry on my business. 'Oh, well,' says one, 'a man may preach very faithfully and yet he may have no souls saved.' Yes, a fisherman may fish and never catch any fish, but he is not much of a fisherman; and so, if there were no souls saved, perhaps I might find some way of satisfying my conscience, but it is unknown to me as yet! I have never sought such solace and hope I never shall. With me it is, 'Give me children or else I die.' If you are not saved and brought to Christ, I feel I must give up my work of preaching to you. I cannot stand here beating the air. If my hearers are not converted, I have lost my time—I have lost the exercise of brain and heart! I feel as if I have lost my hope and lost my life unless I find for my Lord some of His blood-bought ones—and I must find some of them by this sermon!"[525]—C. H. Spurgeon

"God uses it [preaching] to *change lives.* It is hard for any mortal to tell, either of himself or of others, what forces have worked upon him to issue in some dramatic change of life; but many affirm that the occasion, and no small part of the cause, was one sermon. It would be wearisome to set out the names even of the most notable of these who have conspicuously served God and who traced the real beginnings of their life of surrender and service to meeting Him while a man preached."[526]—W. E. Sangster

---

[522] Duewel, *Revival Fire,* 90.
[523] Raymond Barber, "I Am Ready to Preach."
[524] Gibson, *Preaching the Old Testament,* 187.
[525] Spurgeon, "An Urgent Request."
[526] Sangster, *Craft of Sermon Construction,* 25–26.

10
Summary
Evangelistic Preaching

In addition to the minister being saved, much depends on the call to preach, therefore make sure; much on the heart, therefore stay clean and holy; much on integrity, therefore don't be a hypocrite; much on preparation, therefore study diligently.

Much depends on subject, therefore select prayerfully; much on proficiency in the Word, therefore sharpen this Sword daily; much on the recipients, therefore know the audience; much on energy, therefore properly rest; much on health, therefore exercise and eat right.

Much depends on confidence, therefore trust God to honor His Word; much on passion for souls, therefore cultivate it continuously; much on humility, therefore die to arrogance and desire to impress; much on a clear conscience before God, therefore do not offend; much on sermon structure, therefore develop for ease in delivery and hearing.

Much depends on simplicity, therefore preach with such clarity that a child could comprehend; much on music, therefore voice your preferences; much on method, therefore select according to the audience; much on tone of voice, therefore make sure it is pleasing to the ear; much on length, therefore preach shorter sermons.

Much depends on annoying mannerisms in the pulpit, therefore avoid them; much on calmness, therefore relax by taking several short, deep breaths prior to preaching; much on authority, therefore preach with certitude; much on making it personal, therefore speak in such a manner that it comes "home" to all who hear; much on language, therefore use words that connect.

Much depends on freedom in preaching, therefore know the sermon well; much upon practice, therefore rehearse the sermon upon bended knee; much on state of mind, therefore, if down, get "pumped up" by fixing the eyes upon Jesus and remembering this may be the sinner's last sermon; much on family union, therefore love your wife as Christ loves the church.

Much depends on discernment, therefore stay sensitive to the Spirit; much on maintaining focus with the sermon delivery, therefore don't drift; much on vitality, therefore avoid being mundane; much on boldness, therefore do not be "afraid of their faces"; much on persuading men to be saved, therefore work hard at preparing and giving the invitation calling for a verdict.

But preaching depends ALL upon the Holy Spirit; therefore, totally submit to His guidance from start to end, praying for His power to work in and through you to accomplish God's purpose. ALL depends on Truth; therefore, preach the Bible without compromise. In all and through all, remember that "it pleased God by the foolishness of preaching to save them that believe" (I Corinthians 1:21). Preaching puts this statement to the test, one it has passed tens of thousands of times. God honors the right kind of preaching to the salvation of souls. Preach with a fire in your bosom for men to be saved.

Adam Clarke comments, "A dull, dead preacher makes a dull, dead congregation."[527] Writing of the Methodist preachers during the Great Awakening, John C. Ryle states, "They preached fervently and directly. They cast aside the dull, cold, heavy, lifeless form of delivery which long had made sermons a very proverb of dullness. They proclaimed the words of faith with faith and the story of life with life."[528] Evangelistic preaching of this same mode is the great need of the hour.

Regarding evangelistic preaching, Roland Q. Leavell said, "Preachers come and go, and the popularity of evangelistic

---

[527] Clarke, *Letter to a Young Preacher*, 46.
[528] Ryle, *Christian Leaders.*

preaching may wax and wane, but great preaching will never lose its power to draw and to win. 'For the preaching of the cross is to them that perish foolishness; but unto us which are saved it is the power of God....It pleased God by the foolishness of preaching to save them that believe' (I Corinthians 1:18, 21). In spite of the busy tension of present-day life, men yet will stop to hear the impassioned pleas of a burning heart, whether he be a courtier like Isaiah or a rustic like Amos or Micah. Men's hearts yet may be melted by the loving appeals of a modern Hosea or by the sobering prophecies of a present-day Jeremiah. Men will be arrested and gripped by forthright and rugged preaching like that of John the Baptist in the wilderness or that of Paul on Athens' Acropolis. Preachers of truth yet are being heard gladly by the multiplied thousands."[529]

The Preacher's Accountability

As a young boy, the preacher Harry Ironside worked for a Christian named Dan Mackay in a cobbler shop. He had the tiring task of hammering water out of wet leather that had soaked in a tub of water all night until it was dry enough to use as a sole. One day Ironside noticed a cobbler in another shop attaching "wet leather" to shoes and inquired why he did not first pound the water out of the leather. The dishonest cobbler replied, "They come back all the quicker this way, my boy!"

Young Ironside conveyed what this cobbler said to his boss, who instantly stopped his work and explained to him that as a preacher was called to preach, he was called to repair shoes, and that only as he did this to the best of his ability would God receive glory. Further, he told Ironside that he imagined a scene at the Judgment of Christ when all the shoes he made would be heaped into one pile and Jesus would examine each. "Dan," He would say, holding up a pair of shoes, "that's not up to par. You didn't do a very good job there." But with others He would say, "Dan, that was a splendid job." He continued by

---

[529] Leavell, *Christ's Imperative Commission,* 103–104.

telling Ironside that he wanted to make shoes that would pass the inspection of Christ at the Judgment.[530]

Preachers, envision with me all your sermons piled high at the Judgment to be examined by Christ. What might be our Lord's finding? Will He say, holding up a sermon, "This one was below par. You didn't hammer it out in the study and in prayer as it warranted"; or, in holding another, declare, "Your content was good, but it was delivered with lack of soul passion." Might He, with yet another in hand, say, "This message had great evangelistic possibilities, but it was delivered without total reliance upon the Holy Spirit, and therefore it availed nothing." Or may the Lord say of another, "I know you felt this was preached poorly, having no response, but decisions were made known not to you"; or of yet another, "This sermon was an evangelistic jewel, but a poor invitation was extended, hindering souls from responding." Or at this time of accountability, may He be grieved over how few genuine evangelistic messages were preached.

A judgment is coming for the preacher (II Timothy 4:1). God help us to discharge our duty in preaching passionately, preparedly, and prayerfully with pure motives, ever depending upon the power and guidance of the Holy Spirit, so that at the day of divine reckoning both our self and sermons will be pleasing in His sight. J. C. Ryle exhorts the minister, "You preach the Gospel of Jesus Christ so fully and clearly that everybody can understand it. If Christ crucified has not His rightful place in your sermons and sin is not exposed as it should be and our people are not plainly told what they ought to be and do, your preaching is no use."[531]

I read the story of a father who took his son to the church where he was saved many years earlier through loud gospel preaching. Inside the church the boy noticed a rope hanging from the ceiling and asked his dad what it was. The father

---

[530] Stedman, "Accountability of the Preacher."
[531] Larsen, *Company of the Preachers*, 578.

shared that it was the rope that pulled the bell in the steeple that called the people to church to hear the Gospel and to get saved. The boy looked up to him and said, 'Daddy, ring it again!'[532] O Preacher, ring the bell of salvation. Ring it again and again and again.

I close with a most fitting reminder and challenge from C. H. Spurgeon, "O brethren [he said to his pastors' conference], we shall soon have to die! We look one another in the face today in health, but there will come a day when others will look down upon our pallid countenances as we lie in our coffins....It will matter little to us who shall gaze upon us then, but it will matter eternally how we have discharged our work during our lifetime."[533] So preach, brother, preach and preach Jesus Christ and Him crucified, resurrected, and soon to come again.

---

[532] Roloff, "The Family Altar," Number 4, 8.
[533] Spurgeon, *An All Round Ministry*, 69.

Bibliography

Adam, Peter. *Speaking God's Words*. Vancouver: Regent College Publishing. Cited by Danny Akin, Southeastern Baptist Theological Seminary, Contours of a Great Commission Resurgence, Part 17: The Crisis in 21st Century Preaching: A Mandate for Biblical Exposition, Part E, October 3, 2008, www.betweenthetimes.com/category/ministry/page/8/ (accessed May 17, 2009).

Adler, Bill. comp. *Ask Billy Graham*. Nashville: Thomas Nelson, 2007.

Allen, Kerry James. *Exploring the Mind and Heart of the Prince of Preachers.* Oswego: Fox River Press, 2005

Allen and Gregory. *Southern Baptist Preaching Today.* Nashville: Broadman Press, 1987.

Appelman, Hyman. *Appelman's Sermon Outlines and Illustrations*. Grand Rapids: Zondervan, 1953.

———. "Four Rights and One Wrong." *The Sword of the Lord*, 22 August 2008.

Augsburger, Myron. "Preaching Evangelistically." http://www.christianitytoday.com/outreach/articles/preachingevangelistically.html (accessed May 27, 2009).

Autrey, C. E. *Basic Evangelism*. Grand Rapids: Zondervan, 1962.

———. *Evangelistic Sermons*. Grand Rapids: Zondervan, 1962.

Bailey, E. K. and Warren Wiersbe, *Preaching in Black and White*. Grand Rapids: Zondervan, 2003. http://www.books.google. com/books?isbn=0310240999 (accessed June 24, 2009).

Barber, Raymond. "I Am Ready to Preach." http://www. swordofthelord. com /onlinesermons (accessed May 23, 2009).

Barber, Wayne. "Ephesians 4:11–13: Preserving the Unity of the Spirit—Part 3." http://www.preceptaustin (accessed May 28, 2009).

Barclay, William. *The Letters to the Corinthians*. Daily Study Bible Series. Philadelphia: The Westminster Press, 2000.

———. *The Promise of the Spirit*. Louisville, Ky.: Westminster John Knox Press, 2001.

Baxter, Richard. *The Reformed Pastor* (reprint). Montana: Kessinger Publishing, 2006. http://books.google.com/ books?isbn=1428622896 (accessed May 28, 2009).

Beecher, Henry Ward. *Lectures on Preaching*. London: T. Nelson and Sons; Paternoster Row, 1872.

———. "If a Man Sleeps under My Preaching." Preacher's Corner, http://www.preacherscorner.org/illustrations.htm (accessed May 28, 2009).

Berkley, J. D. ed. *Preaching to Convince*. The Leadership Library, Vol. 8. Carol Stream, Ill.: CTi, 1986. "A Leadership/Word book"—T.p. verso. Waco, Tex.: Word Books (accessed May 27, 2009).

Bisagno, John. *The Power of Positive Evangelism*. Nashville: Broadman Press, 1968.

———. *Letters to Timothy: A Handbook for Pastors*. Nashville: Broadman and Holman Publishers, 2001.

———. Personal Correspondence, June 17, 2009.

Blackwood, Andrew. *Evangelism in the Home Church*. New York: Abington Cokesbury Press, 1942.

———. *The Preparation of Sermons*. Nashville: Abingdon Press, 1948.

Bibliography

Bodey, Richard Allen. *Inside the Sermon*. Grand Rapids: Baker Book House, 1990.

Bounds, E.M. *Power through Prayer*. Cosimo, Inc., 2007. http://books.google.com (accessed May 28, 2008).

Bristow, Wayne. "Full-Time Evangelists Called Gift from God." Baptist Press, June 15, 1998.

Broadus, John A. *The Preparation and Delivery of Sermons*. New York: A. C. Armstrong and Son Publishing, 1898.

————. *On the Preparation and Delivery of Sermons* Fourth Edition, Revised. New York: Harper and Row, 1979.

Carroll, B. H. *Evangelistic Sermons*. Grand Rapids: Fleming H. Revell Company, 1913.

Carroll, Lewis. *Alice in Wonderland*. Digital Scanning Inc., 2007.

Cave, Doy. "Olford: Preaching Is Much More Than Just Giving a Sermon." Baptist Press. http://www.jmm.aaa. net.au/articles/ 8407.htm (accessed June 23, 2009).

Clarke, Adam. "A letter to a preacher on his entrance into the work of the ministry." London: William Tegg, 1868.

Coffin, Henry S. *Evangelistic Preaching*. New York: Board of National Missions of the Presbyterian Church USA, Evangelism Division, Undated.

Comfort, Ray. *The Evidence Bible*. Gainesville, Fl.: Bridge-Logos, 2002.

Cox, James. *Handbook of Contemporary Preaching*. Nashville: Broadman Press, 1992.

Criswell, W. A. *Criswell's Guidebook for Pastors*. Nashville: Broadman Press, 1980.

————. "The Effectual Calling of God." The Bible Kind of Salvation, W. A. Criswell Sermon Library (June 5, 1983), http://www.wacriswell.com (accessed June 3, 2009).

————. "The Way Made Plain." The W. A. Criswell Foundation (2009). Reproduced by permission from The W. A. Criswell Sermon Library, www.wacriswell.com (accessed May 25, 2009).

————. "The Secret of the Preacher's Power." http://www. preacherscorner.org/illustrations.htm (accessed May 24, 2009).

————. "Saving Faith." The Criswell Sermon Library, http://www.wacriswell.org (accessed May 26, 2009).

————. ed. *The Criswell Study Bible*. Nashville: Thomas Nelson Publishers, 1979.

Crosby, Fanny. *Songs of Devotion.* New York: Biglow and Main, 1870.

Daniels, E. J. *Dim lights in Dark World.* Orlando: Daniels Publishers, 1971.

————. *Fervent, Soul-Stirring Sermons*. Orlando: Daniels Publishers, 1971.

Day, Richard Elsworth. *Rhapsody in Black: The Life Story of John Jasper*. Valley Forge, Pa.: Judson Press, 1976.

Dixon, Francis. "Flash-Back to Iconium." Bournemouth, England: Lansdowne Magazine, Spring, 1975.

Douglas, J. D., ed. *The Work of the Evangelist* . Minneapolis: World Wide Publications, 1984.

Dowdle, Thad. Personal Correspondence. March 4, 2009.

Drummond, Lewis. *Spurgeon: Prince of Preachers*. Grand Rapids: Kregel Publications, 1992. http://www.books. google.com/books?isbn=0825424720 (accessed June 9, 2009).

Duduit, Michael. ed. *Handbook of Contemporary Preaching.* Nashville: Broadman Press, 1992.

Duewel, Wesley L. *Revival Fire.* Grand Rapids: Zondervan, 1995.

Earle, Ralph. *Proclaiming the New Testament: The Gospel of Luke.* Grand Rapids: Baker Book House, 1968.

Edwards, Tryon. *A Dictionary of Thoughts: Being a Cyclopedia of Laconic Quotations from the Best Authors of the World, Both Ancient and Modern.* F. B. Dickerson Co., 1908.

————. *A Dictionary of Thoughts.* Read Books: Read Books on-line, 2007. http://www.readbookonline.net (accessed May 27, 2009).

Evangelical Church of Fullerton Newsletter. Date unknown. Cited by Danny Akin, Southeastern Baptist Theological Seminary, Contours of a Great Commission Resurgence, Part 17: The Crisis in 21st Century Preaching: A Mandate for Biblical Exposition, Part E, October 3, 2008.

Fabarez, Michael. *Preaching that Changes Lives.* Nashville: Thomas Nelson Publishers, 2002.

Fasol, Fish, Gaines and West. *Preaching Evangelistically.* Nashville: Broadman and Holman Publishers, 2006.

Finch, Ross. "Baptisms Again Dip in S. Baptist Churches." *The Washington Times* (April 25, 2009), http://www.rockrunner. blogs.com/rock_runner/2009/04/baptism-trend-in-the-sbc.html (accessed June 8, 2009).

Fish, Roy. "Roy Fish [Exhorts] Pastors to Preach Christ Crucified, Resurrected." *The Florida Witness,* 2005, http:/www.florida baptistwitness.com/4516.article (accessed May 29, 2009).

Fletcher, Lionel B. *The Effective Evangelist.* London: Hodder and Stoughton, 1923.

Fordham, Keith. *Evangelism in the Heart of God.* Fayetteville, Ga.: KFEA Publications, 2002.

Funk, I. K. and Newell W. Wells. ed. *The Homiletic Review.* New York: Funk and Wagnalls Co., 1892. http://books. google.com/ books?id=VdEnAAAAYAAJ (accessed July 13, 2009).

Gadsby, William. *The Things Most Surely Believed Among Us: William Gadsby's Catechism.* Harpenden, England: Gospel Standard Publications, 1995.

Gericke, Paul. *The Preaching of Robert G. Lee: Adorning The Doctrine of God.* Orlando: Christ for the World Publishers, 1967.

Gibson, Scott M., ed. *Preaching the Old Testament.* Grand Rapids: Baker, 2006.

"Gospel Attitudes." http://www.thelivingwordtbc.com/ 1cor29.htm (accessed May 28, 2009).

Graham, Billy. *Life Wisdom from Billy Graham.* Kansas: Hallmark Books, 2006.

———. "Experience before Preaching." http://www.SermonIndex.net (accessed May 28, 2009).

———."The Narrow Gate." The Coliseum Sermons from Billy Graham's 1958 Charlotte Evangelistic Meeting, http://www. wheaton.edu/bgc/archives/docs/bg-charlotte/charlotte.htm (accessed May 25, 2009).

———. "Heaven or Hell." The Coliseum Sermons from Billy Graham's 1958 Charlotte Evangelistic Meetings, http:// www.wheaton.edu/bgc/archives (accessed May 27, 2009).

Green, Michael P. ed. *Illustrations for Biblical Preaching.* Grand Rapids: Baker Book House, 1991.

Bibliography

Gugliotto, Lee J., *Handbook for Bible Study.* Hagerstown: Review and Herald Publishing Association, 2000. http:www.books.google.com/books?isbn=0828014612 (accessed June 3, 2009).

Gunther, Peter F. "The Fire Sermon." *Great Sermons by Great Preachers,* Chicago: Moody Press, 1960.

Gurnall, William. *The Christian in Complete Armour*. London: William Tegg, 1862.

———. *The Christian in Complete Armour*, vol. 2. Edinburgh: The Banner of Truth Trust, 1995.

Harrison, E.M. *How to win Souls*, Wheaton, Ill.: Van Kamper Press, 1952.

Havner, Vance. *Road to Revival.* New York: Fleming H. Revell Company, 1940.

———. *The Sword of the Lord*, November 28, 2008.

———. "Acceptability of Preaching." http://www.sermonindex.net (accessed May 28, 2009).

———. "Sermon Illustrations." http://www.sermon illustrations.com/a-/p/preaching.htm (accessed June 6, 2009).

Hawkins, O. S. *Drawing the Net*. Annuity Board of the Southern Baptist Convention, 2002.

Heisler, Greg. *Spirit-Led Preaching*. Nashville: B and H Publishing Group, 2007. http://www.books.google.com/ books?isbn=0805443886 (accessed June 24, 2009).

Henry, Matthew. *Matthew Henry's Commentary on the Whole Bible: Complete and Unabridged in One Volume*. Peabody: Hendrickson, 1991.

———. *The Young Christian*. Christian Focus Publications, 1994.

Hill, Junior. "The Greatest Preacher." The Christian View Online, http://www.thechristianview.net/Bill_Stafford.html (accessed July 15, 2009).

Holloway, David. "J. C. Ryle—The Man, The Minister and The Missionary." http://www.biblebb.com/files/ryle/ j_c_ryle.htm (accessed June 11, 2009).

Homiletic Review. Vol. 49. New York: Funk and Wagnall's Company, 1905.

———. Vol. 59. New York and London: Funk and Wagnalls Company, 1910. http://www.books.google.com/books (accessed June 17, 2009).

Hunt, Johnny. Personal Correspondence. December 9, 2008.

Hurst, John Fletcher. *John Wesley the Methodist* . New York: Eaton and Mains, 1903. http://www.books.google.com/ books?id=LOJpAAAAMAAJ (accessed June 15, 2009).

Hutson, Curtis. *Salvation Crystal Clear II*. Murfreesboro: Sword of the Lord Publishers, 1991.

———. *Some Things I Have Learned.* Murfreesboro: Sword of the Lord Publishers, 1995.

———. "The Danger of Delay." *The Sword of the Lord*, 6 Feb. 1998. http://www.swordofthelord.com/onlinesermons/ DangerofDelay.htm (accessed May 29, 2009).

———. "Evangelistic Preaching." *The Sword of the Lord*, July 11, 2008.

———. ed. *Great Preaching on Hell*, Vol. XIV. Murfreesboro: The Sword of the Lord Publishers, 1989.

Hybels, B., D. S. Briscoe, and H. W. Robinson. *Mastering Contemporary Preaching*. Portland, Or.: Multnomah, 1990.

Hyles, Jack. *Teaching on Preaching*. Hammond, IN: Hyles Anderson Publications, 1986. http://www.fbbc.com/ messages/hylestoptoc.html (accessed July 13, 2009).

Bibliography

Jefferson, Charles E. *Quiet hints to growing preachers in my study.* New York: T.Y. Crowell and Company. http://www. books.google.com/books?id=sv8SAAAAYAAJ (accessed June 5, 2009).

John, J. "Evangelistic Preaching (from a British Angle)." *SermonCentral,* March 17, 2008, http://www.sermoncentral. com/article.asp?article=a-WhatsNewTableOfContent (accessed May 29, 2009).

John Mark Ministries. "Pastor Dropout Rate." http://jmm.aaa. net.au/articles/8084.htm (accessed June 1, 2009).

Johnston, Tom. Personal Correspondence. 19 May 2009.

Jowett, J. Henry. *Apostolic Optimism.* "The Secrets of Effective Preaching: Sin & Sympathy." London: Hodder and Stoughton, 1901.

————. *The Preacher: His Life and Work, Yale Lectures.* New York: George H. Doran Company, 1912.

Kipling, Rudyard. *Just So Stories.* Doubleday Page and Company, 1912.

Knight, Walter. *Knights Illustration for Today.* Chicago: Moody Press, 1970.

Knott, Harold E. *How to Prepare an Expository Sermon.* Cincinnati, Ohio: The Standard Publishing Company, 1930.

Koessler, John. *The Moody Handbook on Preaching.* Chicago: Moody Publishers, 2008.

Koller, Charles. *Expository Preaching Without Notes.* Cited by Danny Akin, Southeastern Baptist Theological Seminary, Contours of a Great Commission Resurgence, Part 17: The Crisis in 21st Century Preaching: A Mandate for Biblical Exposition, Part E, October 3, 2008.

Koonce, Brian. "Fish: Evangelistic Preaching Is a Must." *The Pathway* (Dec 13, 2005), http://www.mbcpathway.com (accessed May 29, 2009).

Larsen, David L. *The Company of the Preachers.* Grand Rapids: Kregel Publications, 1998, http://www.books. google.com/books?isbn=0825430860 (accessed May 29, 2009, and June 11, 2009).

————. *The Evangelism Mandate.* Grand Rapids: Kregel, 2002.

Leavell, Roland Q. *Evangelism, Christ's Imperative Commission.* Nashville: Broadman Press, 1951.

————. *Effective Evangelism.* Nashville: Broadman Press, 1955.

Lee, R. G. *R. G. Lee Sermonic Library.* Vol. 14. Orlando: Christ for the World Publishers, 1962.

————. "Why I Extend the Gospel Invitation." The Sword of the Lord, Murfreesboro: The Sword of the Lord Publishers, 13 Nov. 1981.

Lewis, Ralph and Gregg Lewis. *Inductive Preaching.* Wheaton: Good News Publishers, 1983.

Lloyd-Jones, Martyn. *Evangelistic Sermons at Aberavon.* Carlisle, Pa.: The Banner of Truth Trust, 2001.

Long, Michael G. *The Legacy of Billy Graham.* Louisville, Kentucky: Westminster John Knox Press, 2008.

Lorentzen, Melvin E., ed. *Evangelistic Preaching.* Minneapolis, Minnesota: World Wide Publications, 1990.

Luther, Martin. "Qualifications for Preaching." http://www.sermonindex.net (accessed May 27, 2009).

————. http://www.preacherscorner.org/illustrations.htm (accessed June 16, 2009).

Bibliography

————. http://www.quotationsbook.com/quote/32030 (accessed June 16, 2009).

MacArthur, John. *Rediscovering Expository Preaching.* Nashville: Word Publishing Group, 1992.

————. *The MacArthur Study Bible* (electronic ed.). Nashville: Word Pub., 1997.

————. "Question and Answer Session at the Preach the Word Conference." Riverside, Ca.: Harvest Ministries, 1999.

————. *The Vilification of Jesus,* Part 2. http://www.Gracetoyou.org (accessed May 28, 2009).

Maclaren, Alexander. *Maclaren's Expositions of Holy Scripture*. Vol. 17. Grand Rapids: Baker Book House, 1977.

Martin, Roger. *R.A. Torrey: Apostle of Certainty.* Murfreesboro: Sword of the Lord Publishers, 2000.

Matthews, C. E. *A Church Revival*. Nashville: Broadman Press, 1955.

————. *The Southern Baptist Program of Evangelism.* Nashville: Convention Press, 1956.

Mayhue, Richard and Robert L. Thomas. *The Master's Perspective on Pastoral Ministry*. Grand Rapids: Kregel Publications, 2000.

McConkey, James. *The Three-Fold Secret of the Holy Spirit.* Pittsburgh, Pa: Silver Publishing Society, 1975.

McDill, Wayne. *12 Essential Skills for Great Preaching.* Nashville: B and H Publishing Group, 2006. http://www.books.google.com (accessed May 28, 2009).

M'Cheyne, Robert M. *Sermons of Robert Murray M'Cheyne.* Carlisle, Pa: The Banner of Truth Trust, 2000.

Michael, Larry. *Spurgeon on Leadership.* Grand Rapids: Kregel Publications, 2003.

Miller, Donald G. *The Way to Biblical Preaching*. Nashville: Abingdon Press, 1957.

Miller, Norm. "Warren on Criswell: How to Last in Ministry." Ministry Toolbox, Issue #68, http://www.pastors.com (accessed May 27, 2009).

Mohler, Albert. "Expository Preaching and the Recovery of Christian Worship (Part One)." (Tuesday, August 09, 2005), http://www.AlbertMolher.com (accessed May 28, 2009).

————. "Expository Preaching and the Recovery of Christian Worship (Part Two)." (Wednesday, August 10, 2005), http://www.AlbertMohler.com (accessed May 28, 2009).

Moody, D. L. "Tomorrow May Be Too Late." *The Sword of the Lord*, 30 October 1998. http://www.swordofthelord.com (accessed May 22, 2009).

Morgan, G. Campbell. *Evangelism*. Grand Rapids: Baker Book House, 1976.

Morgan, Robert J. *Nelson's Complete Book of Stories, Illustrations and Quotes* (electronic ed.). Nashville: Thomas Nelson, 2000. (accessed June 16, 2009).

————. ed. *Nelson's Annual Preacher's SourceBook*. Nashville: Thomas Nelson Publishers, 2006.

Morris, Lee. "Pastoral Care in Revival Preaching: Billy Graham." http://www.springerlink.com/index/ Q523086XJX476547.pdf (accessed May 28, 2009).

Munger, Robert. "Sermon Illustrations." http://www.sermon illustrations.com/a-z/p/preaching.htm (accessed June 6, 2009).

Murray, Andrew. *Absolute Surrender*. Springdale, Pa.: Whitaker House, 1981.

Nettles, Tom. *Ready for Reformation?* , Nashville: Broadman and Holman, 2005.

Bibliography

Newton, John. *The Gift of Preaching: Advice to a Young Preacher.* http://www.puritansermons.com, 25 July 1772 (accessed October 12, 2008).

Packer, James. *Your Father Loves You.* Colorado Springs: Harold Shaw Publishers, 1986. http://www.higherpraise. com/illustrations/preaching.htm (accessed June 15, 2009).

Pastoral Care, Inc. "Statistics." http://www.pastoralcareinc. com/WhyPastoralCare/Statistics.php (accessed May 28, 2009).

Pentecost, George F. "Book of Famous Quotes." http://www.famous-quotes.com/author.php?aid=5644 (accessed June 3, 2009).

Perry, Lloyd M. and Faris D. Whitesell. *Variety in Your Preaching.* New Jersey: Fleming Revell Company, 1954.

Piper, John. *The Supremacy of God in Preaching.* Grand Rapids: Baker Books, 1990.

———. "Charles Spurgeon: Preaching through Adversity." http://www.desiringgod.org/ResourceLibrary/Biographies/1 469_Charles_Spurgeon (accessed May 28, 2009).

Quayle, William. *The Pastor-Preacher.* Grand Rapids: Baker Books, 1979.

"Quotes on Preaching." http://www.sermonindex.net (accessed May 28, 2009).

Ravenhill, Leonard. *Why Revival Tarries.* Minneapolis: Bethany House, 1987.

———. *Heart Breathings.* Harvey Christian Publishers, 1995.

Rice, Bill. "Platform Leadership." *The Sword of the Lord,* 20 and 27 March 1970.

Rice, John R. *Soulwinner's Fire.* Murfreesboro: Sword of the Lord Publishers, 1941.

———. *Revival Appeals.* Murfressboro: Sword of the Lord Publishers, 1945.

———. "The Kind of Preaching We Need." *Sword of the Lord,* 18 Jan. 1956.

———. *The Evangelist.* Murfreesboro: Sword of the Lord Publishers, 1968.

Riley, W. B. "The Soul-Winning Sermon." *The Sword of the Lord,* Murfreesboro: Sword of the Lord Publishers, 7 Nov. 2003.

Robinson, Haddon. *Biblical Preaching: The Development and Delivery of Expository Messages.* Grand Rapids: Baker Publishing Group, 1980.

———. "The Church Needs Scholarly Evangelists and Evangelistic Scholars." Gordon Cornwell Theological Seminary, Podcast Broadcast, Preaching Point # 16. http://www.gordonconwell.edu/lifelong_learners/preachingp oints (accessed June 13, 2009).

———. "An Interview with Haddon Robinson." Preaching Today Sermons, http://www.preachingtoday.com/skills/ audioworkshops/pt14b.html (accessed May 29, 2009).

———. "An Interview with Haddon Robinson." Preaching Today Sermons, http://www.preachingtodaysermons.com/ evprinloch.html (accessed May 29, 2009).

———. "Preaching the Old Testament." http://www.preaching.org/reviews/display_review/48 (accessed June 24, 2009).

Rogers, Joyce and Paige Patterson. *Love Worth Finding.* Nashville: B and H Publishing Group, 2005.

Rogers, Tim. "Book Review – Franchising McChurch.*"* http://www.sbctoday.com/2009/03/.../book-review-franchising-mcchurch (accessed June 24, 2009).

Bibliography

Roloff, Lester. "The Family Altar Newsletter." Vol. 29. Corpus Christi, Tex.: The Roloff Evangelistic Association, 2009.

Rosscup, James E. (John MacArthur and the Master's Seminary Faculty). *Preaching: How to Preach Biblically.* Nashville: Thomas Nelson, 2005.

Ryken, Leland. *Worldly Saints: The Puritans As They Really Were.* Grand Rapids: Zondervan, 1990.

Ryle, J. C. *The Christian Leaders of the Last Century.* London: T. Nelson and Sons, 1869. http://www.books.google.com/books(accessed May 28, 2009).

———. "Simplicity in Preaching." http://www.gracegems.org/18/Ryle-%20Preaching.htm (accessed June 5, 2009).

———. *Wikipedia Encyclopedia.* http://en.wikipedia.org/wiki/John_Charles_Ryle (accessed June 11, 2009).

Ryrie, Charles. *Ryrie's Practical Guide to Communicating Bible Doctrine.* Nashville: B and H Publishing Group, 2005.

Sangster, W. E. *The Craft of the Sermon Construction.* London: Marshall Pickering, 1954.

———. *Power in Preaching.* Nashville: Abingdon Press, 1958.

Scarborough, L. R. *Prepare to Meet God: Sermons Making the Way to Christ Plain.* Nashville: Sunday School Board of the Southern Baptist Convention, 1922.

———. *How Jesus Won Men.* Nashville: Sunday School Board of the Southern Baptist Convention, 1926.

———. *With Christ after the Lost.* Nashville: Broadman Press, 1952.

———. "Lost!" *The Sword of the Lord,* 13 Apr. 1973.

Smith, Gipsy. "Are You Still Unsaved?" *The Sword of the Lord,* 31 Oct. 2008.

Smith, J. Harold. *God's Three Deadlines*. Orlando: Daniels Publishers, 1968.

Smith, Oswald. "Sermon Illustrations." http://www.sermon illustrations.com (accessed May 28, 2009)

Sorenson, Austin L. "The Pulpit and the Pew," *The Sword of the Lord,* 7 Nov. 2003.

Sprague, William B. *Lectures on Revivals of Religion*. Carlisle, Pa: The Banner of Truth Trust, 2007.

Spurgeon, C. H. *Spurgeon's Gems.* New York: Sheldon, Blakeman and Co. 1859, http://www.spurgeon.org/sermons/0034.htm (accessed May 28, 2009).

———. "When the Preacher Has No Burden for the Souls of Men." *The Metropolitan Tabernacle Pulpit,* 1863, http://www.books.google.com/books(accessed May 28, 2009).

———. "The Approachableness of Jesus." *The Metropolitan Tabernacle Pulpit*, May 3, 1868, http://www.iclnet.org/pub/resources/text/history/spurgeon/web/ss-0007.html (accessed June 9, 2009).

———. *Flashes of Thought.* London: Passmore and Alabaster, 1874, http://www.books.google.com/books?id=2AEDAAAAQAAJ (accessed June 9, 2009).

———. *The Soul Winner*. New York: Revell, 1895.

———. *Lectures to My Students.* Grand Rapids: Zondervan, 1970.

———. *12 Sermons on Decision*. Grand Rapids: Baker Book House, 1972.

———. *C. H. Spurgeon: Autobiography,* vol. 2. Edinburgh: The Banner of Truth Trust, 1973.

———. *Come Ye Children*. Scotland: Christian Focus Publications, 1989.

Bibliography

———. *The Soulwinner*. Grand Rapids: Wm. B. Eerdmans Publishing, 1989.

———. *Morning and Evening*. Great Britain: Christian Focus Publications, 1994.

———. *Spurgeon's Sermons on Soulwinning*. Grand Rapids: Kregel Publications, 1995.

———. *An All Round Ministry*. BiblioBazaar, LLC, 2008. http://www.books.google.com/books?isbn=0554398842 (accessed May 29, 2009).

———. "The Ascension of Christ." http://www.biblebb.com/files/spurgeon/0982.htm (accessed May 28, 2009).

———. "Intelligent Obedience." http://www.apibs.org/chs/3263.pdf (accessed June 9, 2009).

———. "Our Omnipotent Leader." Metropolitan Tabernacle: Sermon #2465, http://www.spurgeongems.org/vols40-42/vols40-42.htm (accessed June 10, 2009).

———. "Prayer-Meetings." Bible Bulletin Board, http://www.biblebb.com/files/spurgeon/3421.htm (accessed May 29, 2009).

———. "Preach the Gospel." The Spurgeon Archive No. 0034, http://www.spurgeon.org/sermons/0034.htm (accessed May 28, 2009).

———. "Search the Scripture." The Spurgeon Archive No. 172, http://www.spurgeon.org/sermons/0034.htm (accessed May 28, 2009).

———. "To Lovers of Jesus." http://www.spurgeongems.org/vols31-33/chs1834.pdf (accessed May 28, 2009).

———. "An Urgent Request for an Immediate Answer." http://www.spurgeongems.org/vols37-39/chs2231.pdf (accessed May 28, 2009).

Stanfield, V.L. *Effective Evangelistic Preaching*. Grand Rapids: Baker Book House, 1965.

Stedman, Ray C. "The Church's Building and Maintenance Service." Discovery Publishing, a ministry of Peninsula Bible Church, PC Library, 1976.

———. "The Accountability of the Preacher." http://www. expository.org/expository3.htm (accessed June 10, 2009).

Stemple, Joseph C. Personal Correspondence. 10 Feb. 2009.

Stewart, James. *Heralds of God.* Grand Rapids: Baker Book House, 1972.

Stott J. R. W. "Fundamentalism and Evangelism." London: Crusade Booklets, 1956.

———. *Preacher's Portrait*. London: Tyndale Press, 1961.

———. "Paralyzed Speakers and Hearers." *Christianity Today*, 13 Mar. 1981.

———. *Between Two Worlds.* Grand Rapids: Eerdmans Publishing Co., 1982.

———. *I Believe In Preaching*. London: Hodder and Stoughton, 1982.

Streett Alan R. *The Effective Invitation: A Practical Guide for The Pastor.* Grand Rapids: Kregel Publications, 2004.

Sunday, Billy. *The Sword of the Lord.* Murfressboro: Sword of the Lord Publishers, 12 Dec. 2008.

Sweazy, George. *Effective Evangelism.* New York: Harper, 1953.

Tan, Michael. *Hearts Aflame.* Singapore: Armour Publishing, 2008.

Tan, P. L. *Encyclopedia of 7700 Illustrations: A Treasury of Illustrations, Anecdotes, Facts and Quotations for Pastors,*

Bibliography

Teachers and Christian Workers. Garland, Tex.: Bible Communications, 1996.

Taylor, Chad. *Why Revival Still Tarries*. Shippensburg, Pa.: Destiny Image Publishers, 2005.

"The Preacher," http://www.gurgaonchurch.wordpress.com/2008/11/29/the-preacher-roy-felix-joshua (accessed June 6, 2009).

"The Revival Labors of Charles G. Finney (Part 2)". Seelyville, IN: Herald of His Coming, July, 2009.

Tozer, A. W. *Tozer on Worship and Entertainment, Selected Excerpts*. Harrisburg, Pa.: WingSpread Publishers, 2006.

Trent, John Scott. *Evangelists in Action.* Orlando, Fla.: Daniels Publishers, 1964.

Truett, George W. *A Quest For Souls*. New York: Harper and Brothers, 1917.

———. *We Would See Jesus*. Chattanooga: AMG Publishers, 1998.

———. "The Door to Heaven." *Sermon and Studies by Godly Men*, BibleTeacher.org, http://www.woundedheart.org/sermons2b.htm (accessed June 1, 2009)

Vines, Jerry. *Exploring 1, 2, 3 John*. Neptune, New Jersey: Loizeaux Brothers, 1989.

Vines, Jerry and Jim Shaddix. *Power in the Pulpit*. Chicago: Moody Press, 1999.

Walden, Viola. *Sword Scrapbook*. Murfreesboro: Sword of the Lord Publishers, 1980.

Walker, Alan. *Standing up to Preach*. Nashville: Discipleship Resources, 1983.

Wallace, Tom. Illustrations on Preaching. www.preacherscorner.org/illustrations.htm.

Wesley, John, *John Wesley: A Representative Collection of His Writings* New York: Oxford University Press, 1980. http://www.books.google.com/books. (accessed May 29,2009).

Whitesell, Faris D. *Sixty-Five Ways to Give Evangelistic Invitations*. Grand Rapids: Zondervan, 1945.

———. *Evangelistic Preaching and the Old Testament*. Chicago: Moody Press, 1947.

———. *Basic New Testament Evangelism*. Grand Rapids: Zondervan, 1949.

Whitsett, Tom. South Carolina Baptist State Evangelism Conference, Feb 24, 2009.

Wiersbe, Warren W. *The Bible Exposition Commentary*. Vol. 1. Wheaton, Ill.: Victor Books, 1989.

———. *The Dynamics of Preaching*. Grand Rapids: Baker Book House, 1999.

———. "Your Preaching Is Unique." Christianity Today Library, www.ctlibrary.com/lebooks/theleadershiplibrary/preachingtoconvince (accessed May 28, 2009).

Wiersbe, Warren W. and D. Wiersbe. *The Elements of Preaching: The Art of Biblical Preaching Clearly and Simply Presented*. Wheaton, Ill.: Tyndale House Publishers, 1986.

Williams, Jerome O. *Sermons in Outline*. Nashville: Broadman Press, 1943.

Yates, Kyle M. *Preaching from the Prophets*. Nashville: Broadman Press, 1942.

Biographical Sketches

Robert Murray M'Cheyne (1813–1843) was known as the holiest man in all of Scotland and for his urging to have others live a devoted life to Christ. Writing to a friend, he said, "I feel there are two things it is impossible to desire with sufficient ardor—personal holiness and the honor to Christ in the salvation of souls." His fervency for purity of heart is heard loudly in his praying, "O God, make me as holy as a pardoned sinner can be." Just seven years into his ministry, M'Cheyne died just short of the age of 30. His life was one plagued with much sickness. At his death in 1843, all Scotland mourned, and seven thousand attended his funeral.

L. R. Scarborough (1870–1945) went from a cow-camp preacher to the presidency of a great theological seminary. He had few equals as an evangelist. He served as professor of evangelism at Southwestern Theological Seminary from 1908 until 1915, when he became its president. He served in this position until 1942. He influenced many in the classroom, church pew, and crusade arena by his lectures and sermons to win souls.

George W. Truett (1866–1944) became pastor of the First Baptist Church, Dallas, Texas, September, 1897, which he served for forty-seven years. He was the predecessor to Dr. W. A. Criswell. Under his leadership the church saw 18,124 additions and 5,337 baptisms. Its Sunday school soared to 4,000, and it became the largest church in the world. His book *A Quest for Souls* pulsates with this great man's passion for God and heartbeat for souls. He was a man on fire who ever preached for a decision.

Hyman Appelman (1902–1983) was a Russian-born Jew who was converted to Christ at age twenty-eight. He graduated from

Southwestern Baptist Theological Seminary in 1933. His ministry was global; he traveled around the world eight or nine times preaching the Gospel. Appelman entered into evangelism in 1942.

Charles Haddon Spurgeon (1834–1892) is a name recognized by most ministers, and various volumes of his sermons find housing upon their library shelf. Known as the "Prince of Preachers," he began preaching at age sixteen and at age twenty became pastor of the New Park Street Chapel in London. Shortly after his ministry began at New Park Street Chapel, attendance grew so much that work started on the construction of a 6,000-seat sanctuary. In 1861, Spurgeon and his church family moved into the Metropolitan Tabernacle. His heart for ministers is keenly seen in his formation of the Pastor's College which yet continues. His heart for the unsaved is manifest in the numerous volumes of sermons he authored. Spurgeon greatly influenced men who became giants for God in America, including B. H. Carroll and John R. Rice. Charles, his son, said, "There was no one who could preach like my father. In inexhaustible variety, witty wisdom, vigorous proclamation, loving entreaty, and lucid teaching, with a multitude of other qualities, he must, at least in my opinion, ever be regarded as the prince of preachers."[534]

John R. Rice (1895–1980) was an author, evangelist, radio host, editor who touched millions in his eighty-five years on earth. He authored more than 200 titles and was the founding editor of the *Sword of the Lord.* Rice died in 1980.

John A. Broadus (1827–1895) in 1858 became a member of the faculty of Southern Baptist Theological Seminary as professor of New Testament interpretation and homiletics. He served in this position for 36 years. During the Civil War, the seminary

---

[534] Spurgeon, *Autobiography,* Vol. 2, 278.

closed, and he served as a chaplain in Lee's army. Following the war, the school had grave difficulty reopening, and had it not been for his and James Boyce's effort, it would not have. It was during this pressing time that he wrote the Magna Charta on preaching, *On the Preparation and Delivery of Sermons* (1870). In 1889, he was invited to give the Yale Lectures on preaching. He remains the only Southern Baptist to do so. He died in 1895. Spurgeon called Broadus "the greatest of living preachers."

Stephen Olford (1918–2004) was one of the world's most dynamic Christian leaders of the 20th century. Throughout his life, he taught boldly and effectively about the importance of expository preaching, evangelistic teaching, and spiritual growth. Many of his sermons, lectures, and books can be found on the Union Theological Seminary website where this bio was found.

William E. Sangster (1900–1960) was a popular Methodist minister of his day and a gifted preacher. His sermons were skillfully prepared and true to the Scripture.

C. E. Matthews (1887–1956), upon departure from his pastorate at Travis Road Baptist Church, Fort Worth, Texas, became the Secretary of Evangelism for the Home Mission Board of the Southern Baptist Convention. Under Matthews' leadership, baptisms skyrocketed nearly fifty-one per cent in the convention. It is impossible to read any of his numerous books on evangelism and revival without noting the tremendous burden for lost souls that he possessed.

C. E. Autrey (1904–1993) was professor of evangelism at Southwestern Baptist Theological Seminary prior to assuming the post of Director of the Division of Evangelism, Home Mission Board of the Southern Baptist Convention. I cut my teeth in evangelism through studying the classic book on evangelism *Basic Evangelism* which he authored.

John Bisagno (1934–) has been in the ministry 57 years, pastoring for 42 years. Now retired from the pastorate of First Baptist Church, Houston , Texas, he continues preaching both in the United States and abroad. Bisagno is well renowned for his evangelistic passion. As a nineteen-year-old pastor, I was instructed and inspired through his book *The Power of Positive Evangelism.*

Adam Clarke (1762–1832) was a British Methodist theologian and biblical scholar who wrote a commentary on the whole Bible which took him forty years to complete.

Faris Whitesell (1895–1984?) was an instructor in Evangelism, English, Old Testament, Pastoral Theology at Northern Baptist Theological Seminary, Chicago, Illinois, for many years. He wrote extensively on evangelistic themes.

Gipsy Smith (1860–1947), a year after his conversion (1876), was invited by William Booth to join the Salvation Army evangelistic team, a post which he held until 1882. He served as an itinerant evangelist from this point in his life until his death in 1947. He was born in a gypsy tent and raised in a gypsy camp, never attending school for even a day, yet God used him to touch millions through his powerful preaching.

Herschel Hobbs (1907–1995) received his Ph.D. from Southern Baptist Theological Seminary, Louisville, Kentucky. He was the chairman of the committee which produced the 1963 version of the *Baptist Faith and Message.* He served two terms as President of the Southern Baptist Convention. Many knew him as "Mr. Baptist Hour" from the many years he preached on the radio program *The Baptist Hour.* Hobbs stated that he was first and foremost a pastor and would remain one if he had 10,000 lives to live. He died in 1995.

W. A. Criswell (1909–2002) was pastor of the First Baptist Church, Dallas, Texas, for 50 years during which time he preached more than 4000 sermons from its pulpit. He published 54 books and received eight honorary doctorates. Criswell was twice elected President of the Southern Baptist Convention. He was widely known for his deep-rooted biblical stance on the inerrancy of Scripture and boldness in its proclamation.

Roy Fish at age 19 knew God was calling him to teach evangelism. This call became a reality in 1965 when he began teaching evangelism at Southwestern Baptist Theological Seminary, Fort Worth, Texas, a post he held for over 44 years. He is regarded by many as the "expert" on evangelism. Distinguished Professor of Evangelism emeritus (SWBTS) and L. R. Scarborough Chair of Evangelism (1965–2006); Roy Fish School of Evangelism and Missions; NAMB ambassador-at-large and former interim president of NAMB (June 2006–May 2007).

John H. Jowett (1864–1923) came to America from Halifax, England, in 1909 to speak at Moody's Northfield Conference. While here, he preached twice at First Presbyterian Church, New York. The people immediately asked him to be pastor, an offer he declined. The invitation was extended twice more, and finally he consented to assume the pastorate there in 1911. He began preparing his sermons on Tuesday in meticulous fashion and was known to read them in delivery. Upon G. Campbell Morgan's resignation from Westminster Chapel in London, Jowett crossed the seas to assume that pastorate, a post which he held until 1922. He died in 1923.

J. C. Ryle (1816–1900) was described by Spurgeon "as the best man in the Church of England."[535] James Packer states Ryle's agenda was "… aimed at four things: the evangelising of English people; the purging of the English national Church; the uniting of English Christians; and the holiness of English believers."[536] "Thoroughly evangelical in his doctrine and uncompromising in his principles, J. C. Ryle was a prolific writer, vigorous preacher, and faithful pastor. He was born at Macclesfield and educated at Eton and Christ Church, Oxford."[537]

---

[535] Holloway, "J. C. Ryle."
[536] Ibid.
[537] Ryle, *Wikipedia Encyclopedia.*